I0606112

LIGHTNING

FROM INCEPTION TO PRESERVATION

LIGHTNING

FROM INCEPTION TO PRESERVATION

RICHARD HALL

FONTHILL

Front cover: *Cold War Intercept,* Keith Aspinall, oil on canvas 2002. (© *The copyright holder; image: RAF Museum*)

Rear cover: Lightning F.6 XS904 'BQ' showing the halo that forms in the intake duct when a high throttle setting is applied. This is due to the sudden drop in pressure in the intake, causing water in the air to condense out and form a mist. (*Richard Hall*)

First published in Great Britain in 2025 by
Fonthill
An imprint of
Pen & Sword Books Ltd
Yorkshire – Philadelphia
www.fonthill.media

ISBN 978-1-78155-950-5

A CIP catalogue record for this book
is available from the British Library.

The Publisher's authorised representative in the EU for product
safety is Authorised Rep Compliance Ltd., Ground Floor,
71 Lower Baggot Street, Dublin D02 P593, Ireland.
www.arccompliance.com

For a complete list of Pen & Sword titles please contact
PEN & SWORD BOOKS LIMITED
47 Church Street, Barnsley, South Yorkshire, S70 2AS, England
E-mail: enquiries@pen-and-sword.co.uk
Website: www.pen-and-sword.co.uk
Or
PEN AND SWORD BOOKS
1950 Lawrence Road, Havertown, PA 19083, USA
E-mail: uspen-and-sword@casematepublishers.com
Website: www.penandswordbooks.com

Foreword

From the 1960s to the 1980s Lightnings were the ultimate performers at British air shows. That distinctive shape, phenomenal turn of heel and spine-chilling sound are fondly remembered and much missed. My early years as an enthusiast involved trips from Liverpool on a draughty Ribble bus to Warton where I could watch test flights from the lane that ran down the airfield's western perimeter. I felt great pride that my native county, Lancashire, had produced such a thoroughbred. (Liverpool was within Lancashire's boundary in those days.)

I read all that I could find on Freddie Page's masterpiece and made a beeline for any air show where Lightnings were expected to tear up the sky. When I became a full-time wordsmith, I wrote on the subject with relish. Covering the end of the line at Binbrook in 1988 was tinged with sadness, surely a never to be repeated era. At Cape Town in 2001 I basked in the fleeting reprieve provided by the determined and visionary Thunder City team.

Love of the Lightning is frequently compared with the adulation generated by the Spitfire. In the purest sense both had the same role: defence of the nation and stirring the blood. Spitfire books and articles proliferate, but very few take the reader into new territory. Tomes on the Lightning are tending the same way…

Now here's *another* Lightning book…so what's new? Richard Hall writes in a highly readable style and from a rare point of view: he *owns* a Lightning, a two-seater XS420 on show at Farnborough. This gives him a novel perspective: he knows every inch of the sublime interceptor and he's got the skinned knuckles and denuded wallet to prove it. Richard's depth of knowledge extends to the Lightning's development and service life; he has diligently accessed first-hand sources and presented them in an original manner. He is as adept at explaining the gestation of the AIRPASS airborne interception system as he is at revealing squadron life on a Missile Practice Camp.

Each chapter added to or refined my own knowledge of the subject and I wager it will do the same for you. Congratulations Richard, you have created a worthy addition to Lightning literature.

Ken Ellis, People's Republic of Rutland

Acknowledgements

Firstly, I would like to thank my long-suffering wife Sarah for her patience and understanding while I was writing this book and for my constant forays to Lincolnshire in pursuit of all things Bomber Command.

I also thank the following for their help in contributing memories, technical information, photographs, proofreading, moral support, answering my constant questions and assistance with XS420. Without your kind support, it would not have been possible to complete this work or keep Lightning T.5 XS420 in one piece:

Al Stepney, Alan Hazelton, Andrew Lee, Andy Wootten, Brian Clifford, Brian Luff, Charles Ross, Chris Graver, Chris Norris, Clive Hammond, Colin Collis, Colin Murray, RAF Coltishall Visitor Centre, Craig Wise, Darren Swinn, Dave Blissett, David Gibson, David Rowberry, David Tylee, Dennis Brooks, Derek Bradshaw, Derek Parks, Farnborough Air Sciences Trust, Graham Rood, Heather Airey, Hugh Trevor, Ian Black, Ian Brett, Janine Potten, Jeff Bell, Jo Deebank, John Ward, Ken Ellis, Kevin Matthews, Laura Downes, Malcolm Warren, Mark Seabrook, Martin Blades, Martin Goodwin, Martin Johnson, Mike Drew, Mike Patterson, Mike Potten, Murray Flint, Neil Aiery, Neil Marshall, Neville Spencer-Beck, Nick Forder, Paul Ridgwell, Paul Tuininga, Phil Wallis, Ray Whiteley, Richard Norris, Richard Scarborough, Roy John Abraham, Russell Carpenter, Scott Bouchard, Scott Sullivan, Simon Jakubowski, Steve Downes, Steve Gyles, Steve Hurst, Steve Mills, Steve White, The Radar Museum Neatishead, Tony Dowland, Tony Hulls and Valerie Eggleton.

Contents

Glossary

A&AEE:	Aeroplane and Armament Experimental Establishment
AAM:	Air-to-Air Missile
ADEN:	Armament Development Enfield
ADIZ:	Air Defence Identification Zone
AFDS:	Air Fighting Development Squadron
AI:	Airborne Interception
AIRPASS:	Airborne Interception Pilot Attack Sight System
AM:	Air Ministry
APC:	Armament Practice Camp
AS:	Armstrong Siddeley
AVM:	Air Vice Marshal
BAC:	British Aircraft Corporation
BAe:	British Aerospace
CAA:	Civil Aviation Authority
CAP:	Combat Air Patrol
CAS:	Chief of Air Staff
Cat:	Category
CFE:	Central Fighter Establishment
C-in-C:	Commander-in-Chief
CLE:	Cambered Leading Edge
CO:	Commanding Officer
COW:	Coventry Ordnance Works Ltd
CWP:	Contractor Working Party
DB:	Development Batch
DFCS:	Day Fighter Combat Squadron
DWP:	Defence White Paper
EE:	English Electric Co Ltd
FAA:	Fleet Air Arm
FAST:	Farnborough Air Sciences Trust
FEAF:	Far East Air Force

Fg Off: Flying Officer
FIP: Fire Integrity Programme
Flt Lt: Flight Lieutenant
GCI: Ground Control Interception
Grp Capt: Group Captain
HCU: Heavy Conversion Unit
IAF: Interceptor Alert Force
IFR: In-flight Refuelling
ILS: Instrument Landing System
IWC: Interceptor Weapons Instructor
LAF: Lightning Augmentation Flight
LCS: Lightning Conversion Squadron
LCU: Lightning Conversion Unit
LFC: Lightning Flying Club
LPG: Lightning Preservation Group
LTF: Lightning Training Flight
M: Mach
MAP: Ministry of Aircraft Production
MAEE: Marine Aircraft Experimental Establishment
Mineval: Station Evaluation Exercise
MoD: Ministry of Defence
MoS: Ministry of Supply
MPC: Missile Practice Camp
MU: Maintenance Unit
NATO: North Atlantic Treaty Organization
OCU: Operational Conversion Unit
ORB: Operations Record Book
ORP: Operational Readiness Platform
PI: Practice Interception
Plt Off.: Pilot Officer
PSI: Pounds per Square Inch
QRA: Quick Reaction Alert
RAE: Royal Aircraft Establishment
RAF: Royal Air Force
RAFG: Royal Air Force Germany
RAFM: Royal Air Force Museum
RFC: Royal Flying Corps
RSAF: Royal Saudi Air Force
R/T: Radio Telephony
SAGW: Surface-to-Air Guided Weapons
SBAC: Society of British Aircraft Constructors
SoTT: School of Technical Training
Sqn Ldr: Squadron Leader

SWP:	Standard Warning Panel
TACAN:	Tactical Air Navigation System
TACEVAL:	Tactical Evaluation
TFF:	Target Facilities Flight
UECCL:	United Electric Car Co. Ltd
UHF:	Ultra High Frequency
USAAF:	United States Army Air Force
USAF:	United States Air Force
VHF:	Very High Frequency
Wg Cdr:	Wing Commander

1

English Electric: Origins, Formation and Personnel

Picture the scene. It's autumn 1949 and the popular pastime for many in Britain is a visit to a local smoke-filled cinema to view the latest film release. This year among the favourites are Robert Hamer's *Kind Hearts and Coronets*, Henry King's *Twelve O'Clock High* and Henry Cornelius' *Passport to Pimlico* starring Alec Guinness, Gregory Peck and Stanley Holloway respectively. Rationing is still in place, but restrictions on clothing have been lifted and life is slowly returning to normal after a decade of strife and turmoil. So, for the average cost of 1s 6d, a delightful afternoon or evening of entertainment was on the cards.

Undoubtedly the assembled crowd is keen for its chosen film to start, but proceedings are opened with a second feature followed by a black and white Movietone newsreel. Before the age of mass television ownership such media kept the British public up to date with current affairs and recent events. On this occasion the subject is the Society of British Aircraft Constructors (SBAC) Air Show at Farnborough, the music is uplifting, and the commentary by Leslie Mitchell is clear and concise, if not a little 'plummy'.

The age of the test pilot had arrived, and many within the audience would have looked in awe upon those who flew to the extreme edges of performance and flight envelopes. There had been rapid advances in design in the past few years, and with the advent of the jet engine the public was beginning to see aircraft in the sky bearing no resemblance to what had gone before. The quest to attain ever-higher speeds and altitudes was on, and for the time being Britain was well and truly one of the forerunners. Throughout the recently ended Second World War the aerial sounds had included the raucous bellow of the inline Rolls-Royce Merlin piston engine or the more subdued note of the radial Bristol Hercules and Wright Cyclone, but now the high-pitched whistle of the turbojet often drew the public's attention skywards to catch a glimpse of futuristic machines. With this heightened interest, maybe some of those awaiting the start of their feature film paid a little more heed to the ten-minute newsreel as the best of British aviation was put through its paces.

Manufacturers such as Avro, Bristol, de Havilland, Handley Page, Hawker, Short and Supermarine would be reasonably familiar to those in the audience. After all, their products had helped win the war, but early in the footage a sleek, twin-engine aircraft is seen being put through its paces. The narrator quotes: 'Outstanding among the bombers, the Canberra B.1 made by the English Electric Company, a medium-range turbojet of tremendous speed and manoeuvrability.' Marked with the serial number VN799, this was the first public outing of a design that would remain in Royal Air Force service and many others for decades.

At the controls of the sky-blue-liveried VN799 on this day was the company's chief test pilot Roland 'Bee' Beamont. He was an aviator with an impressive track record, having flown Hawker Hurricanes and Typhoons operationally in the Second World War. Bee was a master of his craft, shown to good effect as he displayed the Canberra. Those watching could not fail to be impressed by its speed and agility, more like a fighter than a bomber, but maybe some thought 'English Electric, who are they?' However, they could be forgiven as this was not a name freely associated with the world of aviation. Such thoughts, however, were a misconception as the company had its roots firmly embedded in the pioneering days of powered flight, although initially under different names and entities. English Electric also made an immense contribution during wartime, acting as a subcontractor to Handley Page and post-war de Havilland. So who were English Electric, and from whence had the company evolved?

The Pioneering Years

In the latter years of the nineteenth and early twentieth centuries significant technological strides were made in the realms of heavy engineering and manufacturing processes. The power of steam was harnessed during the Industrial Revolution with the evolution of the Newcomen engine, the Cornish Cycle and the emergence of the steam turbine. In addition, use of electricity was in the ascendancy and all manner of uses were found for this new form of power with its application becoming widespread.

For many years railways had been ruled by the steam locomotive, but around the turn of the century thoughts were turning, in some cases, to electric traction. After all, this was a cleaner and more efficient means of propulsion.

One of the electrical equipment suppliers for the railway and tram industry was Dick, Kerr & Co. Ltd, an enterprise set up by W.B. Dick and John Kerr in Glasgow in the latter part of the 1800s. As the company's workload grew within mechanical and electrical engineering, a factory was acquired in Strand Road, Preston, its purpose being to build tramcars.

In 1898 a separate company was formed to manage the facility named the Electric Railway & Tramway Carriage Works Ltd. Five years later Dick, Kerr took over the English Electric Manufacturing Company Ltd, a locally based concern with a new factory specializing in the construction of electrical components for rail and tramways. A further change occurred in June 1905 when the Carriage Works became the United Electric Car Co. Ltd. All of Dick, Kerr's electrical work was concentrated in Preston and its mechanical arm in Kilmarnock.

As electricity usage became more widespread in the early 1900s, there was a requirement to increase generation. Often this was achieved by coupling a steam engine to a dynamo. Two companies specializing in this field were Willans & Robinson of Rugby and the Phoenix Dynamo Manufacturing Co. Ltd from Bradford, both of whom will feature in the ongoing story of English Electric.

With reference to Willans, in 1903 a young student named Geoffrey de Havilland worked for the company for three years. In time he became one of the most lauded names in British aviation, and his activities would cross paths with those of English Electric.

The first decade of the 1900s was a period in Britain when the pursuit of aviation began to get into its stride. Knowledge of Orville Wright's first sustained heavier-than-air flight on 17 December 1903 at Kill Devil Hills, Kitty Hawk, North Carolina, USA undoubtedly encouraged the enthusiasm. However, the military could see very little need or use for the skies. One British army officer, Field Marshal Sir W.G. Nicholson, proclaimed: 'Aviation is a useless and expensive fad advocated by a few individuals whose ideas are unworthy of attention.' Thankfully others were more enlightened, and while the military sat back and observed from the sidelines, civilian companies and individuals set about their quest for the skies. One who pursued this aim was Howard Theophilus Wright.

Wright had served his apprenticeship at his father's works in Tipton, Staffordshire. Part of this business was sold to Hiram S. Maxim (later Sir and inventor of the first fully automatic machine gun) in 1889, with the 22-year-old Wright taken on as engineering manager. The company was named Maxim Electrical & Engineering Export Ltd and manufactured boilers and steam generators. Maxim was also interested in aviation and worked with Wright on a whirling arm to study aerodynamics. The association lasted until the end of 1904 when the company was liquidated.

Wright had two younger brothers, Warwick and Walton, whose interests rested within the burgeoning motor trade. After his time with Maxim ceased, in July 1905 Howard went into business with his siblings as Howard T. Wright Brothers Ltd. The venture was short-lived and soon went into voluntary liquidation. However, the brothers subsequently formed Warwick Wright Ltd in Marylebone in 1906 to work in the automotive industry. Incidentally, one of the executives involved with both companies was J.T.C. Moore-Brabazon, the first officially recognized Englishman to achieve sustained powered flight in Britain. On 2 May 1909 he piloted a Voisin biplane over ever-increasing distances at Eastchurch.

Shortly after the new company was formed, Howard Wright received a letter from Federico Capone, an Italian inventor with a keen interest in flying. He asked if a twin-rotor helicopter could be built for him, and an offer was accepted at an agreed cost of £2,500. In November of the same year, work started on the machine in a shed at the company's premises and was completed at a workshop in Battersea in March 1908. The helicopter was tested at Norbury Golf Links, but failed mainly due to a lack of engine power and undersized rotors. Subsequently it was sent to Italy, becoming Britain's first heavier-than-air export. However, not all was lost as this was the start of Howard Wright's career in the burgeoning aviation industry. In time, he would be rubbing shoulders with names such as Avro, Bristol, Blériot, Deperdussin, Hanriot, Handley Page, Short and Samuel Cody, all pioneers of early flight. Cody – then an American citizen – achieved the first sustained powered flight in Britain at Farnborough on 18 October 1908, piloting British Army Aeroplane No. 1.

While his interests in aeronautical concerns continued, Wright also carried on working within the electrical field, predominately generation. During this time he crossed paths with William Oke Manning, an electrical engineer with a keen interest in aviation. In December 1908 Manning was taken on to work with Wright, who continued to be commissioned to build aircraft and another helicopter for Capone.

Over the coming years Wright, who qualified as a pilot in October 1912, would become one of the nation's leading aeronautical manufacturers and Manning became his chief designer. One of their most successful designs was the 1909 Avis, an Anzani-powered monoplane built for the Scottish Aeroplane Syndicate, and the 1910 Wright Biplane which won the £4,000 Baron de Forest prize for the longest flight into Europe, on that occasion flown by T.O.M. Sopwith. However, after building around thirty-five machines and despite their success, the company's aviation activities were short-lived.

In August 1911 Warwick Wright sold his shares in the company to SA L'Auto Métallurgique of Belgium, with the name Warwick Wright Ltd changing to Métallurgique. Howard disposed of his interests to the Coventry Ordnance Works Ltd (COW) three months later. At the time COW's business was manufacturing naval guns, field artillery and associated war matériel, but there was also a desire to create an aeronautical department. It was slowly being recognized in official circles that aircraft would have a military role in the future. However, there were concerns that Britain might have to rely on foreign-built machines in the event of war, a highly unsatisfactory situation. Therefore trials were arranged by the War Office at Larkhill near Salisbury in August 1912, known as the Military Aeroplane Competition. This event aimed to choose the best aircraft from entrants for flight training and, if necessary, to go to war.

Wright and Manning were now in COW's employment, and the path was open for the company to compete in the trials. The pair designed and built two biplanes, Trials No. 10 and 11, at Battersea, one powered by a 100hp Gnome and the other a Chenu engine. Neither distinguished itself, with a variant of Samuel Cody's biplane winning the trial. Wright left COW in August 1912 and continued working as a designer, technical advisor and consultant in the aviation industry. He died in retirement in 1944, a true if somewhat unknown pioneer of British aviation.

The First World War

Aircraft production was always a secondary consideration to COW's main work areas. However, with the outbreak of war in 1914 the company was manufacturing small quantities of machines for the Royal Flying Corps, including Royal Aircraft

Factory BE. 2a, BE. 2b and BE. 8a. As the conflict progressed, the importance of airborne assets was fully understood and demand grew. An eye in the sky allowed for reconnaissance of enemy lines and to direct the fall of shot. Soon scouts (fighters) were aloft to intercept those who could bring down devastating fire upon enemy positions, leading in turn to dogfights and the creation of aces. In time bombers appeared in the skies, bringing a whole new dimension to warfare, not just to troops on the ground but also to civilians in their homes. Many companies in Britain were now building ever more advanced aircraft, and for COW further orders came for BE. 12a, RE. 7, RE. 8 and later Sopwith Snipe.

With the upturn in manufacturing, more firms were called upon to subcontract and diversify into aviation and other areas of war matériel production. One was Phoenix, whose core business had been producing electrical equipment. However, in 1915 the company received instructions from the Ministry of Supply (MoS) together with Mann Egerton & Co. of Norwich, Frederick Sage & Co. of Peterborough, S.E. Saunders of East Cowes and Petters Ltd of Yeovil to take up aircraft production. Although the enterprise had no experience in this area of work, it delivered its first subcontracted Short Type 184 seaplane by the start of January 1916, followed by eleven more by June of the same year. The requirement for seaplanes was to become ever more demanding as Germany's U-boats sought to blockade Britain's supply routes, thus placing a stranglehold on the nation's imports. Anti-submarine capabilities were paramount, driving the need for more airborne assets to counter the threat.

One drawback for Phoenix was that it had no local access to open water to test fly its completed aircraft. However, the problem was overcome by transporting the components for final assembly to Blackburn's flight shed at Brough on the Humber Estuary, a site requisitioned by the government. From here, completed machines were tested and flown off the River Humber. In addition to the seaplanes, the company also built twenty Maurice Farman Longhorn trainers, six Short Bombers and a pair of Armstrong Whitworth FK. 10s.

Manning left COW in November 1914 and joined the Royal Naval Air Service. In September 1916 he was sent to join Phoenix as the Admiralty's technical representative. The company was considering forming an aeronautical design and manufacturing team to utilize its in-house facilities. Manning was approached and offered the post of chief designer, which he accepted once his release from the Admiralty had been agreed. He then put his considerable knowledge to good work designing the Phoenix P.1 floatplane, which unfortunately didn't get further than the drawing board. However, orders for the Short Type 184 Seaplane continued, and expansion came in anticipation of ever more aeronautical work. This foresight was rewarded in late 1917 when an order for fifty Short Felixstowe F.3 flying boats was placed, with further examples procured of both the F.3 and F.5 variants. The first F.3 was test-flown at Brough in February 1918. However, not all the contracted aircraft were delivered due to the cancellation of the order owing to the war's end in November 1918.

In November 1917 Phoenix was awarded a contract for two experimental twin-engine flying boats designated P.5 and later named the Cork. The hulls were built by May, Harden & May Ltd of Hythe, Southampton, with Manning and his team responsible for designing the flying surfaces and undertaking final assembly. The machine first took to the skies at Brough on 4 August 1918, but although the Cork flew and performed well, it did not go into production.

Dick, Kerr's activities in wartime rapidly expanded to cope with the demand for munitions and other military products. By 1916 the company had acquired a controlling interest in Willans & Robinson (whose wartime output included the manufacture of aircraft engines) and later in 1917 the United Electric Car Co. Ltd (UECCL). Like Phoenix, Dick, Kerr was also subcontracted to build Felixstowe F.3 flying surfaces at the UECCL factory in Preston, again to be mated with hulls built by other contractors in the country. However, the increase in production brought the need for additional space and capacity and the problem of not having open water near the factory. This conundrum was solved by procuring a site on the North Sea coast at South Shields where two hangars and a slipway were built for the final assembly of the flying boats. The distance between Preston and South Shields by road was around 135 miles, necessitating transportation of the airframes from the west to the east of the country for erection and flight-testing. Towards the war's end land was requisitioned at Lytham, where two hangars and a slipway were built and then utilized to assemble some of the last Felixstowes constructed by the company.

The work undertaken by Phoenix and Dick, Kerr was similar so there was a degree of collaboration between the two firms as they progressed with their ventures, possibly encouraged by the Admiralty, which would put them in a good position for future joint working.

In late 1917 a specification, N.4, was issued for a very large flying boat powered by four Rolls-Royce Condor engines to undertake fleet cooperation and open-seas reconnaissance. Fairey won the order to build three machines with work subcontracted for a pair of them to Phoenix and Dick, Kerr. The latter two companies received one hull each from the Gosport Aviation Company and May, Harden & May respectively. However, only one was completed by Dick, Kerr at Lytham, named *Atalanta* and serialled N119. It first flew from an experimental site on the Isle of Grain on 4 July 1923. Phoenix did not complete their example (serialled N118) as it was cancelled and did not progress further than the construction of the hull. The Fairey-built aircraft, named *Titania* (N129), was completed and first flew in 1925 from Felixstowe. Contemporary photos of the two flying boats show them to be of monumental proportions, rightly being recognized at the time as the largest in the world.

While the war continued, all those constructing military equipment were kept fully employed, upscaling their workforces and premises to keep up with demand. Finally, however, on 11 November 1918 the Armistice was signed, ending the First World War. Although this was good news for the world, it presented difficulties for the many companies involved in the war effort. The manufacturers' once-full order books were quickly emptied and contracts were cancelled before their fulfilment. Such a situation was bad for business and something needed to be done.

Interwar Years

Britain was war-weary after the cessation of hostilities and its military had suffered severe losses throughout. The future for the RAF looked grim as a drastic reduction in its squadrons and personnel was implemented, impacting aircraft manufacturers and all those who supplied spares and equipment. The RAF's existence was also in peril from the Chief of the Imperial General Staff (Head of the Army) Sir Henry Wilson and the First Sea Lord Admiral David Beatty, who wanted to see an end of the fledgling force altogether. Thankfully for the nation neither man got their way, partly due to Marshal of the Royal Air Force Sir Hugh Trenchard, who successfully fought for his young force. He was a man of vision who could foresee the course airpower was likely to take and its importance.

In the meantime, none of this boded well for the aviation industry. Therefore measures were needed to try to help mitigate the situation, impacting not just the manufacturers and shareholders but also their workforces and the many families who relied upon employment and the income generated. Redundancies were inevitable as the workflows contracted, but ways were found to keep at least some workers employed.

Towards the end of the First World War the Lloyd George government created the Ministry of Reconstruction, whose task was to oversee the rebuilding 'of the national life on a better and more durable foundation' in post-war Britain. Phoenix, for one, was finding it difficult to adjust to the peacetime market as most of its manufacturing was dedicated to war matériel. One of the committees set up to discuss the ministry's plan was chaired by P.J. Pybus, managing director of the company, and recommended product diversification. For Phoenix, this would mean making furniture for both home and office. However, the change in direction was not restricted to this one enterprise. Even Avro, one of the nation's foremost aircraft manufacturers in the war, was forced to seek a change of direction by designing and marketing its own automobile, the 10hp Avro Car, and producing toys and tin baths, bassinets (prams) and high-quality billiard tables. Such activities may appear to be going from one extreme to another, but they kept companies solvent and workers employed.

After the Armistice Dick, Kerr set upon expanding its traditional pre-war electrical manufacturing. Accordingly the business spread its net into France and Japan to further its railway and tram equipment construction activities. The anticipation of future orders led the company into an options agreement with COW to use its modern factory to manufacture electrical equipment (the drop in demand by early 1919 saw COW close its aeronautical activities altogether).

It was not long before Dick, Kerr and Phoenix concluded that the pooling of resources and knowledge would ensure the best chances of survival in these most challenging economic times. Therefore discussion began between Dick, Kerr, Phoenix, COW, Willans & Robinson and UECCL. The talks resulted in an agreement to form the English Electric Co. Ltd (EE), the amalgamation coming on 14 December 1918. The new company with so much potential expertise had many strings to its manufacturing bow including mechanical, hydraulic, railway, electrical engineering and, not least, an interest in aviation.

The next period for EE was one of consolidation and a return to its normal peacetime engineering activities. In 1920 the company acquired Siemens Bros Dynamo Works at Stafford, an enterprise recently involved in manufacturing electrical equipment for railway locomotives.

EE's approach to its business activities was successful even in depressed times for industry as profits continued to be declared. While all this was happening Manning, still employed by Phoenix at the merger, continued in his role and was now the chief aircraft designer at the company's London office. He was working at the time on a concept for a large passenger-carrying flying boat, the Eclectic, and several others of both a civilian and military nature, but none of the designs made it any further than the drawing board.

With the new company's activities up and running and returning a profit, in the late summer of 1921 thoughts turned to the aeronautical side of the business. Manning's small team, including Henry Knowler previously employed by Vickers, continued to work on his designs and devised the M.1 single-engine biplane flying boat in response to an Air Ministry (AM) specification for a fleet spotting and gunnery aircraft. However, before embarking on large-scale work, a model was built to allow water tank and wind tunnel tests. The outcome was promising, attracting AM interest, who ordered two 450hp Napier Lion powered prototypes (serialled N148 and N149) and designated M.3 Ayr. Only N148 was completed in 1925. The machine was graceful in appearance with some innovative design features, including the lower wings acting as sponsons. However, it refused to take off from the water on trials at Lytham. Therefore it is no surprise that this spelled the venture's end.

Additional work came for the team when drawings were required to allow the fitting of Napier Lion power plants to the Cork II flying boat, which became the III variant. A further AM specification, 23/23, was issued in August 1922, stating a requirement for a coastal patrol and anti-submarine flying boat. Manning, at the time, was considering further development of the Cork. This specification gave him the impetus to move his ideas forward, which were later pitched to the AM who, in January 1923, gave the go-ahead to construct a prototype named the P.5 Kingston.

However, Manning also had another idea: how to achieve flight with the minimum of power. This thought led to an aircraft very different from what he had recently been designing and more akin to the pioneering days of aviation, the Wren. In August 1922 the *Daily Mail* newspaper offered a prize of £1,000 for the longest duration flight of an unpowered heavier-than-air aircraft. The Royal Aero Club organized the competition on the Sussex Downs at Itford between 16 and 21 October of the same year. The event was won by the Peyret Tandem glider flown by French Aviator Alex Maneyrol with a flight time of 201 minutes. Manning was in attendance in an official capacity, and it was here that the inspiration for the Wren came to him.

Powered by a small 3hp 398cc ABC twin-cylinder motorcycle engine, the envisaged wood and fabric monoplane was simple in concept, looking more like a powered glider. Accordingly, the idea gained interest from the AM when Manning offered to build the diminutive ultra-light machine for £600. Hence a contract was awarded with a specification for an extremely light training aircraft capable of half an hour's flight endurance. Construction was undertaken at Dick, Kerr's works in Preston, where it was completed on 5 April 1923. The prototype was named Wren (retrospectively designated Mk I) and given the serial number J6973. On the day of completion, it was transported by road to Ashton Park in Preston where several short flights were made in the hands of Sqn Ldr Maurice Wright, a test pilot assigned from the AM. Three days later, the Wren was taken on longer flights at Lytham. Finally, on 14 June of the same year, it undertook a flight lasting over an hour with a height of 2,352ft and a speed of 52 mph attained. The Wren clearly met Manning's expectations, leading to the decision by EE to put it into production at the cost of £350 for sale to the public.

In October the *Daily Mail* launched a competition to find a machine capable of flying not less than 50 miles on 1 gallon of fuel and the prize money offered was £1,000. In addition, the Duke of Sutherland pledged a further £500 to establish the most economical light single-seat aircraft. Two slightly modified Wren Mk IIs (designated No. 3 and No. 4) flown by Sqn Ldr Wright and Flt Lt Longton competed in the event held at Lympne, known as the Light Aeroplane Competition. Longton shared the £1,500 prize with A.H. James in his ANEC monoplane with both men achieving 87.5 miles per gallon.

Despite the success and promising potential, the Wrens saw little further use and no orders were forthcoming. So instead the prototype went to the Aeroplane Experimental Establishment at Martlesham Heath where its fate became unknown. Wren No. 3 was stored at Lytham, but eventually found its way onto the civil register as G-EBNV. No. 4 was displayed by EE at the British Empire Exhibition between April and November 1924, after which it took up residence at the Science Museum in South Kensington where it stayed for the next twenty-two years.

Wren No. 4 was returned to EE in February 1946, where it remained until a request came from the Shuttleworth Trust at Old Warden in 1954 to restore the aircraft to an airworthy condition. Using some engine parts from No. 3, the Wren made its first post-restoration flight in the hands of test pilot Peter Hillwood on 25 September 1956. A memorable photo was taken in 1957 of Hillwood flying the Wren at Warton with the futuristic-looking English Electric P.1 and test pilot Roland Beamont in the foreground. The separation between the two machines is incredible: one can barely reach 50 mph, while the other is capable of speeds well in excess of the speed of sound.

Today the Wren is in the care of the Shuttleworth Trust and is kept in airworthy condition. On calm days with wind speeds not exceeding 10 mph and a minimal crosswind component, it can be seen puttering down the grass airstrip, slowly gaining enough momentum to leave the ground and showing surprising agility in the Old Warden circuit. Such a display is rare, but one to be cherished when seen as the observer is taken back to a bygone age of flight. The Wren was the first aircraft designed solely by EE to fly.

The next design to become a reality was the twin Napier Lion IIb powered P.5 Kingston flying boat. The prototype N168 was completed by mid-May 1924 at Preston and transported by road to Lytham for final assembly. Test-flying was put into the hands of Maj. H.G. Brackley, but unfortunately all did not go well as irreparable damage was caused to its hull by flotsam in the Ribble Estuary at the point of take-off on 22 May. Luckily the crew escaped with no injuries.

Five further Kingstons were delivered and flown between late 1924 and early 1925, running through the serial range of N9709 to N9713. Kingston N9712, known as the Mk II, was completed in March of the same year, differing from the others as the hull was constructed from metal. Trials with N9709 at the Marine Aircraft Experimental Establishment (MAEE), Felixstowe concluded it was pleasant in the air and handled well, but its seaworthiness left a lot to be desired. The aircraft met its end when it crashed while taking off on 25 May 1925; thankfully, again, the crew sustained no serious injury. N9712 also flew trials with MAEE, which again proved disappointing. The last Kingston, N9713 and designated Mk III, emerged in March 1926 and, after tests, proved superior to the other marks. However, despite this, no further orders were forthcoming.

Of note, the hull of the original N9712 was sent to the Royal Aircraft Establishment (RAE) at Farnborough for crush testing, which in the end did not occur. Subsequently, after a period of storage on the Basingstoke Canal, the hull was taken at the outbreak of war in September 1939 to Great Bottom Flash in Ash Vale after the AM instructed that it be used as an obstruction to enemy seaplane landings under the Defence of the Realm Act. So even though the Kingston was not to see active service, it did assist the British war effort in a somewhat static way. Here it remained, suffering the effects of time, the elements and souvenir hunters until RAF officer cadets in 1970 rescued a small piece which is now displayed at the Royal Air Force Museum (RAFM), Hendon.

With the failure of the Kingston to gain further interest from the AM, EE could see that the writing was on the wall for them regarding their place in Britain's peacetime aviation industry. The company concluded that it could not hope to compete with the major aircraft manufacturers for the small number of orders being placed. So on 16 March 1926, the day the final Kingston made its first flight from the River Ribble, EE closed its aeronautical department.

Unsurprisingly Manning was made redundant, but went on to work for FIAT in Italy as a consultant for racing seaplane designs and later Simmonds Aircraft, who built small numbers of their Spartan biplane at Woolston near Southampton.

Before the outbreak of war in 1939 he headed up the Airworthiness Department of the British Gliding Association, and a year later he joined the RAE, producing and editing technical papers. After this he was employed by Flight Refuelling Ltd, where he co-invented the hose and drogue inflight refuelling system still in use today. Interestingly, the Lightning made good use of this system during its service career due to its well-known thirst for fuel. Manning retired in 1946 and died on 2 March 1958 after a long and creative period in the aviation industry stretching back to its pioneering days.

The years following the closure of the aircraft department for EE were turbulent as world trade conditions led to losses for the company. As a result COW was sold off and closed along with part of the Dick, Kerr works at Preston. However, never a company to be defeated, and under the leadership of George H. Nelson (Sir George from 1943, Lord Nelson of Stafford from 1955), in the mid-1930s EE were back in the game with the full reopening of their premises at Preston to manufacture diesel locomotives and domestic appliances at Bradford. However, more sinister moves were afoot on the Continent, leading to a conflict the likes of which had never previously been witnessed by the world.

Rearmament and the Second World War

Britain's spending on defence during the 1920s and early 1930s was limited mainly because the government assumed that the British Empire would fight no significant war for ten years, 'The Ten Year Rule'. However, in 1932 the rule was abandoned and thoughts turned to strengthening the nation's military power. Those with an eye on Europe could see the momentum being gained by Hitler and his Nazi Party and the threat to peace posed by this. There was also unrest in the Far East as Japan sought to expand its empire. Furthermore, Britain's position would be perilous if war broke out due to its woefully ill-equipped armed forces. Such a situation existed for the RAF, whose depleted squadrons, years of underfunding and outdated aircraft were significant causes for concern.

As the 1930s progressed, Britain began to rearm and aircraft production became the focus of various manufacturing programmes, many of which fell behind schedule and failed to deliver the required outputs. In addition, EE could see the direction of travel and the threat posed to peace, including the potential for conflict to break out. Therefore the company offered its services to the government to assist in supplying war matériels. Moreover, it was clear that existing manufacturers were struggling to keep up with the demand to produce ever-expanding quantities of aircraft. To overcome this, in 1935 subcontract work was issued to selected companies to form a shadow industry to supply parts, assemblies and, in some cases, complete machines.

In April 1938, Scheme L was implemented to build 12,000 aircraft in two years, allowing EE to come in as one of the companies assisting with production.

Initially it was envisaged that the firm would undertake the final assembly of components and flight-testing. However, it decided to carry out the entire process as a one-stop shop, constructing the complete airframe through to delivery. While floor space was freed up and expansion took place at the Preston factories, the problem of not having a suitable site from which to test-fly was addressed by building an airfield at Samlesbury, 6 miles east of the manufacturing plants.

As EE geared up to receive its first orders, the AM decided in mid-1938 that the company would construct Handley Page Hampden I medium bombers. Powered by two 1,000hp Bristol Pegasus XVIII radial engines, the Hampden, Armstrong Whitworth Whitley and Vickers Wellington formed the backbone of Bomber Command's operations from the earliest days of the Second World War.

The initial contract for seventy-five aircraft came into effect on 6 August 1938. The first, serialled P2062, was delivered by specially built articulated tractor trolleys to the flight shed at Samlesbury on 31 December 1939. Test-flying commenced on 22 February of the following year. Deliveries began in March, and by the close of production in 1942 EE had constructed 770 examples of the 'Flying Suitcase', a nickname given to the type by its crews due to its narrow fuselage and restricted internal space. Sadly the career of P2062 was short. After an initial stint with the Aeroplane and Armament Experimental Establishment (A&AEE), it joined No. 14 Operational Training Unit and crashed on approach to RAF Woolfox Lodge on 31 March 1941; all on board were killed. The Hampden is one machine of which very few survive today. However, one that does is AE436 of No. 144 Squadron, built by EE and under restoration at the Lincolnshire Aviation Heritage Centre, East Kirkby following salvage from Tsatsa Mountain in Sweden where it crashed on 5 September 1942.

Following the Hampden, Handley Page designed the Halifax, a heavy bomber powered by four Rolls-Royce Merlin or Bristol Hercules engines. Some years earlier, it had been recognized that bombers capable of longer range and increased load-carrying capabilities would be required to effectively take the fight to the enemy. The Short Stirling was the first to go into production, followed by the Halifax and Avro Lancaster. Like the Hampden, work was again subcontracted, with EE receiving an order for 200 Halifaxes on 30 April 1940. The initial batch of main assemblies arrived at Samlesbury on 24 June of the same year, and test-flying commenced on 15 August with Halifax II V9976 first taking to the air. The aircraft went on to serve with the Airborne Forces Experimental Establishment and was lost flying with No. 138 Squadron while undertaking an operation for the Special Operations Executive on 21 April 1942. Flying in fog over Bavaria, it crashed into a hillside at Kreuth and all eight crew members were killed.

By the time production of the Halifax ceased the company had manufactured 2,150 machines. Like the Hampden, few of the type have survived into preservation, but Halifax II W1048 'TL-S' of No. 35 Squadron has. This aircraft was shot down by flak onto Lake Hoklingen in Norway on 27 April 1942, flying from Kinloss while conducting a raid on the battleship *Tirpitz*. A skilful landing by Plt Off. D.P. McIntyre ensured minimal damage; six of the seven crew were able to evade capture, but one was taken prisoner due to a broken leg. W1048 was one of a batch delivered between November 1941 and September 1942 by EE from Samlesbury, and today it can be seen at the RAF Museum Hendon following recovery from the lake in 1973.

With the production of the Halifax well under way, on 23 December 1942 EE acquired D. Napier & Son Ltd, a long-established engineering company that also manufactured aero engines. Its Lion powerplant was fitted to many aircraft, including the prototype Kingston. At the outbreak of war the company was developing the Sabre, a complex H-format twenty-four-cylinder, sleeve-valve engine destined to be fitted to Hawker Typhoon and Tempest fighters. However, production did not go as planned at the company's Liverpool factory. The Ministry of Aircraft Production (MAP) was concerned about the delays and asked George Nelson to step in as an advisor to the company in November 1942. The placement led to EE's acquisition of the company and the in-house ability to produce their own aero powerplants was gained.

In the years before the Second World War, thoughts were turning to a new type of airborne propulsion, and the practicalities of the jet turbine were being explored. One young RAF officer, Frank Whittle (later Sir), displayed genius in his endeavours to create a viable jet engine. However, a lack of vision, officialdom and infighting within the AM and government ensured that any lead held by Britain in the field would be lost. If matters had been handled more efficiently, the jet fighter, in all likelihood, could have entered RAF service two years earlier than it did.

Germany was also developing its own form of turbine propulsion. So when intelligence was received from reconnaissance photos showing evidence of the jet-powered Heinkel He 280, panic ensued and all efforts were made to ensure that Britain was not left behind. Finally, towards the end of the Second World War, a new form of propulsion regarded as suitable for powering service aircraft began to emerge. In time, the jet engine ushered in an era where the quest for speed, altitude and performance surpassed anything seen before.

Jet interceptor operations for the Luftwaffe began with the Junkers Jumo 004-B1 axial flow turbojet-powered Messerschmitt Me 262 *Schwalbe* (Swallow) in July 1944, when *Erprobungskommando* 262 began testing the aircraft in the combat environment. In October of the same year, under *Kommando Nowotny*, the M262A-1a became operational with the primary task of intercepting the United States Army Air Force (USAAF) bomber fleets then marauding across Europe. Its sinister shark-like appearance in the skies caused alarm and concern due to its potent firepower (four Rheinmetall-Borsig 30mm cannons) and high speed. Contemporary Allied fighters of the day, who were no slouches, could not hope to catch the new German jet in level flight, but maybe stood a chance in a dive or when one was caught on a final approach to land. Had there been more of the type in service, the outcome of the daylight bombing raids mounted by the USAAF and later Bomber Command could have been very different. Thankfully for the Allies, the German production of military matériel could never match the British, American and Soviet war industries. In time, losses were difficult to make good in equipment and, in the case of the Luftwaffe, pilots. The Germans also tended to over-engineer their war-making products. Granted they had formidable weapons on land such as the Tiger tank, at sea the battleships *Tirpitz* and *Bismarck*, and in the skies the *Schwalbe* and *Komet*, but they never had them in bulk due to their complexity of construction and the technology, unlike the Allies who produced simpler weapons in vast numbers and, in most cases, of a more straightforward design.

This war of attrition was only going to go one way and, in essence, came down to the battle of the war factories with EE playing an essential part in this role. The company was building not only aircraft but also tanks, diesel generators, steam turbines, electrical components, bombsights, rangefinders, munitions, cockpit instruments and even aluminium tee pieces for high-altitude oxygen equipment. The list of products was impressive, but by no means exhaustive as more and varied works came EE's way.

In the war's later years Britain developed two jet fighters, the Gloster Meteor and the de Havilland Vampire. The former, powered by two Rolls-Royce Derwent centrifugal flow (CF) turbojets, began equipping No. 616 Squadron at Culmhead in July 1944, but saw only limited operational use. However, it did achieve some success against Hitler's vengeance weapon, the V-1 flying bomb.

The Vampire was propelled by a single CF Halford H-1 (later Goblin) turbojet and, like its famous stablemate the Mosquito, the diminutive twin-boomed fighter was partially constructed of wood. On 13 May 1944, the MAP notified EE that they had been awarded a subcontract to build 120 Vampires at Preston. Further orders came over the following months; the first, F.1 serialled TG274, flying from Samlesbury on 20 April 1945 piloted by Geoffrey de Havilland Junior. The Vampire entered RAF service with No. 247 Squadron at Chilbolton in April 1946. The company delivered 1,376 examples, including exports to Australia, Canada, France, India, Sweden, Switzerland and South Africa through to 1952, a helpful order keeping EE busy during the cuts that would inevitably come post-war. A survivor of early EE Vampire production, F.1 VF301, can be seen today at the Midland Air Museum Coventry.

Teddy Petter and the Westland Connection

On the day TG274 first flew, Nelson announced that EE was setting up an aircraft division to create machines of its own design. This was a bold initiative, as with the war nearing its end and well-established manufacturers already up and running the move was risky. Undeterred, in July 1944 the company hired the gifted if somewhat eccentric 35-year-old designer and Cambridge graduate William Edward Willoughby 'Teddy' Petter, the son of Sir Ernest Petter, as chief engineer to head up their new venture.

Ernest and his twin brother Percival and their company Petters Ltd were the manufacturers of oil engines. However, during the First World War their enterprise was tasked by the MoS, similarly to Phoenix, to build Short Type 184 seaplanes, leading to the opening of the Westland Aircraft Works at Yeovil in Somerset (renamed Westland Aircraft Ltd in 1935). Teddy Petter joined Westland in June 1929 as an apprentice in the factory before moving to the drawing office and, in time, he became the company's technical director.

His first design was drawn up to meet Specification A.39/34, a replacement for the RAF's Hawker Hector army cooperation aircraft. The result was the Bristol Mercury-powered (Bristol Perseus on the II) Lysander, which first flew in June 1936. The type entered RAF service with No. 16 Squadron at Old Sarum in May 1938 in the army cooperation role. It had an impressive war record, notably with the Special Operations Executive, delivering and retrieving Allied agents from Occupied Europe. Today around fourteen Lysanders survive, with two remaining airworthy in Britain, both IIIA variants: V9367 with the Shuttleworth Collection, Old Warden, and V9312 at Duxford with the Aircraft Restoration Company.

While at Westland, Petter also designed the Whirlwind and Welkin. The former was in response to Specification F.37/35, calling for a single-seat day and night fighter armed with four cannons. Two 885hp Rolls-Royce Peregrines powered the machine, which first flew in October 1938. The aircraft was pleasing to the eye and had an unusual design. It also possessed a devastating armament of four 20mm Hispano cannons and was later adapted to carry bombs, from which it gained the nickname 'Whirlibomber'. If it had been available earlier, the Whirlwind would have been a formidable bomber destroyer in the Battle of Britain. However, development and delivery problems coupled with problematic engines ensured that only 116, including prototypes, were built.

The initial three (L6845, P6966 and P6967) were delivered to No. 25 Squadron at North Weald in May and June 1940 for evaluation as night fighters. However, their stay was brief and the trio had left the squadron by July of the same year. The Whirlwind entered operational service in July 1940 with No. 263 Squadron at Grangemouth and, in September 1941, with No. 137 Squadron flying from Charmy Down. It was put to good use as a fighter, together with ground attack and in anti-shipping roles. In combat it acquitted itself well, but was hampered by a drop-off in performance above 20,000ft, let down by the Peregrine's superchargers. Production ceased in 1941, meaning it was only a matter of time before attrition reduced the aircraft's ranks. With no replacements coming online, it had retired from service by the end of December 1943 with Hawker Typhoons taking its place. Today there are no complete examples in existence.

Both the Lysander and Whirlwind were unusually configured machines. However, when the P.1 appeared some years later, it too was very different from what had gone before, a clear sign of its designer's individualistic and innovative way of thinking.

Petter's third design for Westland was the Welkin (meaning sky or upper air), drawn up to meet Specification F.4/40 and later F.7/41 for a high-altitude fighter with a pressurized cockpit to counter the Luftwaffe's Junkers Ju 86P reconnaissance/bombers, which flew at heights that made them virtually immune to interception. Powered by two 1,560hp Rolls-Royce Merlin 61 engines, the first of two P.14 prototypes (DG558 and DG562) flew in November 1942, but by the time the machine was set to go into production, official interest had waned as the threat from the Luftwaffe failed to materialize. In total seventy-five Welkin Is were constructed, but none went into squadron service; most were flown into storage and subsequently broken up. A further twenty-six engineless airframes were also built and later scrapped, none of which have survived into preservation. However, two Welkins did see service with the Fighter Interception Unit at Wittering, and one was taken from the production line for conversion to a two-seat radar-equipped NF.II night fighter (PF370), which first flew in October 1944.

During test-flying the Welkin was experiencing problems when diving from high altitude at high speed due to the effects of compressibility on the wing's upper surfaces. Westland's chief test pilot Harold Penrose reported that the machine shook as if bumping over cobblestones. As aircraft speeds increased, additional aerodynamic effects came into play, which could create unwanted control inputs and lead to handling difficulties. In some cases the forces could be destructive. In one instance Supermarine Spitfire IX EN409 was dived at RAE Farnborough to ever-increasing Mach numbers, whereby the propeller came off at an estimated speed of Mach (M)0.91. Luckily the pilot, Sqn Ldr Tony Martindale, was able to make a dead stick landing. Many pilots of high-speed piston-engined fighters experienced the effects of flying at higher Mach numbers, but the Welkin encountered problems at a lower speed.

The issue was attributed to the aircraft's thick wing design where aerodynamic forces created a turbulent wake, affecting airflow to the tailplane and elevator surfaces. Petter offered a solution. However, due to official disinterest the proposal was not implemented. Although the Welkin programme failed to make it to an operational status, the project undoubtedly gave Petter a good understanding of high-altitude flight and some of the issues to be expected when flying at higher Mach numbers. With ever-greater speeds being achieved and the as yet unknown effects of the sound barrier approaching, such experience was priceless for Petter's future endeavours.

By anyone's standards Petter was a complicated man; he was also very religious, and in times of stress he would often take long absences from his work. However, towards the war's end he was looking into a twin-engine jet fighter bomber to replace the de Havilland Mosquito in line with Specification B.1/44. The AM called for an aircraft capable of carrying a 4,000lb payload at a top speed of 530 mph with good manoeuvrability at a low level. Petter's early drawing showed a design incorporating twin jet engines mounted side by side and intakes at the front of the fuselage. He was also involved in designing a single-engine naval fighter to Specification N.11/44 which became the Wyvern, but his time working for Westland was ending and he resigned from the company in July 1944.

Various reasons have been cited for his departure, including Westland's cancellation of the proposed jet bomber so that efforts could be put into progressing the Wyvern. Whatever the actual cause, Petter joined EE after a meeting with Nelson, in all likelihood instigated by his contacts at the AM, which included its director Air Marshal Sir Wilfrid Freeman. He may have been a somewhat awkward character, but he had powerful friends who recognized his considerable skills. Westland had no further interest in B.1/44, and it was agreed that he could take his jet bomber concept to his new employer. Around the same time, the AM had selected EE along with Avro, Handley Page and Vickers to develop Britain's first jet bombers, so the timing for Petter to join the company was fortuitous. Furthermore, those in officialdom had recognized EE's eye for detail and quality in all the aircraft manufactured under subcontract during the war and were keen to see the enterprise continue. Such thoughts could be attributed in no small part to the fact that not one of the almost 3,000 machines produced by the company was lost in flight-testing before delivery to the RAF, an achievement not to be underestimated.

With his appointment confirmed, Petter moved north to Preston and an office/development workshop on Corporation Street, around a mile from the Strand Road facility. Barton Motors used the site before the war, and the government later requisitioned it as a training centre. In April 1944 EE took it over to house its new design and development office. Locally it was known as 'TC' from 'Training Centre'. Although it was a bit of a grim place to work spread over two floors, the move was considered only temporary before more suitable premises could be found, but as ever with best-laid plans, this took a bit of time.

One of Petter's first recruits in April 1945 was Frederick William Page (Sir Frederick from 1979), who became chief stress-man and came from Hawker where he had worked as a senior aerodynamicist. As the name of Mitchell will always be linked to the Spitfire, Chadwick the Lancaster and Camm the Hurricane, Petter and Page would, in time, become forever entwined with the P.1 and Lightning, although the latter deserves the true credit.

As for Westland, the company became Britain's leading manufacturer of helicopters and today still exists at its home in Yeovil, although following various mergers it is now part of the Italian Leonardo company.

Post-War

The war in Europe ended on 8 May 1945, and with the dropping of atomic bombs on Hiroshima and Nagasaki, Japan signed the official Instrument of Surrender on 2 September of the same year. The conflict caused untold misery to millions of ordinary people, both within the military and civilians. When hostilities ceased, EE recorded its wartime activities by publishing a book, *War Diary of The English Electric Company Ltd, March 1938 to August 1945*. The work lists the company's achievements and output throughout the war chronologically and makes for compelling reading. The conflict left few people untouched and EE's workers were no exception. Towards the end of the work, details are given about the 3,511 men and women from the firm who served, 102 of whom were lost. In addition, a Roll of Honour lists those who served in all branches of the military and failed to come home to their loved ones. Some of the casualties served with the RAF and Bomber Command.

One EE employee who made the ultimate sacrifice was Fg Off. J.H. Powner, who flew with No. 115 Squadron based at Witchford. On 15 November 1944 he was the navigator on board Avro Lancaster NN706 'KO-B', which took off for an operation to Dortmund. There is no clear evidence of what happened, but the aircraft failed to return to its base. Possible causes could have been a night fighter, flak or a technical issue. The crew of seven all now lie in the Reichswald Forest War Cemetery. Powner's parents William and Florence, who lived in Stafford, would have received notification that their son was missing, but there was hope he was still alive. However, in time his loss was confirmed and he became one of 55,573 aircrew from Bomber Command who didn't come home.

The predicted downturn in aircraft production came into play as the war ended. As a result, the manufacture of the Halifax by EE ceased, although Vampire output proceeded at a reduced rate. As 1945 progressed, Petter continued to work on his ideas for a jet-powered bomber. He also strove to build his team. Coming to EE were Harry Harrison (chief engineer formerly at Westland, joined 1945), Bernard Heath (graduate stress-man, 1945), Don Crowe (chief draughtsman, Handley Page, 1945), Glen Hobday (stress-man, Westland, October 1945), Dai Ellis, Ray Creasey (specialist aerodynamicists, Vickers, mid-1945 and mid-1946), Denis Smith (administration, former RAF Wg Cdr), Frank Roe (graduate, September 1946) and A.E. Ellison (assistant chief designer, Airspeed, 1948). The talent within this group of young engineers and visionaries was soon to reap considerable rewards. They were undoubtedly the new kids on the block, or to some those upstarts in the north who built refrigerators and cookers. Although some may have considered this the case, the team had a distinct advantage in being unbridled by traditional thinking and were willing to challenge preconceived ideas. At the dawn of the jet age, such radical thought would be very much in demand.

Prototype A1

The AM had previously expressed an interest in Petter's design for a jet bomber, so one of the fledgling team's first tasks was to produce a brochure detailing their ideas. In June 1945 a study contract was awarded, allowing more staff to be recruited under Ministry of Labour regulations. The work was to centre on the requirement for an experimental high-speed, high-altitude jet bomber to Specification E.3/45. The original design was for an aircraft with a 12,000lb-thrust Rolls-Royce Nene turbojet housed within the fuselage. Air would be drawn in through wing root intakes and exhausted to the rear. However, there was a problem as such a configuration impinged on bomb and fuel-carrying capabilities. Therefore Petter was fortunate that Rolls-Royce informed him of their proposal to produce a 6,500lb-thrust axial-flow turbojet, the AJ65 (later named the Avon). The availability of the new engine sparked a design revision with the powerplants moved to the wing roots and later to nacelles outboard of the fuselage. Consideration was given to having a swept wing, but Petter decided that a loss of manoeuvrability would ensue and only a slight increase in speed from M0.8 to 0.9 was achieved. Therefore he retained a more conventional wing.

In January 1946 the MoS awarded a contract for four prototypes to meet the now formalized Specification B.3/45. This called for a high-speed, high-altitude unarmed twin-engine jet bomber with a radar bomb-aiming system, crewed by a pilot and navigator and known as the A1.

During 1946 and 1947 detailed design work continued with full-scale mock-ups of the cockpit, nose areas, and the aircraft itself built. However, the design team was outgrowing their Corporation Road home and required something more extensive and appropriate, preferably with facilities to allow test-flying. The present site at TC had a small wind tunnel available in the cellar, but it was recognized that more substantial facilities would soon be needed requiring far more space. The problem was solved when permission was granted to EE to lease a hangar and office block at Warton on the Ribble Estuary, around 7 miles west of the Strand Road factory.

Here a large airfield with three asphalt runways had been built during the Second World War. The original intention was for it to be used by the RAF, but in 1942 allocation went to the USAAF as Base Air Depot 2. The aerial campaign over Europe required a constant stream of replacement aircraft and equipment, with many shipped from the USA by convoy. The depot at Warton specialized in the assembly, major repair and modification of Boeing B-17 Flying Fortresses, Consolidated B-24 Liberator bombers, Republic P-47 Thunderbolts, North American P-51 Mustang fighters and a host of other USAAF types. After the Americans had left the site, EE moved into Hangar No. 25 and in 1947 began building a low-speed wind tunnel and a structural test rig. In the following year testing of A1 models commenced. Conditions at Warton were somewhat primitive and in a fair state of dilapidation. However, it offered space and, not least, runways suitable for the ever-increasing demands inherent in experimental jet flight-testing.

The EE team made good progress during 1947, but external forces came into play and began causing problems. First the MoS advised that the proposed radar in development (H2S Mk 9) was too large to fit in the A1's nose and instead would be allocated to the larger V-bombers destined to come into service later. There was concern at EE that this situation could spell the end of the project, but this was not to be. Instead changes were made to the design, including adding a third crew member to allow for visual bomb-aiming and a reduction in range to 1,000 miles but with an increased bomb load. Specification B.5/47 was issued to encompass the alterations, although the four prototypes continued to be built to B.3/45. The second problem related to the development of the AJ65 now designated Avon RA1, which was not proceeding satisfactorily. In time the issues were resolved and the first flight would take place using the proposed engines, although it was planned for the second prototype to be fitted with Rolls-Royce Nene powerplants just in case problems persisted with the Avon. Such a course of action was prudent to cut down on the potential of delays in flight-testing.

Further uses for the A1 were also put forward, one for high-altitude photoreconnaissance and another for a navigational trainer. It was fortunate for Britain that a modern jet-powered bomber was under development as the country's existing types were becoming obsolete, a situation of great concern as the world had entered the stand-off between East and West known as the Cold War. The Soviet Union was developing its own jet-powered fighters and bombers, therefore it was vital for the country not to be left behind in the race for modernization. Accordingly, in an unusual show of confidence in the A1, the MoS placed an order in March 1949 for ninety B.5/47 bombers, thirty-four PR.31/46 photo-reconnaissance aircraft and eight T.2/49 trainers.

While work at TC progressed, EE continued with the day job of manufacturing Vampires at Samlesbury, supplemented by a contract to modify and upgrade Avro Lincoln heavy bombers. The design and technical team was now firmly established, but one final vital ingredient was missing: a dedicated test pilot. It could be expected that either of EE's two in-house test pilots, J.W.C. Squier or R. Blythe, would be utilized, but they were under the control of Preston's works manager Arthur Sheffield who, to put it mildly, didn't see eye to eye with Petter. The latter expected any pilot working within his experimental programme to report directly to him and no one else. He was determined to do things his way and set about recruiting a suitable candidate. One in the running was Sqn Ldr Tony Martindale of Spitfire with detached propeller fame. The other was Wg Cdr Roland Prosper 'Bee' Beamont DSO*, DFC*, who had served three tours of fighter operations in the Second World War and had test-flying experience gained when working for Hawker, Gloster and de Havilland. He had also flown jets. Petter and Page were keen to ensure that the test pilot was a vital team member whose input was to be valued, and after due deliberation Beamont was chosen for the job in May 1947. From the available evidence, his operational experience swung the decision to employ him.

Beamont was soon put to work as EE had been awarded an MoS contract to investigate compressibility and manoeuvrability at altitudes above 40,000ft. The test-flying was undertaken from Warton utilizing Meteor IV EE545, which had been loaned to the company by the ministry for the duration of the programme and concluded in July 1948. Although Beamont had three crew to service and maintain his aircraft throughout this time, he flew in relative solitude and even flying control was absent. Nevertheless, month after month, he took the Meteor into the high blue yonder, a test pilot in his natural element, alone probing the envelope, taking the risk and yielding the results.

By the end of the same year most of the design team had completed the move from Preston to their new home on the Ribble Estuary. The company continued to develop the facilities at the new site with the construction of a second wind tunnel powered by a Rolls-Royce Nene turbojet allowing testing up to M0.9, and the following year a water tunnel. It was now just under four and a half years since Petter had joined EE, and his efforts at establishing a world-class team of designers and technicians were about to come to fruition. Beamont's workload eased a little, with Peter D. Hillwood joining him as an assistant test pilot in March 1949.

In the spring of this year, parts were under manufacture at TC and Strand Road and brought together at the latter for final assembly and checking. Once this process was complete, the airframe was dismantled and moved to Warton in preparation for reassembly and flight-testing. The first A1 serialled VN799 was ready for roll-out from Hangar 25 in early May. Beamont began taxi trials on the 7th of the month, followed two days later by short and then longer hops. To say that a lot was riding on the upcoming flight would be an understatement. The aircraft was the first design for EE's new team and with the Vampire contract soon to end, the stakes couldn't be higher for reputations and future employment prospects.

Friday the 13th is usually a day best avoided due to its association with bad luck. Not so for EE's chief test pilot, who stared superstition firmly in the eye and prepared for the A1's maiden venture into the skies. On the chosen day the weather was good with no clouds and a light wind. Lining up with Runway 08, Beamont called 'Tarnish One' to Warton. 'Ready to go,' brought the response 'Tarnish One. Clear to take off.' He pushed the twin throttles forward, powering up the Avons and, upon reaching 80 knots, pulled gently back on the control column, taking the machine into Lancashire's sky for the first time. He then flew VN799 for just under thirty minutes, joining up with an FB.5 Vampire chase plane (VV696) piloted by J.W.C. Squier. A problem was noted with the rudder, but apart from this all was well. Preferring to be on the safe side, Beamont descended back to Warton and in his logbook following the flight he wrote: 'Satisfactory, over-balanced rudder.' If these were the only concerns expressed by a pilot of his stature, the company certainly had a winner on its hands. However, there was a darker side to the A1's flight characteristics relating to asymmetric control which could and did catch out pilots, especially when in a low and slow landing configuration.

After modifications to the rudder and further testing in which the A1 was flown to 42,000ft and M0.8, it was allowed to participate at the SBAC Farnborough Air Show in September 1949. Beamont put on a spirited performance, to the extent that the display committee asked him to tone it down at one point. However, it appears that the request went unheeded and the routine carried on in the usual manner. The name Canberra was emblazoned on the aircraft's nose, chosen by Nelson due to Australia's early interest in acquiring the A1 to replace its Avro Lincoln bombers. It was not until January 1951 that an official christening occurred at Biggin Hill.

Following its debut at Farnborough, VN799 was sent to the A&AEE at Boscombe Down in October for a service preview. The Establishment's assigned test pilots from 'B' Squadron commented favourably on the new aircraft, with only minor observations to report. Manoeuvrability tests against a Meteor F.8 were also undertaken at high altitude, where it was found that the Canberra could out-turn and out-climb the fighter. In later annual defence exercises, Canberras were ordered to a lower altitude to give the RAF's defenders of the day a chance to engage. All of this boded well for the first offering from a young and enthusiastic EE team. Stating the well-known aviation adage of 'If it looks good, it flies good', a more accurate comment couldn't have been made. Incidentally, a similar scenario occurred in June 1926 when No. 12 Squadron converted to the Fairey Fox light bomber, which could outpace contemporary fighters. Again, operational restrictions were placed on the Fox in annual defence exercises to give the defenders a chance.

Re-equipping for the RAF with the Canberra began on 25 May 1951 when Beamont ferried B.2 WD936 to Binbrook airfield set high in the Lincolnshire Wolds. No. 101 Squadron, a unit with an incredible wartime record flying Lancasters from Ludford Magna, was the first lucky recipient of this radically different aircraft. The process of replacing the Lincoln had begun, and so started a career with the RAF, Fleet Air Arm (FAA), Ministry of Defence Procurement and RAE lasting until 28 July 2006 when the final Canberra PR.9s serving with No. 39 Squadron were retired at Marham in Norfolk.

In total 925 Canberras were manufactured by EE, Avro, Handley Page and Short, an interesting turn of events with the well-known companies now playing second fiddle to the newcomers. A further 403 were built in the United States as the Martin B-57 and 48 in Australia for the Royal Australian Air Force. It was also exported and served with the air forces of Argentina, Chile, Ecuador, France, Ethiopia, India, New Zealand, Peru, Rhodesia, South Africa, Sweden, Venezuela, West Germany and Zimbabwe.

From the start the Canberra was very capable and set a whole raft of new world records, including flying from Aldergrove to Gander on 31 May 1951 in four hours and eighteen minutes. The machine also achieved a world altitude record of 65,890ft on 29 August 1953.

Today Canberras can be seen preserved in many museums throughout the world. PR.9 XH134 flew in Britain with the Midair Squadron based at Kemble after its RAF career ended until 2015. Anyone at the Abingdon Air and Country Show on 4 May 2014 will recall the stunning display flown by Sqn Ldr Dave Piper (Rtd), where the aircraft's manoeuvrability and grace in the skies were shown to great effect. A final high-speed pass down the runway centre line created a sound truly associated with the early jet designs. Just short of sixty-five years since the A1 first flew, the Canberra could still leave a lasting impression, just as it did at Farnborough in 1949.

The EE team had produced a world-beating design borne out by its sales success and longevity. Its members may have been the 'new kids', but undoubtedly they had wise heads on their shoulders. The Canberra was impressive, but the P.1/ Lightning that followed was even more so.

2

Inception: Prototypes, Development and Armament

'Do you really mean it?' These were the simple words Ernest Beamont uttered to his 6-year-old son Roland when he asked for a flight in an ancient Avro 504. The elderly biplane had landed in a field near the Beamonts' home in Chichester, its pilot offering pleasure flights for 5 shillings. Before he knew it, he and his offspring were strapped in and bouncing across the grass as the machine became airborne; it appeared that yes, Roland really did mean it. During the trip it became very apparent that the young boy was hooked, marking the start of a long and eventful association with aviation that would become the stuff of legend.

In the months following Hitler's invasion of Poland on 1 September 1939, a period known as the 'Phoney War' developed in Europe. There was little fighting during this time, but all this changed on 10 May 1940 when Hitler launched his blitzkrieg against the Low Countries and France. The offensive was a brutally quick, coordinated attack that soon had the defending armies on the back foot, forcing them into retreat.

One unit trying to stem the tide against the Luftwaffe in the air was the Hurricane-equipped No. 87 Squadron from the RAF Component attached to the British Expeditionary Force. Among the squadron's young pilots based at Lille-Marcq was Beamont, now a 19-year-old officer with a passion for nature, fishing, sailing and bird-watching. In a familiar routine, the young aviator raced to the cockpit of his Hurricane, strapped in with the help of a ground crew member and hastily carried out checks in anticipation of scrambling to meet the enemy air fleets. Flying was the young man's obsession, and he must have revelled in having the power of a twelve-cylinder 1,030hp Rolls-Royce Merlin and eight 0.303 Browning machine guns at his fingertips. Granted, its speed of around 320 mph was not that of a Spitfire or Messerschmitt Bf 109E, but nonetheless, for a young pilot, the experience of flying the aircraft must have been exhilarating.

As Beamont primed the engine and pressed the start button, the familiar slow spin of the propeller suddenly changed into a blur of motion with the smell of burned fuel assailing his nostrils. The chocks were waved away and, with a push on the throttle, Sidney Camm's hump-backed creation began its bumpy journey towards flight and the dangers of aerial warfare. His Hurricane was close to the best of what was available to the RAF at the time. The eight-gunned machine was a quantum leap over the Avro 504 in which he had taken his first flight. However, if the young pilot had been told that in a mere fourteen years he would be pressing the start buttons on an aircraft capable of propelling him well in excess of the speed of sound and to heights never before contemplated, he would, in all likelihood, have considered thc thought to be verging on insanity. However, such a scenario was in due course to play out and Beamont would be at its forefront.

Intelligence Received

On 14 May 1941, young naval pilot Eric 'Winkle' Brown RN from No. 802 Squadron of the FAA was tasked to fly a Grumman Martlet from the Royal Naval Air Station Donibristle to Croydon for modifications to the harness system fitted to his aircraft. En route to the south he encountered bad weather over Lincolnshire, and with a lowering cloud base he decided to land at Cranwell and wait for conditions to improve. Once on the ground, he was puzzled by the number of civilians at the airfield and equally by the roped-off hangar with a police guard in place. Despite enquiring, he found no answers forthcoming to his questions.

The next day the situation had not altered to any extent, but as evening approached the weather began to change for the better. As he observed the activities on the airfield he became aware of a small aircraft being wheeled out of the previously closed hangar. Nothing unusual in that, one might think; however, it had no propeller. Intrigued, Brown watched as the small monoplane took to the skies in the hands of P.E.G. Sayers, Gloster's chief test pilot, with a rather strange whistling sound. By pure chance, he had witnessed the maiden flight of the Gloster E.28/39 W4041, Britain's first jet-powered aircraft designed by George Carter from Gloster. The diminutive machine was propelled by a Power Jets W.1 turbojet of Frank Whittle's design. Little did Brown know that in three years he would be piloting the E.28 and later selected to fly Britain's effort to break the sound barrier, the Miles M.52.

In January 1930 Frank Whittle, encouraged by his close friend Fg Off. W.E.P. Johnson filed papers at the Patent Office to protect his invention of a powerplant capable of propelling aircraft higher, faster and with a degree of relatively simple operation. The process led to the armed services being informed, which was standard practice should security restrictions be required to keep items with a military application secret. However, in an act that can only be described as short-sighted, those in official circles had no interest whatsoever in the new propulsion and deemed it unworthy of being kept confidential, thus allowing foreign countries to purchase copies of the patent. So in due course, with the appropriate fee paid, Whittle's patent was soon winging its way to Berlin to distribute among those with a bit more vision. It would take just over a decade for the realization to finally hit home that, in all probability, not taking Whittle's invention more seriously at the time was a monumental mistake, or it could be said that hindsight is a wonderful thing.

As early as May 1940, the British received intelligence reports that the Germans were developing an experimental jet known as the Heinkel He 280. Alarm bells started ringing loud and clear in the AM, leading to an approach to Carter for the design of a belated home-grown jet-powered fighter, submitted in August 1940 to the MAP. In November of the same year, Specification F.9/40 was issued, paving the way for the creation of the Meteor. This was just as well as by May 1943 it was becoming apparent that the Reich could very soon have a combat-capable jet in production. In due course the twin Junkers Jumo 004 turbojet-powered Messerschmitt Me 262A-1a became operational with the Luftwaffe in October 1944. This was a machine of immense speed with a powerful armament of four Rheinmetall-Borsig 30mm MK 108 cannons. Its sinister shark-like appearance caused great alarm among the Allied aircrews, especially those flying bombers with the US Eighth Air Force who encountered it in daylight.

Even more alarming to those in official circles was the information imparted by a captured German engineer who, under interrogation, stated that work was under way on a supersonic plane capable of flying at over 1,000 mph at a height of 59,000ft. Of note, on 2 October 1941 Heini Dittmar of the German Institute for Glider Flying at Darmstadt had flown the third prototype Messerschmitt Me 163 V3 Komet to 623.8 mph. Clearly, from an early date Germany had its sights set on achieving high speeds through alternatives to the propeller, in this case a Walter RII 203 rocket motor. It is possible to conclude that this is what the engineer was referring to when the figure of 1,000 was mentioned, and miles and kilometres had become muddled. However, the higher speed quoted provided the focus for minds in Britain. The twin 30mm MK 108 cannon-armed Me 163B-1a entered service in May 1944 and again shocked the Allies upon first encounters, its bat-like shape scything so fast through bomber formations that gunners couldn't track it. It had a blistering performance, climbing to 30,000ft in just over three minutes. However, once its fuel supply was exhausted it became a glider. The machine had minimal success and was more dangerous to its pilots than its adversaries due to its highly volatile fuel and vulnerability when the rocket motor stopped. Nonetheless, it showed that an aircraft could take off and reach great heights in minutes, far faster than a piston-engine fighter could ever achieve. Keep this thought in mind as it was a blueprint of what was to come.

Sir Ben Lockspeiser had recently been appointed as the MAP's Director of Scientific Research, and such was the concern in Whitehall that he was tasked to form the Supersonic Committee. Some were sceptical regarding the idea of supersonic flight and made strong arguments that it simply wasn't possible. One was Sir Henry Tizard, a very eminent scientist with input to helping develop radar to his credit. He compiled a list of reasons why supersonic flight was impossible, including the heat generated by friction on an aircraft's skin which, in theory, could boil the pilot. However, at a meeting on 4 June 1943, Whittle presented a paper making it clear that such notions were incorrect and, in all likelihood, the Reich was years ahead of the current thinking in Britain and the United States.

It would not be long before further photographic reconnaissance evidence became available to show that the Germans were making great strides to put a viable jet warplane into the skies. Official concern over the prevailing situation saw increased activity, spurred on by Prime Minister Winston Churchill's input in developing and manufacturing jet engines to ensure that the proposed Meteor could be ready for service in the shortest possible timescale.

In addition, the MAP was also in the throes of drawing up Specification E.23/43 for a supersonic research aircraft capable of reaching 1,000 mph and fuel to climb to 40,000ft and half an hour at 700 mph. A Power Jets W.2/700 turbojet of 2,000lb thrust equipped with the new concept of reheat (injecting fuel into hot exhaust gases and thus increasing thrust) was proposed to provide propulsion. At last the situation was being taken seriously.

Phillips and Powis Aircraft, which later became Miles Aircraft Ltd based at Woodley near Reading, was the company selected to undertake the work of design and manufacture. The contract awarded on 15 December 1943 called for two prototypes, with the RAE and the National Physical Laboratory providing specialist input. The M.52, as it was known, consisted of a 5ft diameter cylindrical fuselage with the pilot housed in a bullet-shaped pressurized cabin that could be jettisoned in an emergency. Wings were unswept, biconvex with wide-cord ailerons and split trailing edge flaps; it also featured a variable incidence tailplane.

Work to build the M.52 was carried out in the utmost secrecy, and by February 1946 a mock-up had been completed. It was hoped to have a prototype flying by the summer of the same year, but then came a bombshell. Coming completely out of the blue, Lockspeiser informed Miles that the project would be discontinued. Part of the reasoning was a concern as to whether the biconvex wing was up to the job following research obtained from German sources. There were also worries over the safety of any pilot testing the aircraft. However, Eric Brown had been lined up to fly the machine and he certainly had no qualms about flight-testing.

Lockspeiser stated: 'The impression that supersonic aircraft are just around the corner is quite erroneous, but the difficulties will be tackled using rocket-driven models. We have not the heart to ask pilots to fly high-speed models, so we will make them radio-controlled.'[1]

The driving force for using this type of propulsion and crewless vehicles appears to have come from no less a figure than Vickers' Dr. Barnes Wallis, who undoubtedly had the AM's ear. His views on risking lives came from the loss of fifty-three Bomber Command airmen during Operation Chastise (the Dambusters Raid) on 16/17 May 1943. As the inventor of the Upkeep mine – the 'bouncing bomb' – used during the operation, he was very badly affected by the loss of so many young men as he felt he was responsible for their failure to return by coming up with the idea in the first place. From then on he was averse to putting humans in harm's way. Subsequent testing by RAE/Vickers of small-scale models of the M.52 carried aloft by a Mosquito was plagued by technical issues, but one did reach M1.38, bearing out what those who had designed the full-size machine probably already knew.

Following the M.52 debacle and as if to rub salt into the wounds, Sir Stafford Cripps, Minister of Aircraft Production, ordered all the project's drawings, research materials and wind tunnel information to be sent to the Americans. To date there has been no satisfactory answer as to why the project was terminated with such haste. However, time would show that supersonic flight was indeed just around the corner as on 14 October 1947, Captain Chuck Yeager USAF flew the Bell X-1 to M1.06 over Muroc air base in California. One wonders how much of Miles' research contributed to this feat as there was a striking resemblance between the M.52 and X-1. Unfortunately, any lead the British had in advancing its aviation knowledge was lost through a lack of foresight from those in power. Sadly, this would become an all too familiar occurrence in the future.

A friendly nation had broken the sound barrier, but as per the usual course of events it wouldn't be long before a hostile country took a similar route. On 26 December 1948 a turbojet-powered Lavochkin La-176 became the first Soviet aircraft to achieve supersonic flight in a shallow dive. The quest for speed was on.

The Supersonic Quest Continues

Although official documents and specifications referred to in the following text detail the term fighter, primarily the Lightning concept was that of interceptor and it will be described as such from here on.

While in official circles supersonic flight was considered far too dangerous to contemplate to any real extent, others, by private means, were looking into ways of addressing the issue. Such a situation was interesting as it will be remembered that in the pioneering days of aviation the government and the military could see no use for aircraft and therefore came up with excuses not to get involved in their development. Individuals were left to take their ideas forward, typically at their own cost and effort. Only when it was seen that potential foreign enemies could gain an advantage and leave the sovereign nation wrong-footed did those in officialdom show a more willing attitude to maintaining the balance. It was therefore fortunate for Britain that 'Teddy' Petter from EE was contemplating thoughts of supersonic flight.

He rightly considered that other countries, notably the United States and the Soviet Union, would likely be planning to send piloted aircraft through the sound barrier. He was also aware that the A1 twin jet bomber – to emerge as the Canberra – which he had designed but was yet to fly had a predicted performance that could outrun and outclimb the RAF's contemporary interceptors, the Meteor and Vampire. With the machines coming off the production lines already approaching obsolescence, there was a real danger that Britain could be left behind and become vulnerable without some radical thinking in re-equipping the modern-day air force. The threat for the moment came from the Tupolev Tu-4 Bull, a copy of the Boeing B-29 Superfortress piston engine strategic bomber that could reach Britain (some potentially armed with nuclear weapons in the future). The Meteor and Vampire could deal with this type of bomber, but one powered by turbojets at high altitudes and speed was a different matter.

The government still seemed unable to grasp that a machine similar to the A1 in an enemy's hands may render Britain's defences ineffective if the RAF could mount no capable opposition. More worryingly, the Soviet Union's first jet-engined bomber, the Ilyushin Il-28 Beagle powered by a pair of Klimov VK-1s turbojets (reversed-engineered Rolls-Royce Nene sold to the Soviets by the Labour Government in 1947), was soon to enter service with performance similar to the Canberra, although without the range capabilities and a lower service ceiling. The Il-28 was not a direct threat to Britain, but from here on Soviet designs would only improve with subsequent increases in speeds, range and performance being attained. In addition, the problem would be further exacerbated if a belligerent power created a supersonic bomber. Even though the swept-wing transonic Hawker Hunter and Supermarine Swift were in development, neither could hope to catch a high-flying supersonic target. Nonetheless, the Meteor and Vampire assisted the RAF in the first steps of the operation of jet aircraft and gave valuable insight into what to expect over the subsequent decades.

Although the Second World War had ended, it was evident that peace might not last as the Soviet Union under Joseph Stalin was seeking to expand its influence within Europe. This situation put the West and the East on a collision course as the two ideologies of capitalism and communism clashed, leading to a period known as the Cold War. As a result, any hopes that conflict would not erupt again were dashed and it was necessary to prepare to defend Britain from possible Soviet aggression.

Slowly the realization began to dawn in Whitehall of a gap in the country's defences regarding a high-speed, high-altitude interceptor and the risk this posed to national security, possibly in part influenced by Petter through his contacts at the AM. As a result, in late 1947 Experimental Requirement 103 (ER.103) was issued by the MoS, which sought to explore ideas for an aircraft in the low supersonic and transonic speed ranges. Interest came from several companies including EE and Fairey Aviation. The latter submitted a proposal to become the Delta 2, a pure research project that would take the World Air Speed Record of 1,132 mph on 10 March 1956 piloted by Lt Cdr Peter Twiss DSC* and later OBE.

Petter and his team began working on their concept in May 1948, although they were heavily involved with the A1 project at the time. From the outset it was clear that they knew what was required in their design for a machine to achieve controlled supersonic flight. The term 'Area Rule' was not yet used, but its principles were understood at Warton partly due to the vast amount of German research available to the company. For example, as an aircraft approaches M1.0, the airflow around the fuselage and wings exceeds M1.0, known as the transonic speed range. As the supersonic flow develops shock waves form, which are pressure boundaries where airflow moves from supersonic to subsonic. In turn wave drag is produced, requiring a significant amount of thrust to overcome. The solution to this problem is to ensure that the aircraft's cross-sectional area changes smoothly and to minimize its frontal area.

While work was progressing at Warton, in May 1948 Beamont found himself in the United States on an official visit to gain experience with the country's latest experimental fighters and bombers. One he flew at Muroc Lake was the swept-wing North American XP-86, later designated the F-86 Sabre. On 21 May he recorded reaching M0.99-1.01 in a dive from 36,000 to 27,500ft. If this were the case he would have been the first British pilot to penetrate the sound barrier. However, it was noted that no one had heard a sonic boom on the ground, which was expected for an aircraft passing through the speed of sound. Subsequent investigation found that the pitot tube was situated in a position liable to be affected by shock waves and turbulence in the airflow. Such a situation could cause errors in the machmeter reading of 0.03 and 0.04, so in all likelihood the speed achieved was M0.98. Nonetheless Beamont, albeit briefly, was now the fastest pilot in Britain.

The accolade of being the first British pilot to exceed the speed of sound went to John Derry who, while flying de Havilland DH.108 VW120 on 6 September 1948, inadvertently reached M1.02. With the aircraft in a dive at M0.85 it began to exhibit unpleasant flight characteristics, which soon developed into a state of control loss at M1.0. Derry had to resort to using the trim tabs to regain stable flight. However, a subsequent investigation found that he had reached M1.02. Luck was on his side as previously on 27 September 1946 Geoffrey de Havilland Jnr had lost his life piloting DH.108 TG306 which broke up in a dive having reached M0.875.

By July 1948 the EE team had produced several drawings. The first sketches showed an aircraft with twin engines mounted in a staggered configuration, one above the other within the fuselage. Such an arrangement reduced drag and eliminated asymmetric problems in the event of an engine failure. Of note, the position of the powerplants changed fore and aft over various revisions to ensure that the most efficient intake duct design could be obtained. Further drawings showed different intake configurations and pilot positions. As the concept advanced, a single air intake in the nose became favoured as it reduced the machine's cross-section. The planform showed swept wings, which in profile were mounted mid-fuselage. A swept tailplane with a delta planform mounted on its tip was also detailed, together with the option of a swallowtail.

On 3 August 1948 the MoS awarded EE a design study contract based on ER.103 entitled 'Transonic Research and Fighter Aircraft'. This enabled the company to begin the work required to submit its formal proposal, which was ready three months later on 1 November as a brochure. The design drawings 'General Arrangement of Transonic Aircraft Mk I Wing EAG 1973 (EE's project drawing number) and Mk II Wing EAG 1974', like the A1, were relatively simple. The company's philosophy was not to overcomplicate designs as such action could result in delays and increased costs.

The submissions showed a simple tubular fuselage with swept-back wings and the delta form's rear section cut away. Freddy Page believed that such a wing layout would offer a more effective way of achieving satisfactory speed and handling throughout the flight envelope and not just when supersonic. In addition, the proposal provided either unarmed or armed variants with cannons mounted in the wing roots and provision for a ranging radar in the intake lip.

Some interesting thought had been given to the tailplane, and when the drawings emerged they showed twin fins mounted rather elegantly at the tip of each extremity. The usual train of thought with high-speed designs was to mount the tailplane on top of the fin, which created aerodynamic problems relating to deep stalling. However, the EE team were known for radical thinking and looked for a more practical way to provide adequate control surfaces and favoured an all-moving tailplane, which created a further problem in that a thicker fin was required on which to hang the assembly. In turn this would induce drag and potentially develop an additional concern. If the pilot abandoned the aircraft in an emergency he could hit the tailplane. To overcome this, the proposal of using twin fins was put forward.

As speeds began increasing, it became apparent that control surfaces could lock due to increased aerodynamic forces, potentially leading to disastrous consequences. The solution was the use of powered controls. To prove the concept, successful trials were conducted by Beamont and J.W.C. Squier in October 1948 from Samlesbury using a Handley Page Halifax fitted with a Fairey Hydraulics Servodyne powered elevator. The use of hydraulic reversible screw jacks removed the feel that a pilot could expect to experience when operating more conventional controls. However, this was replicated artificially to ensure that control inputs capable of over-stressing the airframe could not be applied. Subsequently the P.1 (as the prototype would be designated) was fitted with Hobson hydraulic units when its turn came to fly.

With the external appearance of the proposed design now clear to see, it's time to turn to the method of propulsion. It was well-known that centrifugal-flow jet engines were, overall, more rounded and bulkier than their axial-flow counterparts. There was also an acceptance that the frontal area of a supersonic aircraft needed to be kept to a minimum to reduce drag. Therefore when it came to engine choice, it was proposed to install a pair of axial-flow Armstrong Siddeley (AS) Sapphire turbojets, taking combustion air through the nose and a single central bifurcated simple pitot intake duct. While it was possible for one engine to provide enough power for supersonic flight, the EE team were looking to the future when their design could become a much heavier interceptor and would need more power. Therefore adopting two axial-flow engines which had the scope for increased power output as development continued was a sound course and showed excellent forward thinking.

Unlike the A1, there was no need to keep the fuselage area clear for the carriage of bombs, allowing the turbines to be enclosed internally. The layout, however, was somewhat unorthodox. The lower powerplant was mounted towards the front of the fuselage and the upper further to the rear. Such a configuration resulted in the lower engine having a long jet pipe which, in operation, created extreme heat. With fuel, hydraulic and electrical lines running within the fuselage, it is not difficult to see why leaks, short circuits or wiring faults had more than enough potential to cause fires. In time this would become one of the Lightning's significant weaknesses. The chosen layout was also the bane of many engineers' lives regarding maintenance and servicing, with access limited to vital components. Another issue with the fuselage-installed engines was the lack of internal fuel space, a factor that, in turn, restricted endurance and range. All this aside, the EE team had still come up with a winning design at a time when the difficulties of supersonic flight were still not fully understood. To their credit, not much change was required to their initial design submission other than rethinking the tailplane area and wing sweepback, which was to attract a fair amount of official interest.

Tailplane Trials and Tribulations

While the MoS and the RAF considered the EE submission in December 1948, the team gave further thought to their design for a transonic interceptor. Further drawings showed changes to the wing and tailplane. Drawing EAG 1991 detailed the Mk III wing with a 60-degree sweep, closely resembling the early Lightnings. A large central fin has also been added as a dashed line. The following month the design received its official designation of P.1 (the P denoting Project). By February, drawing EA/5/001 showed that a single fin had been added with the tailplane mounted partway down.

Discussions regarding engine choice continued with the AS Sapphire and the Rolls-Royce Avon in consideration along with suggestions from other manufacturers. There was also talk of the benefits of reheat for the proposed design. However, with this protracted debate EE became concerned about the delay that could ensue.

At the tail end of 1948, the RAF issued a draft of Operational Requirement (OR) 268 for a transonic interceptor. In March 1949 it was decided that EE should be given preliminary approval to develop the P.1 to have operational capabilities. The MoS officially instructed the company to manufacture one-eighth and 4in scale models for wind tunnel tests at the Warton facility. The company had had the foresight previously to invest in this type of transonic/supersonic research equipment, allowing it to be self-sufficient and not rely on others regarding testing needs. Additionally, a quarter-scale model was sent to Rolls-Royce for ducting tests. The approval also called for a full-scale mock-up of the aircraft and if preliminary tests were successful, prototypes would be ordered in around six months.

The situation in Europe was still giving concern, with the Soviet Union continuing to cause instability. Not content with helping to overthrow the democratically elected government of Czechoslovakia in February 1948, further aggression came when access to Berlin was cut off in June, resulting in the famous airlift to keep the city supplied. In April 1949 the United States and eleven other countries, including

Britain, formed the North Atlantic Treaty Organization (NATO) to counter the threat posed by the East. Essentially, if any member state was attacked, all the others within NATO would come to its aid. Later, in 1949 news came that the Soviets had successfully detonated an atomic bomb. Far from becoming safer, the world was becoming a more dangerous place. Consequently, Labour's Attlee government was forced to increase the budget for defence spending.

On the home front, the MoS issued a formal contract titled 'Design Study for a Fighter with Transonic Performance' on 12 May 1949. Around the same time, OR.268 was revised and called for a

> single-seat fighter land plane for day interception duties. Primarily, it is required for operating in Europe, but it is desirable that it is capable of operating in any part of the world. The primary role of this aircraft will be the destruction of high-speed, high-altitude bombers in daylight, as soon as possible after the bomber is first detected on the early warning system. Great importance, therefore, is attached to quick take-off, the highest possible acceleration and highest rate of climb. The Air Staff would like a minimum speed of M1.2 or higher if achievable. The rate of climb should be such that by the time the pilot touches the button to start the first engine, to 50,000 feet, it is not more than 6 minutes. The aircraft is required to carry a minimum of two 30mm ADEN guns, and the possibility of having rocket or long-range armament should be considered. A gyro gun sight is required with radar ranging. To this end, allowance must be made for a small scanner.[2]

Anyone who remembers the Lightning in its service days will be able to relate to OR.268, as the wording matches in many respects how the aircraft was operated during a Quick Reaction Alert (QRA), which will be explained in more depth later. ER.103 and OR.268 fitted well with EE's thinking as their proposal was for a dual-purpose machine for research purposes and countering a high-speed, high-altitude threat.

To allow for procuring an armed variant of the P.1, the MoS issued a draft specification in September 1949, F.23/49, detailing a requirement for a supersonic day interceptor, which closely followed the stated aims of OR.268. Responding, EE submitted a further brochure on 1 October 1949 with a design showing the P.1 now with the wings and tailplane mounted low on the fuselage. However, this was not an end to the tinkering, as further wind tunnel testing showed the optimum position for the wing was higher up the fuselage. Consequently, the tailplane was moved to its lowest possible position. The layout of the engines was also confirmed with the lower to the fore and the upper aft. Finally, a revised general arrangement drawing was issued on 18 October. From this, it is possible to see the classic lines of the Lightning beginning to emerge.

One thing guaranteed to cause an uproar among the 'boffins' is radical thought. So when RAE Farnborough, which already had concerns over the

P.1's design, became aware of the latest revisions, there must have been sharp intakes of breath, head-shaking and eyes looking skyward. Wing sweep of 60 degrees was one thing, but the position of the tailplane, what were those in the north thinking? But Petter was confident that the design was right and, in time, would be proven correct. In a letter to the MoS, he makes his views clear: 'We are studying very carefully the question of sweepback and the pros and cons of 60 degrees compared to 45 and 50 degrees. I think that there may be good reasons for sticking to the present proposal, subject, of course, to the wind tunnel tests.'[3]

In the following years, delta-wing aircraft such as the Dassault Mirage, Convair F-102 Delta Dagger and F-106 Delta Dart began to come into service. These clean designs eliminated horizontal tail surfaces and reduced supersonic drag. However, the price paid was a loss of lift in manoeuvre when pitch control was achieved by the use of elevon. Although fine creations in their own right, the pure deltas lacked the manoeuvrability that could be achieved by aircraft fitted with a low tailplane. Machines with high 'T'-configured tails were also to experience their fair share of aerodynamic problems, notably the Gloster Javelin and Lockheed F-104 Starfighter, and the Hawker Siddeley Trident and BAC 111 airliners.

With work continuing and gathering pace around the P.1, Petter decided to resign from EE's Aircraft Division. In February 1950, he took up a position at Folland where, in time, he designed the Gnat and Midge jet fighters. His place was taken by Page, who became chief designer with overall responsibility for the P.1 project. Although Petter is often credited with the creation of the Lightning, it was Page who had the most involvement in seeing the design off the drawing board and into service.

On 1 April the company received a contract, 6/Acft/5175/CB.7(a), to construct three airframes, two prototypes, WG760 and WG763, and a third, WG765, for static test work. One was to be fitted with only the equipment essential for aerodynamic testing and handling, while the second would be kitted out to reflect what is expected of an operational machine. The two trains of thought proposed for the P.1, supersonic research aircraft and, ultimately, supersonic interceptor, can clearly be seen.

Behind the scenes, the RAE still expressed concern over the design of the P.1 and its potential low-speed handling due to sweepback and low-mounted tail. As a result, the MoS decided a research aircraft should be built to allay these fears. The company chosen to fulfil the task was Short Brothers and Harland Ltd of Belfast. Designated the SB.5, this was a flying full-scale aerodynamic testbed of the P.1, fitted with a fixed undercarriage and the option for the wings to be swept to 50, 60 or 69 degrees. It also featured a tailplane that could be mounted on the top of the fin or under the rear fuselage. There was an element of forward thinking being applied as it was hoped the SB.5 would be able to highlight any issues with the P.1's handling characteristics before its first flight, reducing the chances of delays occurring.

Interestingly, an amendment to an earlier RAE report from June 1952 concluded that following transonic wind tunnel testing at Warton of a 1/8th scale P.1 model, previous concerns over the low tailplane were not entirely justified.

However, the SB.5 was to go ahead under the insistence of the MoS, with WG768 first flying in the hands of Short's chief test pilot Tom Brooke-Smith at Boscombe Down on 2 December 1952. To cut a long story short, the aircraft was flown in the various configurations, and it was concluded EE had been correct in its assumptions all along. The proposed wing sweep and tail positioning gave the predicted satisfactory handling characteristics.

The test-flying the SB.5 did, however, contributed to one aspect of the P.1's wing. Aerodynamicists had predicted there could be air flow disturbance over the ailerons at close to landing speeds caused by a leading edge vortex running outboard as incidence increased. To overcome this, a small notch was cut into the leading edge, alleviating the need for drag-inducing wing fences. In addition, EE was looking for somewhere to position inward vent valves for the P.1's fuel tanks, so the notch provided a dual purpose. In turn, all future Lightnings would incorporate this aerodynamic feature. To some, the SB.5 was a complete waste of money, yielding little useful information to the P.1 project. To others it played an important role in the development of supersonic flight. One suspects that the answers lie somewhere between the two conflicting viewpoints.

Progress, Threats and Future Considerations

The fuselage of the P.1 consisted of three sections and was made up as follows. The front contained the pressurized cockpit with a Martin-Baker ejection seat, part of the intake duct, the forward undercarriage bay and space for equipment. The centre and rear housed the two engines, intake ducts, jet pipes, fin and tailplane. Finally, the wing torsion boxes and wings, each with internal fuel tanks and the main undercarriage bays, were joined at the fuselage centre line close behind the cockpit.

For a protracted period, a debate had been ongoing about the type of engine to be fitted to the prototype. So, with some relief to EE on 20 March 1950, the MoS confirmed that the preferred option was a pair of AS Sapphire AS.Sa.5 un-reheated turbojets rated at 8,100lb thrust each.

During the same year, changes occurred to F.23/49 with requirements stating the proposed machine should be able to fly supersonically in level flight without reheat. Interceptions were to be made by both day and night under ground control.

On the world stage, an alarming event occurred on 25 June 1950 when North Korea, with the backing of the Soviet Union and later China, invaded their southern neighbours. In response, the United States and the United Nations sent forces to counter the North Korean attack. However, during this conflict, the Western allies came up against the Mikoyan-Gurevich MiG-15 Fagot, powered by a Klimov turbojet and often flown by experienced Soviet pilots. This machine was a match for the United States Air Force F-86 Sabres and completely outclassed Royal Australian Air Force Meteor F.8s. Petter's earlier prediction of an unfriendly foreign power developing a potent fighter had come true.

The need for a home-grown supersonic interceptor became increasingly urgent as foreign adversaries pushed ahead with more advanced aircraft. In the interim, to ease concerns in Britain over the lack of an effective resource, 430 Canadair-built Sabre F.2 and 4s, the only fighter capable of countering the MiG-15, were procured for the RAF until the Hunter and Swift were ready to come into service. The Sabre began equipping home squadrons in 1953.

The following year, the Soviets introduced the Tupolev Tu-16 Badger into service, a swept-wing subsonic bomber powered by two Mikulin AM-3 turbojets, which could propel the aircraft to 650 mph with a ceiling height of 42,000ft and a range of 4,500 miles. It could be conventionally or nuclear-armed and, more worryingly, eventually it would be capable of carrying cruise missiles, a stand-off weapon that could be launched many miles from the target.

Also, around the same time, a further Soviet bomber came into use, the Myasishchev M-4 Bison-A. Powered by four Mikulin AM-3A turbojets, the swept-wing aircraft could attain 588 mph with a 5,600-mile range and service ceiling of 36,000ft. It could carry conventional and nuclear weapons, but on the whole, it failed to meet its set mission and could not reach the United States, and few were built. A more powerful navalized version followed, the M-3 Bison-B, which remained in service until 1994. As predicted, the Soviets were advancing their designs, increasing the threat to Britain. In time, the Lightning force would conduct regular interceptions as these aircraft probed the nation's defences and reactions.

As EE continued its quest to build the P.1, in 1951 official thought was given to turning the machine into an interceptor, requiring more powerful engines, navigation aids, radar and an integrated weapons system. In February 1952, the company was informed the MoS intended to order three more prototypes under F.23/49 Issue 2, which now included a Machmeter to M1.8, an airspeed indicator to 750 knots and an altimeter for heights to 70,000ft. Accordingly, the P.1 was redesignated to P.1A (referred to as such from here on in) to differentiate the research aircraft from the proposed prototype interceptor which became the P.1B.

P.1A's First Flight

Work continued during 1954, constructing the P.1A at Strand Road, Preston. Although engineless, functional testing of hydraulics and flight control systems was undertaken.

Before flying for the first time, it was known that the P.1A would have a high landing speed of at least 160 knots due to its weight and wing loading. However, this could be even higher in the region of 180 or 200 knots should there be low speed or stability problems. At 1,900 yards, Warton's runway was considered too short for the P.1A's first flight. Therefore the aircraft was moved by road around June 1954 to Boscombe Down's 'A' Squadron hangar, where it was reassembled and the engines installed, the airfield's 3,000-yard runway giving an additional margin of safety should it be required. Anyone driving down the A303 towards Amesbury will note the impressive ribbon of undulating concrete stretching off in a westerly direction. It is still in use today, although with far less exotic airframes leaving their tyre marks on its surface.

On 2 July 1954 engine testing began, with the first taxiing runs made by Beamont on the 24th; WG760 was briefly airborne at 125 knots on this day. Short hops were undertaken on the 26th, and it was concluded that the aircraft was responsive and stable in all axes at take-off and landing. By 2 August 1954, he was satisfied the P.1A was ready for flight and planned to take to the air the following day. However, nature intervened and cast a thick mist over the Wiltshire countryside. At a loose end, Beamont decided to use his downtime and climbed into the cockpit to review checklists and briefing notes. Unfortunately, with almost comical overtones of 'don't press that button', he did and inadvertently set off the engine bay fire extinguishers. Undoubtedly he vacated the area with a somewhat sheepish expression, followed by the stares and head-shaking from those who had to clean up the resultant mess.

On 4 August there was an air of anticipation at the airfield as the early morning mist lifted, and preparations were made for WG760's maiden flight. Visibility was around 3 to 4 miles with a little thin high cloud. The sleek aluminium lines of the P.1A awaited on the concrete pan to be put through its paces by Beamont. What were his thoughts as he walked out to this machine so different to his past mounts? It was far removed from the Hurricane, Typhoon and Tempest he knew so well and in which he had faced previous dangers. The Canberra and Sabre with which he was familiar were engineering marvels in their own right, but the prototype before him was in a different league altogether. If its performance lived up to that predicted, he was in for quite a ride. Of note it was forty years to the day since Britain had declared war on Germany and the beginning of the First World War. Think of the Avro 504s available to the Royal Flying Corps (RFC) at its outbreak, then consider the P.1A that Beamont was about to fly. Clearly, aeronautical development had moved at pace over the preceding four decades.

Strapping himself in, Beamont went through his pre-flight checks while EE test pilot Peter Hillwood taxied out Canberra B.2 WD937 to act as chase plane. Observing the proceedings undoubtedly with a sense of anxiety was Freddy Page, a man who had put his heart and soul into the project, not to mention his reputation. Accompanying him were Alec Atkins, chief flight test engineer and Don Horsfield, flight test project engineer.

Content that all was in order, Beamont pressed the starter buttons, waved away the chocks, closed the canopy and began his journey towards flight. Lining up to hold at Runway 24 with leading and trailing edge flaps set, Beaumont performed final control checks and was ready to take Britain's supersonic aspirations into the air for the first time. Then, calling up air traffic for clearance, the clear, measured response came: 'Boscombe Tower to *Tarnish* 1. Wind 260 degrees at 8 knots. Air temp 16 degrees [Centigrade]. You are clear all the way.'

Pushing the throttles forward, the idling whine of the Sapphires increased to a roar, and the P.1A began to roll, with back pressure on the stick, the aircraft rotated at 145 knots. As Beamont settled into his schedule of tests, he flew to a height of 13,000-14,000ft, attaining M0.85. However, he was becoming concerned as the weather started to deteriorate with a thick bank of cloud coming in from the north, south and west. He called up Boscombe for radar assistance, but there was no response. The situation became difficult as his radio calls continued to go unanswered, forcing him to consider descending beneath the cloud base to ascertain his position. Finally, a small break in the cover allowed the pilot to see a bend in the River Avon near Amesbury. He now knew where he was and returned to Boscombe below the cloud base, which had no approach or runway lights showing despite the weather conditions. Unperplexed by the events, Beaumont elected to undertake some low-level handling until the weather further hampered his efforts. He decided it was best to land. With the undercarriage indicator showing a welcome three greens, he touched down at 140 knots and streamed the brake 'chute. Although nature had conspired against the flight, it was a success from a technical point of view but a bit of a disaster with regard to communications and procedure. In summary, Beaumont wrote: 'In this short flight, the aircraft proved pleasant and straightforward to fly, with take-off and landing operations lacking in complication. The over-sensitivity in lateral control will require careful observation during subsequent tests.'[4]

So there it was, the day mainly ended well. Of course, through further testing, there would be concerns over certain aspects of handling and equipment functioning, but these would be minor and addressable in the grand scheme of things. To consider the P.1A flew like a dream 'straight out of the box' would be wrong, as there are always teething troubles, especially with a new complex machine. The team was in reasonably uncharted territory, and the whole point of the project was to push boundaries and, in doing so, things would inevitably go wrong. However, progress needed to be made, and it was now time to look at taking the P.1A through an invisible phenomenon, the sound barrier.

Through the 'Barrier'

On 11 August 1954, the P.1A was at 30,000ft over the Solent when Beamont went to full throttle and reached a speed of M0.98. The acceleration paused, but it later transpired from instrumentation records that WG760 had reached M1.0 true, and Britain had its first genuinely supersonic aircraft. The P.1A flew well and was stable with no signs of roughness, although Beaumont later commented that the controls were becoming less crisp, indicating reduced aerodynamic damping. With fuel now a factor, he returned to Boscombe and was content that the 60-degree wing sweep and low tailplane was a satisfactory combination.

Two days later, Beaumont was at 40,000ft over Swanage. Banking to port and heading up the Channel at full throttle, the P.1A reached M0.98 and again hesitated. Then, with little drama or sensation, the Machmeter jumped to M1.01 and increased to M1.08. The transition was so smooth it went almost unnoticed, and the aircraft responded normally with no apparent difficulty. Furthermore, handling was satisfactory, but as ever the fuel state became a factor and Beamont undoubtedly, with reluctance, headed back to Boscombe. With the airfield on the nose, he put WG760 into a gentle dive and, with a burst of power, nudged the aircraft up to M1.02. Those on the ground were treated to a loud double sonic boom; proof, if needed, that supersonic success had been achieved.

Over the coming weeks testing continued, but by the time of the 1954 SBAC Farnborough Air Show held between 6 and 12 September, WG760 did not have the required ten hours of flying needed to allow the prototype to display. However, the machine was not entirely left out as during a routine flight it flew over the airfield at 40,000ft. Eagle-eyed observers on the ground may have noticed the contrail, but did anyone realize what it was? On 23 September 1954, WG760 was returned to Warton where flight-testing continued over the winter.

Elsewhere, world events were unfolding. In May 1955, the Warsaw Pact was formed, bringing Albania, Bulgaria, Czechoslovakia, East Germany, Hungary, Poland and Romania into a military alliance with the Soviet Union. However, unlike NATO whose members retained their own military command structures, countries in the Pact were subordinate to Moscow.

Back at home, a second P.1A, WG763, joined the flight test programme on 18 July 1955 and had a ventral 250-gallon fuel tank, two 30mm ADEN (Armament Development Enfield) cannons and toe brakes fitted. Again, flight testing provided valuable information, leading to further modifications to the airframe. Later in its career, it commenced gun-firing trials, including at supersonic speed, but flew just under half the hours of WG760 before retirement came on 7 December 1959. A third example, WG765, was retained by its manufacturer for static structural test purposes and never flew.

EE was keen to push WG760 into the as yet unknown realms of higher supersonic speeds. Therefore in November 1955 the aircraft was fitted with a basic reheat system, increasing the thrust of each Sapphire to 10,300lb. Unfortunately this modification brought about another problem, as dry thrust was decreased by half. In the event of an engine failure, it was unlikely that the machine could be recovered, but Beamont was unconcerned and felt that careful management of energy in a descent could lead to a satisfactory recovery. In due course WG760 was pushed to M1.53, but directional stability became a major cause of concern and was considered unsafe. An increase in fin size, one of several, helped to alleviate the problem. However, the fin and rudder area seemed to be an Achilles' heel for the P.1A and future variants, especially concerning flutter, an undesired aerodynamic effect that can result in structural failure. To counter this, a small damper was fitted to the rudder, which became a standard feature on subsequent variants of the aircraft.

While Beamont continued to be the lead test pilot for the development of the P.1A, he was soon joined by Peter Hillwood and Desmond 'Dizzy' de Villiers, who ensured continuity would be maintained should anything befall the chief, as after all, test-flying was a dangerous profession. The unexpected could occur at any time. On one flight with the P.1A, Beamont, while at 585 knots over Morecambe Bay, experienced a colossal explosion. Partially blinded, he took stock and realized he was now flying an aircraft more akin to his first flight in an open cockpit Avro 504, although much faster. The locks holding the canopy had failed, and it had sailed off into the Lancashire skies along with his bone dome and visor. Despite the pilot's predicament, normal flight continued, albeit with heavy buffeting. Reducing speed, Beamont returned to Warton, who had been alerted by the radio silence that there was a problem. He landed without further incident, and it was determined the failure occurred due to suction loads on the canopy at high speed, which, in turn, detrimentally acted on the locking hooks, forcing an uncommanded release. In due course, de Villiers was to experience two further such releases, so there was no denying there was a problem.

The canopy malfunction became a bit of an embarrassment for EE, not helped by a cartoon in *Punch* magazine showing it held in place by a rope. Sir George Nelson (who featured in the lampooning) was far from impressed, undoubtedly hastening a redesign of the entire locking mechanism and finally resolving the issue.

As testing progressed, the need for test pilots increased. In time, Jimmy Dell, Johnny Squier and Don Knight joined the original trio and formed the nucleus of test pilots entrusted with moving the design forward towards becoming an operational interceptor.

As could be expected, EE was keen to show its latest creation to a broader audience. Therefore in September 1955 Beamont flew WG763 at the SBAC Farnborough Air Show, although he didn't land due to security restrictions. Also the machine failed to appear in the modestly priced one-shilling official flying programme, undoubtedly adding to the air of mystery. Nevertheless, the aircraft provoked much comment and debate, its futuristic design and spritely performance leaving a lasting impression. More evident at the display were the P.1A's stablemates, Canberra B(I).8 WT328, PR.9 WH793 and the Bristol Siddeley Olympus-powered B.2 derivative WD952 (which attained the world altitude record on 4 May 1953, climbing to 63,668ft above Taunton, Devon).

During the latter part of 1956, WG760 underwent further modification. A new wing was fitted to enhance stability and reduce drag, hoping to increase endurance and improve handling. The previously straight leading edge was kinked to 55 degrees near the chordwise slot, producing a cambered wing with squared-off extended tips, which slightly reduced the aileron span to allow the carriage of tip-mounted stores in the future. Test-flying revealed little detrimental change to supersonic flight characteristics but an improvement when flown subsonically. A report stated the aircraft felt more flexible, more precise and generally more pleasant to fly. Although the new wing configuration had been proven beneficial, it was not adopted for the production model of the Lightning until the introduction of the F.6 variant in 1965. WG760's last flight took place on 18 February 1961, by which time it had achieved 268.17 hours in the air.

Prototype P.1B

Before the first flight of the P.1A, thought was being given to evolving the aircraft into an operational interceptor. Specification F.23/49 Issue 2, released in June 1953, called for a machine that could achieve M1.7 with a rate of climb from engine start to 50,000ft in six minutes or less. A paper by the Vice Chief of Air Staff (CAS), Sir Ralph Cochrane, in February 1952 acknowledged that the Soviet Union had stolen a march on the British with the MiG-15 and detailed the likelihood of a hostile supersonic bomber coming into production at the beginning of the next decade. The country was already behind in military aeronautical development, and the Air Council was recommended to procure three further supersonic prototypes. This proposal was agreed upon, and on 5 August 1953 EE received a contract to construct three P.1Bs serialled XA847, XA853 and XA856. Although this was, in concept, an entirely new aircraft, the company wisely elected to name the prototypes P.1B so as not to draw scrutiny from government circles, whose support for new projects was somewhat variable.

Changes to the P.1A's original design were made and mainly affected the frontal area. The ovoid shape intake changed to circular, and a double-shock intake system took care of the anticipated effects of high supersonic speeds. At one stage, consideration was given to repositioning the engine air intakes to the wing route or chin. However, this did not materialize as EE believed the central positioning was the best option to provide satisfactory results across the speed range and was considered the most practical design.

The shock body, a bullet-shaped fairing, was mounted within the intake and provided a useful place to fit the Ferranti Airborne Interception and Pilot Attack Sight System (AIRPASS) AI 23 – airborne interception Type 23 – X-band fire control radar scheduled for testing in selected (DB) P.1Bs and operational use with the production Lightnings. The radar worked in conjunction with the proposed weapons fit of two de Havilland Propellers Blue Jay (entering service as the Firestreak) infrared-homing air-to-air missiles (AAM). Although there was potential for the AI 23 to pass information to the Pilot Attack Sight (PAS) creating a simple head-up display, it only saw limited use in the production F.1, F.1A, F.2 and F.2A.

The AI 23 was developed using Douglas Dakota III TS423, with the radar mounted in the nose (this aircraft survives in Britain registered as N147DC). The cockpit of TS423 was modified to incorporate all the instruments associated with the radar, including the display, hand controller and PAS. For high-speed trials, Canberra B.2 WJ643 and B(I).8 WT327 of the Ferranti Flying Unit assisted with the development programme. The AIRPASS installation, in time, became the first monopulse radar system to achieve front-line service.

In addition to the missiles, 30mm ADEN cannons (up to four) and spin-stabilized air-to-air rockets carried in removable packs were also proposed as part of the armament. Over time, further consideration was given to the aircraft's offensive capability, including the nuclear-tipped McDonnell Douglas Genie unguided air-to-air rocket, the heat-seeking Naval Weapons Center Sidewinder and Hughes Falcon, and the radar-guided Raytheon Sparrow. None of these options were taken up.

There was also thought of creating other variants, including tactical reconnaissance (P.15), bomber (P.18) and later, in 1962, a navalized version with variable wing sweep. None of these ideas came to fruition.

Further design changes included installing two Rolls-Royce Avon 209 axial-flow turbojets rated at 10,750lb each in dry thrust and 13,720lb with four-stage reheat. Visibility from the cockpit was improved by raising the pilot's ejection seat, leading in turn to the fairing of the canopy into the fuselage central spine, which housed the Plessey LTSA 70 AVPIN (Isopropyl Nitrate) starter system, tank and pumps. In addition, changes were made to the air brakes, flaps (which also acted as fuel tanks) and nose wheel, which now retracted forwards, removing the need to swivel to lie flat as in the P.1A. The result of the alterations produced a design taking on the classic lines of what would become the production Lightning.

With interception, the whole purpose is to get the defending aircraft to a great height in the shortest possible time and it was predicted that P.1B would be able to achieve this, but EE gave thought to enhancing performance even further. A company within the Group, D. Napier and Son Ltd, had developed the Double Scorpion rocket motor, and it was planned to trial this in the new interceptor in the form of a jettisonable pack. Tests were undertaken with the Scorpion fitted to Canberra B.2 WK163 (extant with Vulcan to the Sky Trust at Finningley/Doncaster-Sheffield) and B.6 WT207, but that is as far as the concept went as it was subsequently cancelled. The tests were not without cost as WT207 was lost during the trials on 9 April 1958 after the rocket motor exploded at 56,000ft over Monyash, Derbyshire. The crew, Flt Lt J.P. de Sallis and Fg Off. P. Lowe ejected and survived. The Guinness Book of Records has this as the highest recorded successful parachute escape made from an aircraft to date.

The maiden flight of the first P.1B XA847 took place from Warton on 4 April 1957 in the hands of Beamont. The aircraft behaved exceptionally well, reaching M1.13 in dry power at 25,000ft.

On the day of the first flight of XA847, the 1957 Defence White Paper (DWP), written by Conservative Defence Minister Edwin Duncan Sandys MP, was issued and proceeded to have a marked effect on Britain's future defence thinking. Prime Minister Harold McMillan had tasked Sandys to formulate a new defence policy to substantially reduce expenditure and manpower, together with a plan to reshape and reorganize the armed forces. As Sandys was known to advocate ballistic and surface-to-air guided weapons (SAGW), a chill wind blew through the boardrooms of defence contractors as they waited with bated breath as to what the future would bring.

The nation's defence against a nuclear strike was deterrence, provided by the V-Force (Vickers Valiant, Handley Page Victor and Avro Vulcan) and Douglas Thor ballistic missiles. The latter came into operation in July 1959 and were based at airfields in Cambridgeshire, Leicestershire, Lincolnshire, Norfolk, Northamptonshire, Rutland, Suffolk and Yorkshire. Her Majesty's Government owned the missile bodies, the Americans the warheads. Any decision to launch would be taken jointly by the two administrations. To ensure that the deterrence remained effective, it was imperative that the bomber and missile bases were protected from any attack that would prevent them from launching a counterstrike on a would-be aggressor.

Official thought considered that the day of the piloted interceptor was ending, and SAGWs were the way forward in meeting an incoming hostile threat. This thinking was a marked change from only a year before in the Air Estimates, where it was considered that aircraft armed with air-to-air missiles would provide the backbone of Britain's defence, supplemented by SAGWs. However, Sandys clearly had other ideas which proved very detrimental to the defence industry and the armed forces, especially the RAF, leading to numerous projects being abandoned. However, the P.1B survived as it was a fair way through its development and there was a need to protect Britain's V-Force bomber bases, as can be seen in extracts from the DWP wording below:

> Nuclear Deterrent
>
> It must be frankly recognised that there is at present no means of providing adequate protection for the whole country against the consequences of an attack with nuclear weapons. Though, in the event of war, the Hunters and Javelins of the Royal Air Force would unquestionably be able to take a heavy toll of any enemy bombers, a proportion would inevitably get through. Even if it were only a dozen, they could with hydrogen bombs inflict widespread devastation.[5]
>
> Defence of the Deterrent
>
> Since peace largely depends upon the deterrent fear of nuclear retaliation, it is essential that a would-be aggressor should not be allowed to think he could readily knock out the bomber bases in Britain before their aircraft could take-off from them. The defence of the bomber airfields or rocket launching sites is therefore an essential part of the deterrent and is, we believe, a feasible task. A manned fighter force for this purpose will be maintained and will progressively be equipped with air-to-air guided missiles. These fighter aircraft will in due course be replaced by a ground-to-air guided missile system. In view of the good progress already made the government has come to the conclusion the RAF are unlikely to have a requirement for a fighter more advanced than the supersonic P.1, and work on such projects will stop.[6]

So the P.1B was saved and many other promising projects were axed. Although EE was undoubtedly pleased to have scraped through by the skin of its teeth, plans to extend the range and operational effectiveness of the P.1B were thwarted, at least for the time being. In time it would be seen that the thinking behind the use of only SAGWs was flawed, but the damage was done and the British aviation industry took a severe knock from which it could be argued it never recovered.

Towards the end of October 1957, supersonic handling trials were undertaken with XA847 fitted with Blue Jay missiles and a ventral tank. The aircraft was then sent for testing by service pilots at the A&AEE, Boscombe Down and the Central Fighter Establishment (CFE), West Raynham. One area of concern established during the trial programme was some directional control deficiencies. As a result, improvement was made in May 1958 with the fitting of a Stage 2 fin and rudder, increasing size by 30 per cent to aid directional stability at higher speeds. This fin type would be standard to the production F.1s with the small ventral tank and Firestreak missiles.

In June of the same year, Beamont was invited to fly some of the United States' new 'Century Series' of supersonic jets at Muroc Lake, including the North American F-100A Super Sabre, Convair TF-102 Delta Dagger, Lockheed F-104A Starfighter and Convair F-106A Delta Dart. He flew the Starfighter at M2.0 on the 27th, but was critical of its wing and handling characteristics. In his assessment he considered the P.1B superior in handling and performance to all the Americans had to offer.

The following month and back in Britain, Beamont undertook in-flight refuelling (IFR) trials with a Canberra from Flight Refuelling Ltd, utilizing a side-mounted probe, a piece of additional equipment that became a must-have for the type in the future. Unfortunately he broke off the probe tip during the initial trial upon disengagement. Nevertheless, in time the process was refined and would significantly increase the aircraft's endurance, keeping it aloft for hours at a time, a far cry from the early days of limited flight time.

Finally, on 23 October 1958 at Farnborough, Sir Dermot Boyle, Marshal of the Royal Air Force accompanied by Sir George Nelson, Lord Nelson of Stafford from 1955, EE's chairman, officially gave the company's creation a name. The moniker bestowed was Lightning, celebrated with a bottle of champagne cracked over the forward port fuselage.

It must have been in the minds of those at EE that with the Starfighter already achieving M2.0 and the Dassault-designed Mirage III set to do so on 24 October 1958, the Lightning would soon be called upon to do the same. Until now, the P.1B had been limited to M1.7 as it was unknown if intake buzz, a duct instability characteristic of supersonic flight, would become a problem at higher speeds. There was also concern regarding aerodynamic heating, which at M1.7 was acceptable but could present problems at M2.0. Despite the doubts, it was decided to try to fly at twice the speed of sound when suitable conditions in the tropopause allowed the attempt to be made with a degree of safety.

Such a day came on 25 November when in another first for British aviation, in the hands of Beamont, XA847, flying at approximately 42,500ft off St Bees Head, became the first British aircraft to achieve M2.0 in level flight, the third in the world to reach this coveted milestone. A small commemorative plate was attached to the machine's port side to mark the achievement. The previously expressed concerns did not materialize and the flight was smooth and stable, bearing out EE's confidence in its design.

Speed often comes with a price, and fuel was always in short supply when flying the early Lightnings. Consequently one of the most essential sets of gauges within the cockpit was those showing the contents remaining in the tanks. To try to increase range, ways were sought to lengthen the 'legs' of future variants. In April 1963 XA847 was fitted with a ventral tank of increased size, the forward portion of which could be adapted for the carriage of either cannons or reconnaissance equipment. It also carried two Red Top missiles (to be explored in more depth later), and testing with the installation showed some directional instability, partially counteracted by fitting a fillet to the fuselage and attached to the fin.

Further modification to the tail area was not an option, so two small additional fins were installed to the rear of the tank. XA847 was the only Lightning to have this fin modification as later F.2A, F.3, T.5 and F.6 came with an enlarged Stage 3 fin with a squared top. As for the other two P.1Bs, XA853 spent most of its time conducting cannon trials, while XA856 supported Avon development with Rolls-Royce at Hucknall.

The P.1B prototypes continued with their trials work through into the next decade, with XA856 making the final flight of the trio on 31 March 1967. XA847 survived into preservation and was initially displayed at the RAFM Hendon before being ousted by F.6 XS925. Today the aircraft is in private hands, but is not viewable to the public at the time of writing.

F.1 Development Batch

Following the initial trio of P.1Bs, in February 1954 the Treasury granted funding for a further twenty aircraft to be built as a Development Batch (DB) with serial numbers in the range XG307 to XG313 and XG325 to XG337. The thinking behind procuring the airframes was to accelerate the testing of cannons, radar, missiles, radios and navigation systems, coupled with handling and tropical trials. Spreading the testing of individual systems across many airframes was considered an expedient way of hastening the Lightning into service. However, keeping twenty machines modified to a similar standard would prove problematic.

In June 1957 the AM produced a memo outlining plans to develop Specification F.23, broken down into three phases: Mks 1, 2 and 3. The first of these, F.23 Mk 1, for the early production aircraft, called for Interim Flight Instruments, Mk 13 manoeuvre-holding autopilot, including Instrument Landing System (ILS) couple, Blue Jay Mk 1 and 2, rocket battery, cannons and AI 23.

It was recognized that the proposed Mk 1 had no full all-weather capability and would be of limited operational value. Therefore F.23 Mk 2 sought to address this by calling for an OR946 instrument and control display and cathode ray tube head-down attack display (known as B-Scope). Included within this installation was an attitude indicator, together with navigation (capable of showing compass, off-set TACAN – Tactical Air Navigation – an electronic UHF navigational aid system for aircraft, which measures bearing and distance from a ground beacon and ILS – Instrument Landing System – modes), strip speed/machmeter and height and rate of climb displays. This sophisticated system truly enhanced the aircraft's capabilities in the weather conditions it later encountered over areas such as the cold, cloud-covered, windswept North Sea. It also gave the pilot far more functionality and therefore confidence when taking his machine into hostile environments.

In addition, the memo called for the provision of the later fitting of the Blue Jay Mk 4 infrared homing AAM, which entered service in 1964 as the Hawker Siddeley Dynamics Red Top. It was clear from the memo the ministry was serious about procuring a more capable interceptor. However, to create space for the additional equipment, it was decided the upper cannons were to be removed.

The third phase, F.23 Mk 3, took things even further, calling for Blue Jay Mk 4 missiles, data link (which never became operational on the Lightning), AI coupled to the autopilot for automatic attack (again, this didn't become operational) and higher engine thrust. The Mk 4 Blue Jay allowed for a forward hemisphere attack to be mounted, a clear advantage over that available from the stern-chase missiles.

The DB examples between them featured the AIRPASS radar, 30mm ADEN cannons and pylons to mount AAMs. The fitting of an air-to-air unguided rocket pack was also trialled, but never made it into RAF service. Power was provided by a pair of Rolls-Royce Avon 209 turbojets (the Pilot's Notes, dating around the early 1960s, detail the P.1Bs as being fitted with the Avon RA.24R 210). Fuel load amounted to 7,500lb, which allowed the aircraft to take off on full reheat, reach 30,000ft and effect a single pass interception at M1.5, leaving 1,600lb of fuel on return to base or allowing for a diversion to an alternate airfield. The first of the batch, XG307, made its maiden flight from Samlesbury to Warton on 3 April 1958 piloted by Beamont.

The DBs carried out a multitude of testing and development work during a career spanning just over eleven and a half years. Included within the research programme were trials with AI 23 (including B variant), Firestreak and Red Top, ADEN cannon, 2in rockets, OR946, TACAN, Data Link, Auto ILS, Auto Attack (never entered service), radio equipment, ventral tank, AVPIN starter system and development of the F.3. As well as equipment tests, the DBs were used for fin loading, vibration, stalling, spinning, roll clearance, tropical, target duties and general handling trials. One, XG329, was involved with 'Linesman' trials, a new ground control system offering a fully computerized air defence process.

The last flight for the DB fleet came on 31 October 1969 with the retirement of XG307, which was fitting as it was the first to fly. During its career four – the XG311, XG332, XG334 and XG335 – were lost in accidents, but the pilots – Don Knight, George Aird, Sqn Ldrs Ronald Harding and Andrew Whittaker – were all thankfully able to eject.

Regarding Aird, a photo of his ejection from XG332 on 13 September 1962 at Hatfield shows the aircraft perilously close to the ground in a dive. In the foreground, the driver of a tractor looks on, probably in disbelief, seconds before impact as Aird's parachute begins to open. The release of the camera shutter by photographer Jim Meads resulted in an iconic image that must surely rank highly as one of the best in aviation history due to the drama of the unfolding event. The cause of the crash was an engine fire, rendering the aircraft uncontrollable just short of the airfield's runway.

Upon retirement some of the DBs found their way into other roles, as RAF apprentice Colin Murray recalls:

> My first introduction to the Lightning was in the last few months of my two-year Airframe trade apprenticeship at 1 School of Technical Training at RAF Halton. In May 1970, P.1B DB Lightning XG336 (8091M) was delivered by road and moved into the 'New' workshops at RAF Halton for re-assembly. Being in the senior entry, we were selected to assist the MU [maintenance unit] in reassembling the aircraft. It occurred to me at the time that it was just like a giant Airfix kit. The port and starboard wings were joined together in the middle by large plates, top and bottom, with numerous bolts, the whole assembly then being carefully manoeuvred into the horizontal slot in the main fuselage. After this, the front fuselage, mainly the cockpit, was moved into place and bolted to the main fuselage, effectively closing the wing slot.
>
> With the main fuselage and wings now in one piece, the remaining major parts of the aircraft could be assembled. Major items were the fin (vertical stabiliser) and rudder, the port and starboard tailplanes and the top and bottom engine hatches, and finally, the undercarriage could be lowered to allow the jet to stand on its own again. If I remember correctly, main items like the airbrakes, ailerons, nose and main undercarriage were all left in situ when the aircraft was dismantled. It sounds like a quick and easy job, but rest assured, there was much blood, sweat and tears involved, and a not small modicum of foul language.[7]

Two-Seat P.11

In 1954 a requirement was issued for a two-seat training variant of Specification F.23/49 designated P.11 (T.4 when in RAF service). The aircraft's role was to facilitate pilot conversion and be as close to the single-seat variant as possible while catering for the training need. This entailed a redesign of the cockpit to allow for a side-by-side configuration for a pilot and instructor. A tandem arrangement was considered, but was abandoned at an early stage. The additional Martin-Baker ejection seat was accommodated by widening the fuselage by just over 11in which had no detrimental effect on performance, and in addition the ADEN cannons were removed.

EE was issued a contract in May 1956 for two prototypes. The first, XL628, took to the air with Beamont at the controls on 6 May 1959, followed by XL629 on 29 September of the same year. The design produced a very elegant-looking machine that softened the lines of the more brutish DB. Powered by a pair of Rolls-Royce Avon 210 turbojets, XL628 achieved M1.2 at 32,000ft with reheat engaged on its first flight. Overall, Beamont concluded: 'Within the limitations imposed for this first flight, the aircraft demonstrated excellent handling qualities, which were, in particular cases, improvements over the single-seater standard.'[8]

Further testing showed that the P.11 handled almost identically to the DB at an indicated airspeed of 650 knots at low level and M1.7 at altitude. With testing proceeding well, disaster struck on 1 October 1959 when XL628 lost its fin while piloted by Johnny Squier, forcing him to become the first pilot to eject while flying at supersonic speed. He came down in the Irish Sea, but a failure within the search and rescue (SAR) system resulted in Squier not being found, but he was able to scramble ashore on the Galloway coastline some twenty-eight hours later. His predicament was not helped by the failure of his SARAH (SAR and Homing) distress beacon due to a defective battery. Nevertheless, there was relief at Warton as he had been given up for lost. The inability of the RAF to locate Squier using an Avro Shackleton to seek out the non-working beacon at 2,000ft led to a heated debate regarding SAR processes, and improvements were subsequently made to low-level visual search procedures.

At the time of its loss XL628 was undertaking tests to explore rolling ability under G-forces up to the most severe inertia-coupling conditions within design limits. The speeds were progressively increasing in M0.05 increments above M1.4 and had been flown previously by Beamont to M1.6 on the same day as the loss. However, an investigation of recovered wreckage established that the fin had failed in yaw brought on by the vigorous manoeuvres during the test flight. Subsequently it was decreed that all Lightnings would require a bigger, stronger fin.

Service Preparations

On 23 December 1959 XG334 of the DB was sent to Coltishall, Norfolk for evaluation with the Air Fighting Development Squadron (AFDS), a sub-unit of the West Raynham-headquartered CFE. The Establishment was first formed at Tangmere in September 1944 to enhance the skills and abilities of the best RAF pilots. P.1Bs XG335 and XG336 joined XG334 on 19 January of the following year, with the unit aiming to develop tactics and techniques to allow the new interceptor to be used to its full potential by service pilots.

The first production F.1, XM134, took to the skies on 30 October 1959 (some sources state 29 October or 3 November), piloted by Beamont and flown from Samlesbury to Warton. It then went to A&AEE on 31 March 1960 for service release trials.

In April 1960 runway resurfacing and lengthening work at Coltishall entailed 'A' Flight of AFDS moving to Leconfield, Yorkshire to which the first full production F.1, XM135, was delivered to the RAF on 25 May 1960 by Don Knight. The second XM136, piloted by Beamont, arrived at the airfield on 21 June of the same year. The Lightning's progression to operational status had begun.

Of course the aircraft would be upgraded to more powerful and capable machines over time, but the basic shape throughout would be as Petter and Page had envisaged in the years just after the conclusion of the Second World War. We must honour their vision of giving the nation a true supersonic thoroughbred, one that both young and old still look upon today in awe, the same way they did when it first took to the skies.

The British Aircraft Corporation

As discussed earlier, the 1957 Sandys Defence White Paper profoundly affected Britain's aviation industry. Continued government interference pressured the British aircraft industry to create mergers to reduce the number of manufacturers competing for diminishing contracts. However, in what could be seen as a rather harsh measure, only new companies coming forth from an amalgamation or takeover would be offered the chance to bid on upcoming contracts.

In 1959 the company behind the Canberra and Lightning changed its name to English Electric Aviation Ltd and, in the same year, began negotiations to merge with Bristol and Vickers. The result of the talks was the creation of the British Aircraft Corporation (BAC). Later, in September 1960, the company gained a controlling interest in Hunting Aircraft Ltd and employed 40,000 workers across its manufacturing sites.

In addition to its existing work, BAC was awarded a contract in October 1960 to develop the TSR.2, a promising strike/reconnaissance project that was cancelled by Wilson's Labour government in 1965. BAC also manufactured the Jet Provost trainer, Vickers VC10 and BAC One-Eleven airliners and was involved in the Concorde supersonic airliner with Sud Aviation and the SEPECAT Jaguar with Bréguet.

The Lightning continued to be built with the company's formation, and EE/BAC often preceded its name. In addition it was involved in exporting Lightnings and Strikemasters – developed Jet Provosts – to Saudi Arabia (discussed in more detail later).

On A Different Track

While this work is predominately related to the world of aviation, it is hoped that the reader will allow a little bit of self-indulgence on behalf of the author and a brief excursion onto the 'Iron Road'. In the year the P.1A first flew at the SBAC Farnborough Air Show, the EE factory at Preston was building another machine that would become iconic to many in Britain.

At the end of the Second World War the predicted reduction in aircraft production came into play, forcing manufacturers to look for other revenue streams. As a result the manufacture of the Handley Page Halifax ceased, although de Havilland Vampire output continued at a reduced rate. This situation left the factory at Preston with the capacity to recommence the manufacture of railway equipment, rolling stock and electric motors.

One locomotive constructed at the factory in 1955 was the prototype Deltic, a 3,300hp Type 5 diesel-electric equipped with twin Napier eighteen-cylinder two-stroke engines, a powerplant with a distinctly nautical heritage as it had been designed to propel Royal Navy fast-attack boats. EE built twenty-two production examples at the Vulcan Foundry, Newton-le-Willows, all named after racehorses or military regiments. Entering service with British Rail in 1961, the Deltic hauled 100 mph express trains on the East Coast mainline until the last revenue-earning run on 31 December 1981.

There is no denying that the Lightning has a considerable following among aviation enthusiasts, but the same can be said about the Deltic within railway preservation circles. It is also safe to say that many of those interested in railways are keen followers of what goes on in the air. As if to seal the affection for both Lightning and Deltic, artist Lee Lacey has produced a superb painting entitled 'English Electric Legends', which depicts D9009 Alycidon being overflown by a pair of Lightning F.1As of No. 56 Squadron. The scene is well worth seeking out as it shows the best of British engineering. However, for the time being all this was yet to come.

3

Interception Part One: Lightning F.1 and F.1A

'What General Weygand has called the Battle of France is over. I expect that the Battle of Britain is about to begin.'[1] These were the words Prime Minister Winston Churchill addressed to the House of Commons on 18 June 1940. The British had been forced out of France and awaited Hitler's next moves, and an invasion was feared and prepared for. However, the RAF had put up a valiant fight, holding off the hordes of Luftwaffe fighters and bombers that attempted to stop Operation Dynamo, the evacuation of the British Expeditionary Force and elements of the French army at Dunkirk.

Göring's Luftwaffe had not had things all its own way and had sustained significant losses, as had the RAF, but it proved the latter was more than a match for what was expected to come. In the interim, the Hurricane, Spitfire, Defiant and Blenheim squadrons of Fighter Command drew breath and awaited the next stage of the air war, one that would shape the future of world history.

On 29 June 1940 No. 74 Squadron, based at Hornchurch, awaited the coming storm. After all the recent activity over France it was a relatively quiet day, and the pilots in their Spitfires went about air drills, radiotelegraphy and direction-finding homing, patrol reconnaissance, air tests and No. 2 attacks, a standard flight formation and tactic used for attacking a flight of enemy bombers. Of note, one who was flying on this day was Plt Off. D.H.T. Dowding, son of Air Chief Marshal Sir Hugh Dowding, the latter a man whose vision and determination paved the way for the nation's effective defence during the Battle of Britain.

On this day eleven pilots from the squadron would be flying. Of these, ten would participate in the Battle of Britain, with three not surviving until its official end on 31 October 1940. Three more would not see the war's conclusion and one, Sgt White, was very unfortunate when his Spitfire I K9928 was struck by lightning on 3 July 1940, causing it to crash near Margate and taking his young life. However, four of the eleven flying that day survived to retire from the RAF after long and active careers.

One of the veterans was Wg Cdr John Connell Freeborn, DFC*, a fighter ace who was just 20 years old when he took part in the Battle of Britain. He retired from the RAF in 1946 and lived until the age of 90.

Now this is pure conjecture, but as a former military aviator there can be little doubt that Freeborn watched with interest the development of jet aircraft in the years after the war. What would he have made of the Lightning, a machine that could fly four times faster than and at least twice as high as Spitfire I N3091 which he was piloting on 29 June 1940? Of course his thoughts are unknown, but to think that only twenty years separated the two types and it is suspected that he would have liked to have had the chance to fly one.

So why is the date of 29 June relevant here? Well this is the day in 1960 that his former unit, 74 Squadron, received its first Lightning when F.1 XM165 was delivered to Leconfield by Jimmy Dell. Two decades before, like many others, Freeborn had no idea whether he would survive the war or become another of those oppressed by Nazi tyranny.

Nevertheless he, with many others in the RAF commands, did their duty and prevailed. However, the threat now came from the Warsaw Pact, and like their forefathers, the young pilots of 74 Squadron trained to meet the potential aggressor. The aircraft had changed, but the steadfastness and fortitude remained strong as they took aerial warfare into the supersonic age. For the Lightning, it was the start of a career lasting for just under twenty-eight years.

Lightning F.1

On 25 May 1960 the Air Fighting Development Squadron (AFDS) received the first full production, Lightning F.1 XM135, at Leconfield, flown in by Don Knight. It is not the intention to go into all the instrumentation, equipment and performance statistics relating to the Lightning as this has been more than covered in many other publications. However, a general overview would not go amiss and the differences between the variants will be discussed.

The aircraft was powered by a pair of Rolls-Royce Avon 210 axial-flow turbojets producing 11,200lb of thrust at sea level and 14,400lb in reheat, which came in four stages: first, second, intermediate and maximum. It featured Hobson-powered flying controls with artificial feel and hydraulic duplication. Electrical power was provided by a generator and alternator driven by a turbine taking air from one of the engine stages, backed up by service and emergency batteries.

Slowing the Lightning down on landing was paramount. This was achieved by hydraulically operated disc-type brakes fitted with Maxaret anti-skid units operated by a lever on the pilot's control column. Differential braking to the wheels via the rudder bar and brake lever allowed the aircraft to be steered on the ground. Also a braking parachute was located in a compartment in the lower rear fuselage to aid additional deceleration on landing.

The cockpit was pressurized and fitted with a Martin-Baker Mk 4BS ejection seat. A vital system provided to the Lightning was its fire detection and extinguishing equipment positioned within zones in the fuselage. The pilot was alerted to a fire by indication on the Standard Warning Panel (SWP) and 'attention-getters'; depressing of buttons on the SWP activated the extinguishers. In addition a Mk 13 auto-pilot was fitted giving three-axis auto-stabilization, bank attitude hold and auto ILS coupling. Radio communication was maintained by the use of twin VHF TR1985/86 sets.

The F.1 had a wingspan of 34ft 10in, a length of 55ft 3in, a height of 19ft 5in and a tailplane span of 14ft 6in. The empty weight came in at 25,753lb and the maximum at 35,000lb. Fuel was carried in integral wing tanks, flaps, recuperator and jettisonable ventral, giving a usable supply of 947 gallons. There was no provision for IFR. Therefore the Avon's thirst for fuel presented problems concerning endurance, rather like early variants of the Spitfire and Hurricane which had similar afflictions.

Airspeed limitations, either clean or with missiles and ventral tank, were M1.7 or 650 knots, depending on which was reached first. The minimum speed stated was 180 knots with flaps and undercarriage up or 140 knots with both down. The mention above of speed reached first needs a little explanation, which is detailed by Sqn Ldr Dennis Brooks of Nos. 111, 65 and 56 Squadrons and OC LTF:

> The limit is whichever comes first, the Mach No or the indicated airspeed in knots. The speed of sound is temperature dependent and at sea level, say 20 degrees [Centigrade], is just under 670 knots, M1.0. The aircraft limit is 650 knots, so that is the maximum speed you are allowed to fly, even though you are just under M1.0. The aircraft limit in knots is the Indicated Airspeed (IAS). As you go higher the air density is reduced and the IAS is much less than the True Air Speed (TAS) so at high level you may achieve M1.0 at, let's say 350 knots IAS. If you continue to accelerate, then at 650 knots IAS your Mach Number would be, let's say M1.8, and that would be the limit. The key is the relationship between IAS and TAS as altitude increases.[2]

Limitations relating to g were (positive):

SPEED	VENTRAL EMPTY	FUEL IN VENTRAL
Up to M1.6	5g	4.5g
Above M1.6, the normal acceleration is not to exceed 3g.		

The minimum runway length for operation is detailed as 2,500 yards. The Pilot's Notes state that the aircraft should not be flown above 60,000ft, which had more to do with the restrictions placed on the pilot by his oxygen regulator and personal equipment than its capabilities.

Of note, XM135 was to gain a degree of infamy as being the aircraft in which Wg Cdr Walter 'Taffy' Holden had inadvertently taken off at 33 Maintenance Unit (MU), Lyneham on 22 July 1966. On this day he was trying to locate an electrical fault using the 'lazy' (out of use) runway that seemed to occur only when the machine was accelerating for take-off. As he carried out the checks, reheat was mistakenly engaged, launching the Lightning forwards. Holden was now in a desperate situation. As speed was gained, he narrowly missed a fuel bowser that crossed his path and a de Havilland Comet taking off on the main runway. With tarmac and options running out, he took off with no canopy, radio or flying helmet. Another important factor is that Holden, as a ground engineering officer, only had limited flying experience on the de Havilland Tiger Moth, Chipmunk and North American Harvard, and here he was piloting, obviously not by choice, an aircraft that required considerable experience to master. He considered ejecting, but the pins were in so that option was ruled out.

The whole situation could have ended in disaster, but after several fraught attempts he managed to land the Lightning with nothing more than a tail bump, which caused damage to the cable of the braking parachute. Without this piece of equipment to provide deceleration, the use of the wheel brakes entailed him stopping with just 100 yards to spare. It took some time for 'Taffy' to get over his experience, but he went on to have a long life, dying at the age of 90 in December 2016. The Lightning suffered no ill effects and was returned to service in due course.

In total nineteen F.1s were constructed with serials between XM134 to XM147 and XM163 to XM167, of which four were lost in accidents. The variant made its final flight in November 1974 when Holden's XM135 was flown to the Imperial War Museum at Duxford, making it the only complete F.1 in existence. However, others ended their time as airfield decoys, and the author can remember a time at Wattisham in 1984 when XM139 (maintenance serial 8411M) and XM147 (8412M) were noted performing this role as McDonnell Douglas Phantom F-4J(UK)s of No. 74 Squadron moved around the peritrack in preparation for a training sortie. Of note, XM139 was used by Flt Lt R. Pengelly as the display aircraft for the air shows at SBAC Farnborough in 1970 and 1972 and at Paris in 1971. XM144 was assigned to the Leconfield Station Flight in January 1967 for continuation training and gained the name 'Golden Arrow' due to the markings applied to the nose.

Weapons Fit Upon Entering RAF Service

When the Lightning F.1 entered service with No. 74 Squadron it was armed with twin 30mm ADEN cannons and a pair of de Havilland Propellors Firestreak infrared homing air-to-air missiles. In addition the Pilot's Notes state that two additional cannons or forty-eight 2in air-to-air rockets (which did not enter RAF service) could be fitted internally in an interchangeable armament pack. It was also equipped with an AI 23 and a PAS.

The ADEN cannon was a development of the Mauser MG 213, designed by the Germans towards the end of the Second World War. Ammunition provided 90 rounds each for the upper weapons and 100 each for the lower. In the early days of use the cannons experienced problems due to movement and harmonization, but the fit became a reliable weapon in time. For many fighter pilots a cannon is an important if not essential piece of equipment. However, as will be seen later, common sense didn't always prevail, but for now the Lightning was a true gunfighter.

Upon service entry in 1957 the Firestreak was a first-generation air-to-air guided weapon and the first within the RAF's inventory. Originally code-named Blue Jay, the missile also equipped the Gloster Javelin and the FAA's de Havilland Sea Vixen.

When fitted to the Lightning F.1 a pair was carried on a fuselage-mounted pack below the cockpit. The missile was designed for rear-aspect attack within a cone of 20 degrees to the target's exhaust. It could be conveyed throughout the flight envelope, with launch limited to M1.3 (F.1 and F.1A) manoeuvring to 3g. One drawback of the weapon was that it couldn't be used in cloud, but given the medium- to high-altitude target it sought to engage this wasn't seen as a significant issue.

The Firestreak was 125.3in long with a launch weight of 305lb. It was powered by a solid propellant (cordite) Magpie rocket motor with a range of between 0.75 and 5 miles and could reach a speed of approximately M1.17 over launch at motor burnout (around 1.8 seconds). Once the fuel had been used the missile coasted to the target where a 40lb blast fragmentation warhead was detonated either by a direct hit or a proximity fuze. Should the weapon miss, it would self-destruct. An interesting feature at the front of the missile was the glass nose that covered its homing eye comprising eight triangular pieces converging to a central point. It has been known for this type of item, when rendered redundant, to be turned into a display case for a small model Lightning.

The heart of the Lightning's weapon system was its Ferranti AI 23 radar utilizing valve technology. In the cockpit on the port side the pilot has a radar hand controller (duplicated on the starboard side when fitted to the T.4, T.5, T.55 and T.55K) with seventeen functions at his fingertips. This is a truly remarkable piece of equipment and any reader who has the chance to handle one should do so as the action is a marvel of precision engineering.

Data from the radar scanner was fed to a B-Scope, a small cathode ray tube on the starboard side of the cockpit presenting raw data to the pilot in range and azimuth (horizontal bearing to target). So not only did he have to fly the aircraft, but he also had to work out in three dimensions and with the use of trigonometry what the radar return was telling him to enable a successful interception to be made. To the author's simple mind, doing all this on a sunny day in clear skies would be a difficult enough task, but imagine flying at night in rain with minimal visibility at high Mach numbers with the intended target instigating jamming to hinder your progress. No wonder you had to be a very talented individual to pilot and fight in a Lightning. To that end, only a fundamental explanation of the radar and missile system will be attempted here.

When a Lightning was scrambled to an interception, it used its phenomenal speed and rate of climb to rapidly close on an intruder. A sortie would last from thirty to forty minutes (extended later with IFR, but not available to the F.1), with the aircraft returning to base to rearm and refuel and make ready to repeat the process.

Once airborne, detection of a target could, for the average pilot, be between 20 to 25 miles, which appeared on the B-Scope as a small orange blip shaped like a grain of rice. When using Firestreak the pilot would need to work out how to position his aircraft behind the target as the missile could only be fired from the rear.

While the AI 23 searched, the missile was in a state known as the armed period. During this time the Firestreak was connected to the aircraft's power supply to energize its systems. Hot air at 70 degrees Centigrade (C) was provided from the 8th stage of the No. 1 engine to prevent pneumatic actuators from freezing at high altitudes. Cooling for the missile's electronics and homing eye (kept at zero degrees C) was provided by ammonia fed from a bottle housed within the launch shoe. Ammonia caused corrosion to the missile's infrared photo-cell if it came in direct contact with the chemical, therefore it was conveyed through a heat exchanger where air was cooled and fed to the cell. An air bottle charged at 2,600 pounds per square inch (PSI) for one launch or 3,300 PSI for two was used to propel the ammonia via stainless steel tubes around the missile body and would last for fifteen minutes during the armed period.

With the target located and the Lightning rolled out for a stern attack, the pilot locked on. The radar information was processed by an onboard computer with a steering dot appearing on the PAS as guidance towards the hostile target.

As the interception unfolded and the target aircraft came into view of the missile's homing 'eye', a photocell detected infrared radiation from its engines. In turn a signal was passed to the guidance equipment and an output was then sent to the Lightning's acquisition system. The pilot was then given a 'target seen' indication, and when within range he initiated the launch sequence. The time from pressing the firing button to the missile launching was around one second.

In the early days of operation it was typical for the pilot to lock on to the target as soon as possible after acquisition, which had the disadvantage of warning the prey through its own radar warning receivers of the interceptor's presence, thus allowing jamming and countermeasures to be implemented. Later intercepts were flown with the radar in search mode for longer, allowing lock-on to be achieved at a much closer distance. Recording events for later analysis, a G90 gun camera was fitted beneath the radar bullet. Early missiles were known to have their foibles, but if all else failed there were always the pilot's faithful cannons to fall back on at that time.

The Operations Record Book

The RAF has a long and detailed history spanning times of peace and war. From its earliest days, both heroic and mundane events were recorded within the Operations Record Book (ORB) comprising individual pages of RAF Form 540. Each squadron (and station) had volumes of information written down detailing its activities for a given month and year. Today many of these documents can be viewed at The National Archives at Kew, with some available online.

For the Lightning's days of operation the ORBs hold priceless source information spanning some twenty-eight years. This adds up to a huge amount of typed words for the researcher to sift through, a task undertaken by the author over many weeks. At the time it seems like a thankless, never-ending chore, but in its conclusion the information obtained adds colour and substance to the role of the iconic interceptor. A conversation with Sqn Ldr Dennis Brooks, whose name appears as Compiling Officer on some of 56 Squadron's ORBs in 1974, brought forward the information that this was a secondary duty assigned to squadron members along with other responsibilities.

With so much information at hand it is difficult to know what to put in and what to leave out. In 2000 the first volume of Stewart A. Scott's *English Electric Lightning (Volume One): Birth of the Legend* was published, followed four years later by *Volume Two: The Lightning Force*. Within these tomes Stewart has drawn on the ORBs for his works, and the level of detail looks in depth at all aspects of the Lightning's career. Consequently the two volumes run to many pages of informative and interesting script.

It is noted within the ORBs that each of the Lightning squadrons, on formation, followed a typical route of training, exercises, exchanges and front-line duties that repeated through to the type's retirement. Therefore if one unit undertook certain tasks such as QRA or deployment overseas, the others would likely follow suit in due course and a cycle would begin. Covering all the events within the ORBs through the aircraft's career would require a work of monumental proportions. It would also be repetitive and far in excess of what is allowed within this book. Therefore in the coming chapters each variant of Lightning will be described, together with its entry into service and a description of squadron events drawn from the ORBs. In some cases the latter will be looked at in a little more depth, while in others it will be briefer depending on the notable events that occurred or historical relevance. Extracts from the ORBs are written as detailed in the words of the compiler or the commanding officer (CO). Therefore grammatical errors, punctuation or inconsistencies will not be corrected.

The ORBs will also reference damage to aircraft as Categories, an explanation of which is given below:

Cat.1 – Damage sustained by an aircraft capable of repair on-site by first-line personnel.

Cat.2 – Damage sustained by an aircraft capable of repair on-site by second-line personnel.

Cat.3 – Damage sustained by an aircraft capable of repair on-site but beyond the unit's technical resources. Assistance from a repair and salvage unit or civilian contractor is required.

Cat.4 – Damage sustained by an aircraft that is not repairable on-site but requires removal to an established repair depot or civilian organisation.

Cat.5 – Aircraft damaged beyond repair or missing.

No. 74 Squadron

The first three squadrons to convert to the Lightning were Nos. 74, 56 and 111. The early years of the aircraft's entry into service, training and engineering shaped the future of its role, although this did evolve in time. Therefore the onset of conversion and operational use will be looked at in a little more depth than when the machine had become established in the air defence role, which has been covered in many other works on the subject.

Formed on 1 July 1917 at Northolt, No. 74 Squadron was equipped with Royal Aircraft Factory S.E.5a fighters and fought in France until the German defeat, followed by disbandment in February 1919. Reformation came on 1 September 1935 with Hawker Demons and later Gloster Gauntlets until conversion to the Spitfire I in February 1939. The unit gained a degree of infamy on 6 September of the same year when it was involved in the so-called 'Battle of Barking Creek' in which two of its Spitfires shot down a pair of Hurricanes of No. 56 Squadron in a friendly fire incident. Despite this setback the squadron went on to distinguish itself, fighting in the Battles of France and Britain, in Egypt and the Mediterranean. It finished the war, undertaking close support and escort work equipped with the Spitfire IXe in France and Belgium.

The jet age was entered with the Meteor F.3 in May 1945, followed by the F.4 and F.8 in December 1947 and October 1950 respectively. Conversion to the Hunter F.4 came in March 1957 and the F.6 in November of the same year.

In January 1960 the unit was in residence at Coltishall with No. 23 Squadron's Javelin FAW.7s and 9s all-weather interceptors. However, inclement weather, promotion examinations and runway improvements severely restricted flying for the month. To add to the woes, snow fell between the 12th and 19th, again curtailing activities. Towards the end of the month word of a revision to the training syllabus was received, required to allow the squadron to convert to the Lightning. The ORB stated that introducing the new syllabus would see an increase in night flying.

Also in January of the same year the Lightning Conversion Unit (LCU) was formed at the airfield. In the early days only pilots with 1,000 flying hours were selected to fly the aircraft, but in time this requirement was relaxed to allow younger pilots, or 'First Tourists' as they were known, to be considered. The unit had no machines of its own and borrowed from the AFDS and later No. 74 Squadron, as well as utilizing a Lightning flight simulator. The LCU moved to Middleton St George in August 1961 and was renamed the Lightning Conversion Squadron (LCS).

The man entrusted to bring the Lightning into service, Sqn Ldr John Howe (later AFC, CBE, CB), joined No. 74 in February 1960. Of South African descent, he had flown the North American Mustang with No. 2 Squadron of the South African Air Force (SAAF) during the Korean War, earning a decoration for bravery. His citation recorded that he had demonstrated intrepid aggressiveness and aeronautical skill in pressing home attacks.

After his time with the SAAF, in 1954 Howe travelled to Britain and joined the RAF, qualifying as an instructor on the de Havilland Vampire T.11 and later flying Hunter F.4s with No. 222 (Natal) Squadron based at Leuchars. Upon the unit's disbandment in November 1957, a victim of the Sandys White Paper, Howe joined No. 43 'Fighting Cocks' Squadron as 'B' Flight Commander, again at Leuchars. By the end of February 1958 it had converted to the Hunter F.6, with Howe leaving for the Day Fighter Combat Squadron (DFCS), West Raynham in June 1959. Here he qualified as a fighter combat leader.

Following his time with the DFCS Howe was posted to No. 229 Operational Conversion Unit (OCU) at Chivenor, Devon, where he put into practice what he'd learned at West Raynham. On strength at this time were Hunter F.4s and T.7s, Meteor F.8s, a single T.7 and an Avro Anson. While there he applied for the Junior Command and Staff School course at Bircham Newton, which he began in January 1960 but didn't finish. The reason for this was that he received a phone call the following month advising him of a promotion to the acting rank of squadron leader. Howe was informed that he was to make his way to Coltishall, take over command from Sqn Ldr P.W. Carr of No. 74 Squadron and oversee the Lightning's introduction into service. It is of note that a previous commander of the unit during the Battle of Britain was 'Sailor' Malan, also a fellow South African.

As previously stated, No. 74 Squadron received its first Lightning F.1, XM165, at Leconfield on 29 June 1960. At this time AFDS was based at the airfield, with No. 74 residing at Horsham St Faith while improvement works were undertaken at Coltishall. Upon delivery to Leconfield, the ORB states that the technicians immediately pounced on the Lightning to better understand how to keep this complex machine serviceable and in the air. However, as time will tell, the hard-working ground crews were certainly going to have their work cut out. It would also not be long before the aircraft were adorned with the squadron's Tiger's Head badge on the fin and black and yellow triangles on the nose on either side of the roundel.

In July 1960 the squadron returned to Coltishall with eight pilots actively undergoing Lightning conversion, a task rendered a little more complicated by the lack of two-seat trainers. Again it fell to the AFDS to devise a programme to aid the transition.

In the first instance, pilots attended a five-day aviation medicine course at RAF Upwood where they were acquainted with new flying clothing including g-suits, pressure jerkins and Taylor pressure helmets, unpopular items of equipment due to their size which restricted head movement in the cockpit. Next came a week of lectures from the AFDS covering all aspects of the Lightning plus ten sorties in the General Precision Systems Mk 1 simulator.

Once the above was completed, it was time for the daunting prospect of the first solo. For this it was usual for an AFDS pilot to accompany the soloist in a Hunter chase plane where he would do his best to follow the somewhat quicker Lightning. The first flight usually entailed flying away from the airfield, getting used to the incredible performance and rate of climb, and returning to the circuit to undertake approaches with the AFDS pilot monitoring activities and offering guidance.

Howe flew his first Lightning solo on 14 July 1960, piloting XM165 for a fifty-minute flight. In Bob Cossey's book *Upward and Onward* Howe recounts:

> There were no two-seat Lightnings early in its career, so it was a matter of ten sorties in the simulator, and then away we went by ourselves. I thought the leap from Vampire to the Hunter was pretty big but this leap to the Lightning was huge! I was confident enough on that first occasion until it actually started down the runway – then I began to have doubts! But we were ready for it. In modern parlance, the adrenaline rush we had was quite something. Everyone inadvertently went supersonic (without reheat) at 18,000 to 20,000 feet on their first sortie for we simply weren't used to that sort of power! From brakes off to 35,000 feet, it took three and a half minutes in cold power. No wonder it was considered the most desirable aircraft in the inventory to fly and that competition to get on to a Lightning squadron was fierce.[3]

With the Lightning starting to come on stream, the RAF was keen to show off its new Mach 2 interceptor, resplendent in its bare aluminium finish, to the wider world. The public needed to see where their hard-earned taxes were being spent, and there was also the export potential.

Howe was an exceptional leader and was always ready to face the challenges placed upon him, but it could be said that when he received the signal telling him to fly four Lightnings at the SBAC Farnborough Air Show in September 1960, he maybe thought that this was a tall order. For a start he didn't have four aircraft, and his pilots were new to the machine and flying it in formation had as yet been untried. There was also the added problem that ground equipment and the supply of spares was inadequate. Undaunted, Howe found ways around the latter problem by circumventing the usual RAF Fighter Command channels for parts procurement by going directly to Beamont, Dell or Squier at EE. The required items would be available for collection by one of the unit's Hunters or Meteors the next day. This situation did not please some in officialdom, but as they say, when needs must. In 1961 an ordering process known as 'Early Bird' was brought in, which helped to ease tensions and ensure that spares were available.

During August the ORB states that the squadron had five Lightnings on strength, but four remained mainly on the ground with serviceability issues. Despite the problems Howe prevailed, and on 14 August he and one of the flight commanders flew a formation display at Duxford for a Royal Observer Corps event, although the records do not state how many aircraft took part overall.

Formation practice continued during September with the six Lightnings deployed to Boscombe Down. Four flew from there each day (except one when rain stopped play) to perform at Farnborough, led by Howe and accompanied by Flt Lts A. Wright, J. Cohu and Fg Off. T. Nance. From the available evidence, the Lightnings that appeared at the show were XG332, XM138, XM140, XM141, XM142, XM164 and XM165. The SBAC event was in its 21st year and the official public programme, now priced at one shilling and sixpence, showed several images of Lightnings and, interestingly, one of T.4 XL629, which also participated in the show.

Following their busy flying schedule, the unit returned to Coltishall on 13 September and began preparations for Battle of Britain 'At Home' Days held later in the month at Biggin Hill, Cottesmore, Waddington and Wattisham. Fg Off. Mike Cooke also flew solo displays at Gaydon and Bassingbourn. His brief was to keep the routine low and make plenty of noise, something at which the Lightning would become very adept over the years.

It had been a tough time for the pilots and ground crews, the latter working flat out to keep the Lightnings flying, a feat Howe recognized with genuine admiration. By the end of the month ten Lightnings had arrived out of the expected twelve, but a lack of spares once again kept many of them grounded.

Although display flying was undoubtedly important, it was not the reason for the Lightning's existence; it was a machine designed to fight in the air. As yet there was no firm idea of a date for service entry. In October 1960 the Lightning conversion programme was moving slowly due to aircraft being grounded due to poor serviceability, AI 23 radar issues and inclement weather.

Aside from the problems, on 25 November five members of the US Air Force's 79th (Tiger) Tactical Fighter Squadron based at Woodbridge were entertained in the Officers' Mess at Coltishall. One of the men in attendance was Lt Col Ed Rackman USAF, whom Howe knew well from the days of the Korean War. As a result further ties were implemented between the two units, resulting in the formation of the NATO Tiger Association. In time a French Air Force squadron based at Cambrai, EC1/12, joined, and on 19 July 1961 the first Tiger Meet was held at Woodbridge. Here the three units flew five Lightnings, four North American F-100 Super Sabres and six Dassault Mystères in formation, thus creating a strong bond that still exists today between the current association members that have expanded to include squadrons from eighteen countries.

As the year ended, Howe had some parting words to commit to the ORB:

> 1960 has been a year of challenges to No. 74 Squadron, and the pilots, and especially the groundcrew, have put in a tremendous amount of work to meet these challenges. Morale has fluctuated over the past few months with the introduction of the sophisticated Lightning, but on the whole, it has been high. The Squadron as a whole is 'bedding in' with the new aircraft, and once the spares provisioning improves, there should be a great improvement all round. The Squadron looks forward to the challenge of the New Year and the many varied commitments 1961 is likely to bring.[4]

The New Year started well for the squadron, with 100 hours flown in January and an improvement in AI 23 performance. However, the issue of Special Technical Instruction 23c (jet pipe and reheat removal for X-ray) and other modifications impacted Lightning serviceability. Later in the month it was announced that the unit was now a night and all-weather squadron. In February the AM arranged a three-day media event at Coltishall to showcase the Lightning, giving Howe a chance to make the following quote:

> We know we can catch the bombers and going on past experience we know we can outfight any known fighter in service today. The performance of the aircraft, coupled with the ease with which it is flown, gives the pilots confidence and the fact that it is felt to be the best fighter in operational service gives our Lightning pilots the highest possible morale.[5]

However, things began to go awry as later in February the unit was grounded due to a severe fire hazard being found between the No. 1 engine, the jet pipe and the ventral tank. The removal of the tank offered a temporary fix but curtailed endurance. The manufacturers quickly provided a solution, and after modification works the aircraft were back online by 18 March 1961.

The following month No. 74 Squadron would be declared operational and became part of Britain's air defence against any hostile airborne threats, coming initially under Exercise Halyard. This exercise was a duty that entailed keeping two armed aircraft at cockpit readiness and ready to react if intruders were detected in or approaching Britain's airspace. Squadrons took it in turns to participate in the alert, which lasted for seven days. However, the process was unpopular as it interrupted training and was incredibly boring for the pilots and crews tasked with long hours sitting around and waiting for something to happen. It was usual for two pilots to be held at thirty-minute readiness and a further two at ten minutes, the latter fully kitted up. Two more pilots would sit in their aircraft cockpits parked on the Operational Readiness Platform (ORP) at two-minute readiness. After around ninety minutes they would be relieved by other pilots and return to the crew room to await their next turn. The unpleasantness of sitting out on an ORP on an exposed airfield cannot be underestimated. In addition, it would be mind-numbingly cold in winter and in summer stiflingly hot when wearing a full flying kit.

In time Halyard changed to QRA. Three airfields – Binbrook, Leuchars and Wattisham – were equipped with a QRA hangar or Q-Shed that could house two fully armed and fuelled Lightnings ready to react to any airborne threat at a moment's notice, twenty-four hours a day throughout the year. The hangar was built near the runway's end and connected via a taxi-way. Purpose-built self-contained crew accommodation offered a degree of comfort over that provided by Halyard, with no more sitting at readiness in the cockpit. A Q-Shed was also constructed at Gütersloh in West Germany for Nos. 19 and 92 Squadrons' use when they held Battle Flight.

Britain's Post-War Air Defence System

While those on alert willed away the hours, Britain's early-warning system kept its electronic eyes on the skies in a never-ceasing vigil to ensure nothing of a hostile nature would go undetected. The following briefly overviews the detection system in operation when the Lightning entered service.

As well as the heroic acts of the Battle of Britain's 'Few', many other factors contributed to the Luftwaffe being held at bay and denying Hitler his invasion. These included the ground crews, WAAFs, the Royal Observer Corps, army, Royal Navy, factory workers and the radar system that gave early warning of incoming threats. In many ways this integrated defence measure was instrumental in changing the course of the battle as it allowed squadrons to remain on the ground until needed, saving fuel, airframe life and the nerves of hard-pressed pilots, all vital requirements when resources were being diminished through attrition. However, it was fortunate for the nation that Luftwaffe intelligence did not have a better understanding of the radar utilized by the RAF and its importance to the country's defence. Had they known the vital contribution the Chain Home system would play in the battle, more effort may have been made to destroy it.

After the war ended, Britain's radar systems were wound down as the threat of immediate attack diminished. However, with the Soviets successfully detonating an atomic bomb in 1949 and knowing they also had the means to attack the country with the Tupolev Tu-4 Bull, thoughts changed to upgrading the nation's early-warning system. The threat of nuclear attack necessitated a constant state of readiness to be maintained, and with the expected increase in aircraft speeds it was known that the time between detection and interception would need to be reduced.

Some wartime Chain Home radar stations remained in operation in the post-war years, but a system known as ROTOR was conceived as the threat increased. This was approved by the Air Council in 1950 and required a significant procurement effort to bring the concept into operation. Existing Chain Home installations were upgraded while others that had been mothballed were brought back into use. New underground and semi-submerged Ground Control Interception (GCI) stations were built along the east and south-east coast, which in time extended to cover the north and north-west of Scotland and Northern Ireland.

In 1955 the Decca Type 80 S-Band radar with a range of over 240 miles and the AN-FPS6 Height Finder were introduced at RAF Trimingham on the North Norfolk coast, significantly improving performance and efficiency and rendering many existing radar stations redundant. The Type 80 would prove to be a very useful piece of equipment as it brought the functions of early warning and fighter control together for the first time in the same unit.

Changes in thinking came with the 1957 Defence White Paper (DWP) that placed nuclear deterrence at the heart of policy and how early warning was to be implemented. The detection of an incoming threat was no longer designed to protect the population; it was to provide early warning of a pre-emptive attack by the Warsaw Pact against Britain's V-bomber and Thor ballistic missile sites, allowing the launch of interceptors and also Bristol Bloodhound SAGWs. If the nation's nuclear assets were taken out before being launched, there would be no means of retaliation available should an attack of a non-conventional nature come from the East.

The ROTOR system of early detection greatly enhanced Britain's capabilities. However, there were concerns over gaps in coverage and delays in reporting and control. Therefore in 1958 the Control and Reporting Plan recommended moving away from sector operations and creating nine Comprehensive Radar Stations (later known as Master Radar Stations). These were equipped with the Type 80 radar and had direct links and communications with fighter airfields.

Britain's early-warning system developed and evolved over time to the sophisticated network that is seen today. The Soviets and then the Russians have continued to probe Britain's air defences and reaction times and on each occasion Britain's interceptors are sent to meet them. However, when the Lightning entered service in 1960, the control of interceptions would have been under the ROTOR system as described above.

Towards Operational Status

In April 1961 74 Squadron's role changed from short-range day fighter to night all-weather and was declared operational. Again, with his pilots and ground crew Howe had achieved a remarkable feat by bringing the Lightning into service with no fatal mishaps or significant incidents. When the complexity and advanced nature of the aircraft are considered, this is an accomplishment not to be underestimated. However, some potentially sticky situations did arise, one of which is recounted here.

On 16 May 1961, while being piloted by Flt Lt Jim Burns (Deputy Officer Commanding of 'A' Flight), XM141 was seen to be missing part of its fin and the entire rudder. He had been flying as part of a close finger four formation, practising a high-speed pass along Coltishall's runway. Despite the damage Burns successfully landed the Lightning and, after the incident, with typical RAF humour, gained the nickname of 'Finless Jim'. Until the failure the F.1 had flown a total of eighty-three hours and forty-five minutes. An investigation by EE into the incident concluded:

> The prime cause of the accident was that Lightning XM141 sustained an aerodynamic load which resulted in the structural failure of the fin and rudder. The aerodynamic load was most probably produced by the interaction between aircraft flying at high subsonic Mach number in close formation at low altitude.[6]

Following this incident all Lightning fins were strengthened, including XM141's which was repaired on-site by No. 71 MU. The aircraft was returned to No. 74 Squadron on 22 November 1961. Of note, the remains of the fin survive today, complete with its Tiger's Head marking at Farnborough Air Sciences Trust (FAST) where it is on display.

Also taking place during the month was Exercise Matador, in which the squadron flew nineteen sorties with two scrambles and the claim of twenty-six kills. However, as 1961 progressed, practice was the most important order of the day as the unit was chosen to be the year's RAF aerobatic team, resulting in displays at the Paris Air Show in June and events during the summer culminating in an impressive nine-ship Lightning roll performed at the SBAC Farnborough display in September. Contemporary footage shows a stream take-off, with glowing reheat, rotating to 30 degrees and then near vertical climbs. The spectacle and the noise created are still discussed today when those who attended such air shows recount their memories with a misty eye.

Following the Farnborough displays, the unit performed at Battle of Britain 'At Home' Days at Biggin Hill and Coltishall, with a final commitment for the year coming with the squadron demonstrating their new mount to the Queen Mother at Leconfield. However, it would be November before the real business of operational training could recommence. During this month 276 hours were achieved, the highest number since conversion. A bonus was the good reliability of the AI 23.

Howe's time with No. 74 Squadron was ending, and in November 1961 he relinquished command and took up a role at HQ Fighter Command. For his work in bringing the Lightning into service he was awarded an Air Force Cross. Sqn Ldr Peter Botterill took his place.

The last month of the year saw a visit from a Mr Stevenson and his camera, and he wrote an article about the squadron for *The Eagle* comic. One wonders how many young lads were inspired to seek a life in the RAF or maybe even aspire to become a Lightning pilot from its publication. On a more serious note, Jimmy Dell visited and gave a lecture on the spinning characteristics of the Lightning.

For the first three months of 1962 the unit's aircraft were grounded as an EE Contractor's Work Party modified hydraulic systems. It had been found that the aluminium tubing used was inflexible and cracked, resulting in leaks and the potential for fire. This in turn led to the complete re-piping with high-tensile steel. Such a job was by no means easy and it would be May 1962 before a full complement was back online. With such downtime the pilots had to undergo a reconversion course of three preparation sorties to allow them to fly the Lightning again operationally, consisting of a comprehensive emergencies trip, an air test and a flight profile sortie.

At the end of April HQ Fighter Command deemed the squadron the official RAF aerobatic team for the year. Towards the tail end of the following month, eight Lightnings flew from Coltishall to Västerås in Sweden. On the 26th four aircraft flew a display over Stockholm, followed by eight machines undertaking a flypast of the British Trade Fair. Two days later the pilots were flown to a Swedish Air Force base where they were introduced to the Saab Draken.

Leaving Sweden, the unit flew to Gardermoen in Norway where a display was given on 3 June to commemorate fifty years of the Norwegian Air Force. Three days later the squadron returned to Coltishall and began working up for a display at Upavon. However, a further problem came to light as stick jamming was experienced during practice. The culprit was balance weights at the lower end of the control column fouling the structure beneath the cockpit. Until modifications were made, manoeuvres were limited to 2g and practice ceased, but by July events were back on track.

For the 1962 SBAC show in September the 'Tigers' joined the Hunter display team of 92 Squadron, the 'Blue Diamonds', to perform a synchronized display over the Hampshire airfield. The unit wanted to ensure that its aircraft stood out, and to this end their fins and spines were painted black. Seven Lightnings flew with sixteen Hunters, creating a truly epic ten-minute display routine that won a commendation from the SBAC flying committee, which was quite a feat. The ante was upped even further for the show's final day, with seven Lightnings and eighteen Hunters flying together. On 10 September the squadron returned to Coltishall with twelve F.1s and a T.4 arriving in formation, undoubtedly a magnificent sight for those who witnessed the event. After Farnborough, Battle of Britain 'At Home' Day displays were flown at Biggin Hill, Coltishall and Wyton.

With the show season over it was time to get back to the job for which the Lightning was designed: air defence. It had been a difficult period for the aircraft, its pilots and ground crew, with numerous problems relating to spares, design problems and serviceability issues. However, this was to be expected with such an advanced, complex machine.

Over the coming months pilots got to grips with radar training, cannon-firing and alert commitments. In addition, some aircraft came offline to enable an upgrade of the radio fit to UHF. Then in April 1963 the squadron experienced its first Lightning loss. On the 26th, Flt Lt 'Finless' Jim Burns was piloting F.1 XM142 on an air test after an engine and tailplane change. As the flight progressed, indications on the SWP gave warning of a hydraulic failure. Burns decided to eject and the Lightning crashed into the sea off Cromer. He was picked up safely by an SAR helicopter from No. 228 Squadron and returned to duty shortly after.

On 9 September the squadron participated in Battle of Britain Week with a flypast over Norwich. Accompanying them and in the lead were a Hurricane and Spitfire of the RAF Historic Aircraft Flight, at the time based at Coltishall. This unit was later renamed the Battle of Britain Flight before becoming the Battle of Britain Memorial Flight in 1969. It now operates out of Coningsby in Lincolnshire.

As autumn moved into winter, the unit was engaged in training and practice interceptions (PIs), together with a stint on QRA, which was now twenty-four hours a day, seven days a week. In February 1964, four Lightnings were deployed to Valley to undertake a Missile Practice Camp (MPC). Despite problems with the weather, targets, missiles and their systems, five Firestreaks were fired. After a long association with Coltishall, No. 74 Squadron moved to Leuchars in Scotland on 28 February 1964 and was operational within five hours of their arrival.

In April of the same year it received the first of its Lightning F.3s, with the squadron's last use of the F.1s coming in July. After this retired jets were reassigned to the Target Facilities Flight (TFF) or placed in storage. Some aircraft were transferred to the training role with No. 226 Operational Conversion Unit based at Coltishall.

The F.1 was hampered by its lack of IFR capability, resulting in short-duration sorties. However, it ushered in the age of supersonic flight to the RAF, providing valuable experience to the pilots and ground crews tasked to take the supersonic interceptor into a new era of operations.

Target Facilities Flight

An essential factor for any fighter squadron is the ability to carry out PIs against realistic targets. In the early days of Lightning operations Canberras of No. 85 Squadron provided the means to do this, but above 45,000ft the bomber's effectiveness in performing the role diminished. To overcome the issue Lightnings were used but presented a poor radar picture; however, there was no other option.

Before 1966 Lightning squadrons had provided their own aircraft to act as targets. However, with F.1s becoming surplus to requirements, the AFDS (renamed the Fighter Command Trials Unit – FCTU – on 31 January 1966) evaluated XM137 and XM164 at Binbrook and concluded that their role as targets was appropriate.

When the FCTU disbanded, the two F.1s remained at Binbrook and formed the station's TFF. Further flights were created at Leuchars and Wattisham, each with two to three aircraft on strength. The TFF Lightning's task was to operate at high speed, day and night, and at all altitudes where they simulated the actions, tactics and deceptions likely to be employed by an enemy aircraft. The flight was part of the squadron at each base to which it was assigned but had its own CO (often the full-time pilot) and ground crew. There appears to have been a degree of affection for the old F.1s as two received names while operating with Wattisham's TFF. XM144 was christened Jinx in June 1966 and later Felix in August 1969. XM147 took over the moniker of Felix in May 1969 and later became known as Korky.

The TFFs were very proud of their task and had their own markings applied, often sporting 'kills' painted below the cockpit when the hunted reversed the role and became the hunter. In his first posting following his apprenticeship, Colin Murray of Wattisham TFF recalls:

> Having left RAF Halton after my two-year apprenticeship, I found myself in the wilds of Suffolk at RAF Wattisham. All very new, and after arrival, was internally posted to the TFF, who flew a small number of F.1 and F.1a Lightnings (and either one or two Chipmunks depending if ATC summer camp was on), and with the secondary tasking of looking after all visiting aircraft types. The normal number of our Lightnings on the flight line would be three, with a fourth in scheduled servicing. The Flight's official badge was that of RAF Wattisham itself, but unofficially, we had the 'Clean pair of heels'. This was a stylised rear view of a cat with wings and tailplane, always cut out of dayglo sticky-backed material. It was not only mounted on either the nose or tail of our jets but also on the Chipmunks and vehicles.
>
> The main task of the Flight was to supply supersonic targets for the resident 111 (Tremblers) and 29 Squadrons. Additionally, we were tasked with providing the aeros display jet during the airshow season. For this, we always had two jets

prepped on the line and ready to go. For displays with no landaways involved, both jets would be started with the display pilot in the prime (in my time, this was Russ Pengelly) and, in the backup, one of the other Flight pilots. If the prime went U/S on start, Russ would climb out, move to the backup jet, which had been vacated by the other pilot (still with engines running), climb in and continue with the sortie. I can only recall the one time when I saw this happen.

These 'no land away' displays were usually at the weekend and, as is still the case, involved a working weekend for the selected few. For displays further afield, normally over a two to three-day period, with two jets, we would send groundcrew plus equipment, i.e. spare brake chutes, ladders, oil replenishment rigs, tools, etc., in a Bedford 3-tonner and usually with a Morris 250 JU van or a Land Rover for the groundcrew.

Accommodation in the UK for the groundcrew was always in military barracks, either Navy, Army or RAF; for instance, RAF Waddington and RNAS Yeovilton were on base, but for the Farnborough Airshow, we were nearly 50 miles away at RAF Thorney Island (then less than an hour's drive). I believe we only used air transport once, an HP Hastings of 1066 Flt, for the Paris Airshow in 1971, and possibly Metz in France in 1972.

During station exercises (Tacevals, etc.), our aircraft were either detailed as point defence for the airfield, to defend against attacking incoming bandits, or as bandits themselves. Exercises, either station, command or NATO, were fairly easy-going affairs at that time compared to what was to come towards the end of the decade when NBC [nuclear, biological and chemical] suits and working from a hardened environment were the norm.

We did not distinguish between lineys and second line; where you worked on the flight was dependent on the flying task. In the hangar, we could do all servicing up to and including Minor, cycling through, Primary every 125 hours and 250 hours, Minor 500 hours and 1,000 hours. The duration for each servicing was, of course, dependent on the amount of checks called for on that particular servicing. We were also called on to assist the CWP [Contractor Working Party] with the rebuild of XM163, which had been sitting in the corner of the hangar Cat.3 since October 1968 and had been very much used as a Christmas tree, being robbed for spares for other jets. This rebuild was finally finished by February 1971, and the machine was taken back on the strength of TFF. However, it was a short-lived career, as just a year later, in February 1972, it was flown to 60 Maintenance Unit RAF Leconfield for storage and scrapped by May 1974.

One very alarming incident that sticks in my mind during my time on TFF was one early evening when we took a jet down for a reheat engine run. There was no 'hush house' then and runs used to be carried out in between the old WW2 blast walls at the west end of the airfield.

Aircraft would be double chocked with the normal complement of ground equipment, i.e. power set and CO_2 extinguisher, and for the run itself, we would have a manned fire crash tender pulled up at the front of the aircraft.

This particular evening, everything was set up with the fire crew sitting in their cab facing the jet and ready to watch the ensuing ground run. If I recall correctly, we were only going to be doing runs on the No.2 engine, so with all pre-start checks carried out, the engine start signal was given to the propulsion techie in the cockpit, and we waited for the wheeeee chooosh noise as the starter button was pushed with the engine hopefully starting to wind up. Well, we certainly got the wheeeee chooosh noise, but what we didn't expect was the large fireball that rolled down from near the starter exhaust under the port wing all the way to the wing tip, around the wing tip and along the top surface before extinguishing itself just at the overwing fuel vent valve cover.

Bear in mind that this only took fractions of a second to happen, and the thoughts of what the. ....., and where's the fire extinguisher, I glanced round to the fire truck and the memory of seeing the fireman closest to me in the cab, with the door swung open and his right leg appearing beneath it and getting ready for some real action for a change, but only to be disappointed as the fireball disappeared.

The engine was shut down, and hurried checks were carried out before the brief panic subsided and the realisation of what had happened sank in. What had caused the problem was the port overwing dump valve doing what it was named for: venting fuel. This had made its way down, across, and around the wing, effectively giving a nice trail for any flame to follow, which, of course, is exactly what it did when we started the No.2 engine. The exhaust outlet for the starter is on the port side of the fuselage just beneath the middle of the wing, and occasionally, there would be some residual AVPIN (starter fuel) that would burn briefly at the end of the exhaust outlet. Part of the normal equipment used for engine starts on the Lightning was a fireman's type silver asbestos glove, used to 'pat' out any residual flames from the No.2 starter exhaust after the start cycle had finished, with emphasis on the word 'finished'. If you tried to do it before, you would have had a nasty surprise as the glove would have been blown out of your hand with great force. Tales also abound that people used to use their berets to do a similar job, although I never saw it myself likewise with the residual flame from the exhaust, I never saw it happen apart from that mentioned above. With the best will in the world, an asbestos glove or any other sort of device would not have worked in this scenario. Were lessons learnt, probably, but working on Lightnings, you got used to seeing fuel venting or leaking from many places, along with the associated puddles on the ground.[7]

Lightning F.1A

The Lightning F.1A was similar to the F.1 in dimensions, equipment, performance, propulsion, limitations and armaments, but was fitted with a fixed IFR probe, UHF radio and external cable ducts running along the port and starboard sides of the lower fuselage.

Twenty-eight F.1As were built with serials between XM169 to XM192 and XM213 to XM216. Nine were written off in crashes and accidents. One, XM170, had a short flying career of fourteen minutes after mercury contamination sustained during its construction phase spread while flying, causing corrosion to its systems. The aircraft was written off from further flight but later served with No. 9 School of Technical Training (SoTT) at Newton, ending its days on the fire dump at Swinderby in 1976. One further F.1A, XM168, was constructed but was used as a structural test airframe at Warton and never flew.

Like their F.1 counterparts, when the airframes were retired from front-line use they found further employment with the TFFs and in the training role into the 1970s. Others were placed into storage with No. 33 MU at Lyneham. The MUs mainly involved with the Lightning were No. 33 and No. 60 at Leconfield. The two sites between them took responsibility for major servicing, modifications, Immediate Readiness Reserve and storage.

No. 56 Squadron

Following hot on the heels of the F.1's entry into service came the Lightning F.1A, with XM172 delivered to No. 56 Squadron at Wattisham by EE test pilot Peter Hillwood on 14 December 1960. Like No. 74 Squadron, the unit had an impressive track record with two Victoria Cross holders within its ranks. Both Capts Albert Ball and James McCudden had each been awarded the medal in the First World War, flying S.E.5 and '5A biplanes. During the Second World War the unit had been at the forefront of the action, participating in the Battles of France and Britain, flying Hurricanes and later Typhoons, Spitfire IXs and Tempest Vs as the RAF took the offensive to occupied Europe. Hillwood, who had delivered the first F.1A, had flown with No. 56 Squadron during the Battle of Britain.

In April 1946 the squadron entered the jet age with conversion to the Meteor F.3, followed in June 1948 by the F.4 and F.8 in December 1950. Then in February 1954 it became the only RAF unit to be equipped with the unsuccessful Swift F.1, which was replaced in May 1955 by the Hunter F.5 and later the F.6.

Pilots began their conversion to the Lightning under the command of Sqn Ldr J.R. Rogers in December 1960 and followed the same course as their No. 74 Squadron counterparts. Three aircraft had been delivered by the year end, with Rogers taking the inaugural flight on 3 January 1961.

Over the coming twelve months the squadron worked up on its new charge and, by January the following year, had twelve F.1As on strength. Despite ongoing radar serviceability problems and the need to strengthen the Lightning's fin following Flt Lt Jim Burns' incident with No. 74 Squadron, the unit was declared operational on 14 July 1961 and six days later participated in Exercise Halyard. During this an unfortunate incident occurred when Fg Off. M.J. Moore, who was sitting in his cockpit at operational readiness, inadvertently jettisoned his two

Firestreak missiles. Fortunately he was not held responsible for the incident and a Board of Enquiry concluded that the fault lay with the jettison system.

In mid-August Wattisham was closed for runway works, necessitating a squadron move to Coltishall. An entry in the ORB at the end of the month by Rogers shows that the operational readiness of the Lightnings was far from satisfactory:

> The pilots are now ready to go to subsonic high-altitude work, but unfortunately, the aircraft are still far from operational; there is a total prohibition on using the guns, which are unharmonised and the primary armament quite unproven. Considering the international situation, this is a very disturbing state to be in.[8]

It appears that the international situation referred to by Rogers was the tensions between the Soviet First Secretary of the Communist Party, Nikita Khrushchev, and American President J.F. Kennedy over West Berlin.

Since the Second World War ended, Berlin had been divided between Britain, France, America and the Soviet Union. The city always had the potential to act as a flashpoint between East and West, with Soviet fighters often making their presence felt by harassing aircraft using the air corridors into Berlin. This seems to be a favoured tactic, as even today the modern-day Russian Air Force continues to cause a nuisance in international airspace by flying dangerously, acting provocatively and failing to file flight plans.

The Soviets wanted the American military out of Europe, but this would never happen so the standoff continued, made worse on 13 August 1961 when the border between West and East Berlin was closed, leading to the construction of that most potent symbol of the Cold War, the Berlin Wall. This effectively shut off the escape route for many who wanted to flee the communist regime. Just before the closure it became evident that the Soviet Air Force was introducing new types to its inventory with the appearance at the Tushino Aviation Day of the Tupolev Tu-128 Fiddler long-range interceptor, the Tu-22 Blinder bomber, Yakovlev Yak-28 Brewer fighter, Sukhoi T-5 interceptor (which would develop into the Su-15 Flagon) and Myasishchev M-50 Bounder supersonic strategic bomber (never to enter service).

The problems in Berlin led to NATO reinforcing its air power resources in the area. Fighter Command increased its commitments with No. 14 Squadron based at Gütersloh (80 miles from the East German border) holding dawn to dusk alert with two Hunter F.6s at two-minute readiness, two at five minutes and a further pair at thirty minutes. The Javelins of No. 41 Squadron handled all-weather and night interceptions. In addition, six No. 56 Squadron Lightnings were deployed to Brüggen on 18 September. The unit flew one sortie to show the flag before a return to Coltishall the same day. The arrival, albeit brief, of the RAF's latest supersonic fighter would not have gone unnoticed by the Soviets in their own backyard and, in all likelihood, gave the communist regime something to think about.

On 16 October the squadron returned to Wattisham in a rather odd manner with their wheels down due to a problem with hydraulic pipework in the No. 1 engine bay. This defect necessitated all Lightnings being grounded until modifications had been made. However, Nos. 56 and 111 Squadrons had been given dispensation to return to their home airfield, where the former performed a wheels-down diamond nine flypast.

The short range of the F.1 was a constant headache for No. 74 Squadron. However, on 18 December 1961 XM171 became the first F.1A to receive and fly with an inflight refuelling probe. Soon No. 56 Squadron began practising the art of IFR. Also, in the same month, command changed with Sqn Ldr D.J. Seward taking over the reins.

Highlights in February and March 1962 included a short detachment to Gütersloh and Exercise Kingpin, where close-controlled medium-level supersonic interceptions against USAF Republic F-105 Thunderchiefs were made. On a social level, Nos. 56, 74 and 111 Squadrons held a 'Lightning Users' get-together at the Grange Country Club (the recorder neglects to say where this venue was located).

A hydraulic refit in April limited the number of Lightnings available to the unit, but following this training continued in IFR to enable participation in Operation Tambour, an exercise designed to allow the new interceptor to fly to destinations overseas. This culminated in a non-stop flight by two aircraft from Wattisham to Akrotiri, Cyprus on 23 July 1962 accomplished in four hours and twenty-two minutes. To achieve this feat, Vickers Valiant tankers from Nos. 90 and 214 Squadrons provided the fuel to keep the Lightnings aloft. In October of the same year, four F.1As flew Exercise Dedicate to Cyprus in four hours and thirty minutes. The success of these early long distance flights paved the way for the Lightning's future overseas deployments as it could now be seen that the machine had legs.

In 1963 No. 56 Squadron was tasked to take on the role of Fighter Command's aerobatic team from 92 Squadron who were stood down to convert to the Lightning F.2. Named the 'Firebirds', the team's aircraft were painted with a red fin, spine, wing and elevator leading edges, while retaining the red/white chequered nose markings either side of the roundel. Proudly adorning the tail was the squadron's Phoenix insignia. By the end of March the display manoeuvres included barrel rolls and loops in arrowhead, swan neck and 'vic' formations, with several rolling and looping formation changes.

The unit trained for a display of ten Lightnings and first performed its routine at Waterbeach on 24 May 1963. Formation flying was not without its dangers, as was seen on 6 June when XM179, piloted by Flt Lt M. Cooke, collided with XM181. Cooke managed to eject, but broke his back due to a seat malfunction and was thereafter confined to a wheelchair. Surviving the collision, XM181 went on to fly with Binbrook's TFF, ending its days on the airfield's decoy line with the maintenance serial 8415M and it was scrapped by September 1987.

On 24 June 1963 the squadron was declared QRA operational and, four days later, fully operational. The final Firebird display took place at Wattisham for the Royal Observer Corps on 15 September 1963, with Sqn Ldr I.R. Martin taking over command at the end of the month. In November QRA was held for the first time for a stint lasting two weeks and again in December.

With their display duties behind them, 1964 saw the squadron return to its usual operational responsibilities, including deploying nine aircraft to Akrotiri on 6 February named Exercise Forthright 1 and 2. Six days later the political situation on the island deteriorated as fighting broke out between ethnic Turks and the Greeks. In 1960 Cyprus gained independence from Britain, and both Turkey and Greece claimed the land as their own and had come close to war on several occasions. Following concern due to the rising tensions, No. 56 Squadron placed two Lightnings on QRA at two-minute readiness for the twelve-hour daylight period. Several scrambles were ordered, resulting in one interception of two Turkish Republic F-84 Thunderjets.

The squadron left the island on 27 February, returned to Wattisham and settled into the usual training and operational routines including survival scrambles. The main role at the time for the Lightning squadrons was to defend against nuclear war, and survival scrambles were regularly practised and entailed every available aircraft getting airborne to prevent being caught on the ground should the Ballistic Missile Early Warning System detect a Soviet nuclear strike against Britain.

In April the unit deployed six Lightnings to a Firestreak MPC at Valley where five missiles were successfully fired. On 4 August the unit moved to Coltishall to allow work to be undertaken on Wattisham's runway lighting, with a welcome coming from resident 226 OCU in the form of a barrel of beer. A return to the home airfield was made in early September, followed on 5 October by four aircraft deploying to Akrotiri for a detachment. Also of note this month is the following comment made in the ORB:

> All the Mark 1As have been modified with the lower gun pack and air to air firing has been carried out by both day and night to prove the guns. 1182 rounds have been fired for two stoppages, both of which resulted from link stoppages. All squadron pilots, other than those in Cyprus have been given experience in gun firing by day, and a number by night. First impressions indicate a very stable gun, with very little sight jump or gun flash.[9]

In November night IFR training began, and change was in the wind with the squadron preparing to convert to the Lightning F.3; although there is no mention in the ORB of this, it is alluded to by the CO in his comments for December:

> 1964 has proved to be a remarkably full and eventful year for '56' with two detachments to Cyprus totalling four months, MPC at Valley and one month at Coltishall, together with QRA at Wattisham. For all but two and a half months of the time the squadron was on home territory. Given a slightly less interrupted and more peaceful year in 1965, I have little doubt that the squadron will take the introduction of the Mk 3 in its stride and produce the sort of flying achievement that was indicated by the first nine months of 1964.[10]

The four Lightnings from the Akrotiri detachment returned home in January 1965 and QRA was held in the same month. Also an MOD memo was released identifying issues with a bracket within the Lightning's undercarriage that could crack and cause problems with its safe operation. A maximum number of cycles was applied for undercarriage rotations, with the F.1A assessed at 1,560. Within the squadron, XM172 and XM182 were grounded due to the restriction, followed shortly after by two more. A modification was implemented, which in time would be applied to all Lightnings as part of routine servicing schedules. However, No. 56 Squadron found it had a shortfall of operational aircraft, which was partly made up by the redeployment of three aircraft, XM169, XM190 and XM213, from 111 Squadron, which had begun conversion to the Lightning F.3. The CO commented as follows:

> Although not committed to QRA during February for the first time since September, the flying achievement has been badly restricted by the four F.1As that were grounded in the first week of the month as a result of the number of undercarriage cycles now permitted on all marks of Lightning. The loss of these four aircraft brought the squadron down to a total strength of seven F.1As and has necessitated a major reshuffle in the current dispatch programme for 111 Squadron, bringing the strength back to ten F.1As.[11]

The unit began its own conversion to the F.3 in March 1965, and by the end of June of the same year the squadron's association with the F.1A had ended.

No. 111 Squadron

The second unit to equip with the F.1A was No. 111 Squadron or 'Treble One' under the command of Sqn Ldr K.A.C. Wirdnam. On 30 March 1961 XM185 was delivered to Wattisham, and in April pilots began attending the LCU to enable their conversion. Again, No. 111 had a rich heritage dating back to the First World War and was the first squadron to receive an eight-gun fighter when the Hurricane I entered service at Northolt in December 1937. On 10 February 1938 the CO, Sqn Ldr J.W. Gillan AFC, made history when he flew a Hurricane from Edinburgh to Northolt in forty-eight minutes at an average speed of 408 mph, achieved due to a strong tailwind.

Like its counterparts Nos. 56 and 74 Squadrons, No. 111 participated in the Battles of France and Britain and, in early 1941, began conversion to the Spitfire for offensive operations over occupied Europe. The unit participated in the North African campaign and the Allied invasions of Sicily and Italy. In May 1947 it disbanded to reform again in December 1953 at North Weald, equipping with the Meteor F.8. Conversion to the Hunter F.4 came in June 1955, and in a nod to former glories, CO Sqn Ldr R.L. Topp AFC* flew WT739 at an average speed of

714.504 mph between Edinburgh and London on 8 August of the same year. The squadron gained further acclaim with the formation of the 'Black Arrows' display team. Strangely, a further attempt on the record was not made by the unit with a Lightning, which would have undoubtedly broken it.

In March 1961 Wirdnam and five of his pilots visited Warton and were pleased to see most of their Lightnings in an advanced state of production. By the end of May 1961 the squadron had six Lightnings on strength and four more were delivered in June. However, this number was reduced by one during the month when on the 28th Fg Off. P. Ginger was forced to eject from XM185 after an undercarriage malfunction, his aircraft crashing near Rattlesden, Suffolk. In the CO's comments for the month he made the following observation regarding the ejection:

> Flying Officer Ginger's bale out was done in a very competent manner. It was, of course, premeditated and he was able to make sure of a good posture before ejecting, which greatly assisted in an injury free ejection. Apart from the scare of being chased at one stage by an unmanned Lightning and a stiffness in the nether regions for a few days he had no after effects and is now fully recovered.[12]

Also in June Wirdnam recorded a familiar story surrounding the Lightning's entry into service in his monthly report: 'Radar unserviceability and lack of adequate servicing facilities appear to be one of the biggest headaches in keeping the Lightning fully serviceable as a weapons system.'[13]

However, the situation had improved by the following month, and in August the unit flew temporarily to Coltishall while Wattisham's runway was resurfaced. While there they received their full complement of Lightnings with the delivery of XM216 and were declared operational on 29 September 1961. The CO commented:

> The target for the month was to become operational, this was achieved with one day to spare though it did mean that several of the pilots who had already completed the conversion had to take a back seat while the tail enders were thrust into the air at every opportunity. The squadron reunion held on the 30th September at the Victory Ex-Services Club was a most successful one at which well over 100 members and ex-members were present. It was encouraging to find quite a few of the 1917 vintage members present, and it was interesting to discuss with them the problems of our respective days with the squadron.[14]

The squadron returned to Wattisham in mid-October and flew for the first time with Firestreak acquisition missiles the same month. Six Lightnings deployed to Gütersloh in December and flew twelve sorties before returning home the next day.

With the dawn of 1962 training continued, with experience gained operating the F.1A despite a continued implementation of Special Technical Instructions coming forth to cure various problems which, in turn, curtailed flying activities.

Like No. 56 Squadron, the unit also began losing its Lightnings to a hydraulic refit in April through to when the first aircraft became operational again in July.

Markings were important to the units operating the Lightning, and No. 111's were adorned with a black lightning flash outlined in yellow, cutting through the roundel on the nose and an ornate badge of two swords in saltire charged with three seaxes (short Saxon swords) on the fin.

In October the squadron began working up a new procedure known as Visident, designed to enable a pilot to close to within 800 yards of a target utilizing the B-Scope and then using his eyes to identify the contact. Visident would become a standard interception technique for the Lightning in the future.

Fg Off. P. Ginger was given an interesting task in November 1962 when he was assigned to conduct a practice interception of a Lockheed U-2. Previously AFDS pilot John Mitchell had carried out the first intercept of the high-flying USAF reconnaissance aircraft on 17 October while operating out of Middleton St George. At the time three U-2s were deployed to Upper Heyford and were undertaking air sampling missions near Norway in connection with recent Soviet nuclear weapon tests. With the cooperation of the USAF, it was agreed that the AFDS could intercept the U-2s as they went about their daily missions. The success of the interception would be measured as to whether the Lightning could get into a position where a Firestreak lock could be acquired, which was achieved by Mitchell on the above date at around 65,000ft. The result of the interception showed that the high-flying U-2 was no longer invulnerable to piloted interceptor aircraft. It is reasonably safe to say that the USAF was unlikely to have been impressed that the RAF possessed this capability.

Following the AFDS trial Ginger, operating from Middleton St George, flew three high-altitude profile trials piloting XM191. Finally on 14 November he successfully intercepted a U-2. The Lightnings used were in a standard fit with nothing changed to enhance performance, showing that the RAF had a potent interceptor and a true thoroughbred within its ranks.

In January 1963 the unit began training to conduct IFR and held QRA for two and a half weeks. The former continued into February, resulting in flights of up to six hours. The success of IFR allowed a two-week detachment to Cyprus in March. However, the outward flight was staged through Orange (France), Decimomannu (Sardinia), Luqa (Malta) and El Adem (Libya) to prove that the route to Akrotiri was viable should tanker support be unavailable. The return flight was made non-stop with a Valiant providing fuel.

Squadron life continued over the coming year with QRA commitments fulfilled, together with ongoing training, PIs and routine exercises. In April the CO made the following remark:

> Towards the end of the month, training emphasis was put on supersonic interceptions, followed by visual identifications, and pilots are now getting quite familiar in travelling large distances over the North Sea with rapidly diminishing

> fuel readings. The exercise is very critical because of this and demands a very high degree of cooperation between the pilot and ground controller.[15]

On 27 May 1963 an interesting trial took place with a view to extending IFR capabilities. Three Lightnings deployed to Boscombe Down where they each flew a sortie to hook up with a FAA Sea Vixen from Yeovilton to take on fuel. Pilots commented that they felt the procedure was much steadier than tanking with a Valiant.

Tragedy struck on 18 July when the Lightning Force and No. 111 Squadron suffered its first fatal accident since conversion. Fg Off. A. Garside was killed while displaying XM186 to Imperial Defence College visitors at Wittering when his aircraft entered a low-level spin from which recovery was impossible. He managed to eject, but was too low and his parachute didn't have time to deploy.

A return was made to Cyprus in August, which continued into September with a further stint at home the following month carrying out twenty-four-hour QRA duties. In November night IFR exercises were undertaken, and debate ensued as to whether a probe illumination light would be useful, but the unit decreed that it could do without such a fitment. The month also saw two further accidents. On the 19th, following a heavy night landing, XM187 left the runway after losing its undercarriage and sustained Cat.4, later upgraded to Cat.5, damage. The pilot, Flt Lt Smith, suffered back injuries and was taken to Ipswich Hospital. The Lightning never flew again and was relegated to ground instructional duties at No. 9 SoTT, Newton. Later in the month XM215 caught fire after entering the barrier following a brake chute failure. Flt Lt Mason was unhurt and the aircraft was repairable after sustaining Cat.3 damage.

December 1963 closed with further day and night QRA commitments and a final comment from the CO in the ORB: 'The last day of the month was marked by a present from a tanker of No. 90 Squadron, which presented Chris Carr-Wright with a drogue at 30,000 feet off Yarmouth. He managed to bring it home safely.'[16]

The year 1964 began with command passing to Sqn Ldr George Black AFC. Squadron life continued much as the previous year, with routine training, day and night QRA, IFR, MPC, PI, exercises and Fawn Echo exchanges with the Royal Danish and Norwegian Air Forces. On 11 March Wg Cdr Howard (OC Flying, Wattisham) and Sqn Ldr Black, piloting a Lightning T.4, led a twelve-aircraft flypast over London with participation from Nos. 19, 56 and 92 Squadrons to celebrate the birth of Prince Edward.

In June Exercise Co-op took place, with interceptions against civilian Boeing 707 and HS Trident airliners. The ORB states that these were somewhat disappointing for the Lightning pilots, who were keen to get to grips with actual bombers.

Two further accidents occurred in June. On the 9th a No. 1 engine fire to XM191 resulted in Cat.5 damage caused by a foreign object to the compressor. The aircraft landed safely but never flew again, and for many years the cockpit was used as a travelling exhibit for the RAF Exhibition Unit as a recruiting aid and survives today in private hands. Of note, the next F.1A in the serial range XM192, also flying with No. 111 Squadron, was the subject matter for a 1:72 scale model released by Airfix in the 1960s. Today this aircraft is preserved at Thorpe Camp Visitor Centre, Lincolnshire.

On 26 June Sqn Ldr Black and Flt Lt Graham flew to Brussels to enable the latter to perform a routine before the King of Belgium at the International Air Show the following day. The ORB goes on to state the following:

> A fine afternoon on the 27th allowed a partial rehearsal, but a lowered cloud base resulted in a flat, bad weather show on the Sunday. The hosting was excellent throughout and was marked indelibly on both aircrew and Flt Lt Hitchins and Sgt Chillingworth, who are the ground support party. The large crowd failed to notice, however, the tremendous contrast in ground equipment needed by the Lightning (nil) and the Belgium F-104s (immense).[17]

At the end of July the squadron deployed to Akrotiri. The annual Cypex exercise began on 5 August, but was terminated when internal troubles flared on the island, resulting in one Lightning being placed at ten-minute readiness day and night and another at thirty minutes. The commitment was reduced to dawn to dusk on the 17th when the Javelins of No. 23 Squadron took over the night-time period. Scrambles were undertaken by No. 111, as the ORB describes:

> Before the air-to-ground attacks in the northwest of the islands, both RF-84Fs and F-100s of the Turkish Air Force were identified. During the second stage when the squadron was on day alert, F.84s of the Hellenic Air Force were shadowed. During one identification run on a Greek F-84, the sight of Flg Off O'Dowd's steely grey eyes caused the Greek pilot to jettison both his large overload tanks![18]

It would appear that the QRAs were very popular among the Lightning pilots, but it was just as well the situation didn't turn hot, as the CO explains:

> The frequent QRA scrambles against Greek and Turkish fighters provided plenty of gossip for the crew room and bar, and at one time pilots were volunteering for the QRA roster just to get in on the act. Unlike UK QRA duties however, all aircraft must remain unarmed, a fact which is kept strictly to ourselves![19]

During September the unit began returning to Wattisham, leaving four Lightnings to cover QRA until relieved by No. 56 Squadron in October. The detachment had lasted for twelve weeks.

Once back in Britain the squadron began to settle into its usual routines. A comment in the ORB by Black mentions two F.1s on strength. These were XM140 and XM146, formerly of No. 74 Squadron, and they had been brought in as attrition replacements on loan from No. 226 OCU. The unit rarely flew the pair as their VHF radio fit was not the best way to communicate with GCI stations who, on the whole, used UHF. The stay was brief, and the pair were flown out to No. 33 MU in the following January.

In November the pilots renewed their acquaintance with the ADEN cannon. Day and night air-to-air firing exercises were undertaken from 36,000 to 48,000ft over 84 sorties with 9,414 rounds fired. From this there were 20 stoppages, indicating one round per 487 expended. One aircraft was fired with a four-cannon fit; the others used the ventral pack only. Also night IFR was carried out during the month with XM169 fitted with a probe light. Although this was described as a little too bright, it was considered a useful aid. It will be remembered that such an item of equipment had been dismissed during the previous year, so the thinking had changed sometime in the intervening period. During December the squadron received the first of its Lightning F.3s and the days of the F.1A were numbered.

January 1965 saw great efforts being made regarding conversion to the new Lightning variant. To assist with this the squadron was split into two flights. 'A' Flight left for Coltishall, where it undertook ground school, the F.3 simulator course and four basic conversion flights for each pilot. Later in the month, 'B' Flight followed a similar route to conversion.

A sad day occurred on the 24th as Britain's great wartime leader, Winston Churchill, died. He had seen the country through its darkest hours, so it was fitting that four Lightning squadrons, Nos. 19, 56, 92 and 111, all veterans of the Battle of Britain, were given the honour of performing a flypast at his state funeral. Following a service at St Paul's Cathedral on 30 January 1965, Churchill's coffin was conveyed to the River Thames at the Tower of London to the sound of a nineteen-gun salute. Here he was placed aboard the MV *Havengore*, and as the dockyard cranes dipped their jibs he was conveyed to Festival Pier, where his onward journey to Bladon, his final resting place, began. Overhead, sixteen Lightnings flew in formations of four in line astern at 1,000ft intervals, passing over the bridge at 12:52 hours. It was led by No. 111, with Nos. 56, 19 and 92 following. In February just three hours of flying time was logged for the F.1A, and by the following month its use had ceased altogether.

Lightning T.4

The Lightning T.4 was a side-by-side two-seat trainer with full combat capability. It was powered by a pair of Rolls-Royce Avon 210 axial-flow turbojets producing 11,200lb of thrust at sea level and 14,400lb in reheat, which came in four stages: minimum (with appropriate jet pipe modifications), first, second intermediate and maximum. To all intents and purposes the T.4 was similar to the F.1 and F.1A in dimensions (apart from the twin-seat configuration, which added slightly to the frontal area), performance and armament, but the ADEN cannons were deleted. In addition, the Pilot's Notes show that the T.4 carried 19 gallons more fuel than the single-seater; not much but, as they say, every little helps. The notes also indicate that T.4 could pull slightly more g at all configurations than the F.1 and F.1A.

Configuration	Up to Mo.9	Mo.9 and above
With empty or no ventral	6g	5.5g
With fuel in ventral	5.5g	5g
With single missile	3g	3g

Twenty-two examples were constructed, including the P.11s and the two converted to T.5 standard, with eight succumbing to accidents and write-offs.

The trainer's origins lay with the P.11, with the first production model, XM966, taking to the skies on 15 July 1960. This aircraft did not serve with the RAF and was subsequently converted to T.5 standard. The second T.4, XM967, was also upgraded but again did not enter RAF service and spent its career in the test environment.

In total eighteen T.4s served with the RAF either within the LCS, No. 226 OCU or as a part of a squadron, where it was typical to have one example on strength at any given time. The first trainer for No. 74 Squadron, XM974, was received on 3 August 1962, just over two years after the F.1, and it was soon put to good use in converting new pilots while also checking out all those already qualified. Another popular activity undertaken by the T.4 (and later T.5) was inducting members into the exclusive One Thousand Miles Per Hour Club (also known as the Ten Ton Club). Invited participants flew with their pilot to 1,000 mph to gain the coveted certificate, substantiating their flight. One such instance is recorded in No. 111 Squadron's ORB:

> On 2 April 1964, Air Marshal, Sir Augustus Walker, KCB, DSO, DFC, AFC, MA, visited the squadron. In addition to joining the 1,000mph Club during a T.4 sortie, he was able to observe closely the workload on a Lightning pilot during a supersonic interception, the latter being the primary objective of his visit.[20]

Life on the flight-line of an active Lightning unit could be fraught with peril, and one incident at Wattisham on 23 June 1964 to T.4 XM992 of No. 111 Squadron led to an interesting flight. While standing on the ORP the aircraft's canopy was torn off by jet blast, with Cat.3 damage sustained. To ensure a rapid repair, Sqn Ldr Black flew the T.4 to Leconfield on 7 July minus the canopy. The cold and noisy thirty-minute flight was undertaken wearing a pair of flying goggles with comments relating to the handling characteristics of the journey passed to Boscombe Down.

The T.4 went on to perform an essential role in training and within the front-line RAF squadrons. BAC used one aircraft, XM968, to support the TSR.2 project, while XM989 (Saudi serial 54-650) and XM992 (54-651) were converted to T.54

standard for export to Saudi Arabia. Once retired from service, some examples were assigned to Battle Damage Repair Training, decoy and fire-fighting duties. Just one T.4, XL629, survives in Britain and is displayed within the QinetiQ site at Boscombe Down, while the two T.54s are extant in Saudi Arabia.

No. 226 Operational Conversion Unit

The Conversion Unit (CU) concept can trace its origins back to Bomber Command in the Second World War with the introduction of the first four-engine heavy bombers such as the Stirling, Halifax and Lancaster. In the early days of operation, the heavy bomber squadrons would have specific aircraft allocated to act as a CU to convert crews after their stint on twin-engine bombers at an Operational Training Unit. This process was required to bring the new intakes up to a standard where they could begin operations on the front line. However, in time this led to the creation of Heavy Conversion Units (HCUs) located at airfields away from the operational squadrons and autonomous in their own right. Once crews had passed through the HCU and had reached the required standard, they would be assigned to a unit to begin operations.

The same concept continued after the war with the formation of Operational Conversion Units (OCUs), where pilots were trained to a standard that allowed them to take their place within a squadron.

As previously stated, the LCU was first formed in January 1960 at Coltishall. It was renamed the LCS in 1961 and took up residence at Middleton St George (now Teesside Airport) in August of the same year. The unit had no T.4s and borrowed Lightnings from other sources until XM970 arrived in November. Its stay was brief as it returned to Warton for modifications to hydraulic pipework. It was not until June 1962 that XM970 returned to the LCS, enabling the pilots to begin practising for the commencement of Lightning Conversion Courses (Flying), which started in early September. It was the intention for the T.4 to have an operational role in times of war. To this end it participated in Exercise Matador II in October, flown by pilots from 19 Squadron.

As time progressed, more T.4s arrived with the LCS and eight were on strength by November. On 1 June 1963 the name changed to No. 226 Operational Conversion Unit with Wg Cdr John Severne OC of the Flying Wing. Its aircraft soon sported an exquisite colour scheme of red and white along the dorsal spine, which extended up onto the fin. Gracing the tail, a scarlet cross was drawn upon a white disc cut through by a sword. This was the badge of No. 145 Squadron, a designation that the OCU would have taken in times of national emergency, NATO exercises or war as a shadow squadron. As the T.4s were fully combat-capable, they would have been used to bolster the RAF's resources should conflict have broken out. Finishing off the markings was the application of the last three digits of the aircraft's serial number in large black characters just behind the intake ring.

The squadron from which No. 145 took its number was formed in May 1918, only to disband in September the following year. It reformed at Croydon in October 1939 in the day and night-fighter role equipped with the Blenheim If. The unit converted to Hurricanes in March 1940 and saw action in the Battles of France and Britain. Conversion to the Spitfire I began in January 1941, a type it would fly through several marks until the war's end and disbandment in August 1945. Reforming in March 1952, the squadron became part of Germany's 2nd Tactical Air Force and equipped with the Vampire FB.5. Conversion to the Venom FB.1 came two years later and a further disbandment in October 1957.

With the Lightning F.1 beginning to be phased out of front-line service, examples found their way to No. 226 OCU starting in July 1963. The arrival of the single-seaters allowed weapons and radar training to be introduced to the syllabus, relieving the squadrons of the ab initio task.

In April 1964 the unit moved to Coltishall following No. 74 Squadron's relocation to Leuchars. The OCU consisted of No. 1 Squadron, which carried out ab initio conversion to the Lightning, No. 2 Squadron basic AI 23 radar training and later No. 3 Squadron advanced AI 23B training and Interceptor Weapons Instructor (IWC) courses.

Pilots who had passed through advanced pilot training were converted onto the Lightning. After intensive ground school, the student would be first taught how to fly the aircraft, then in the second phase how to operate the weapon system and, to conclude, ground briefings and airborne exercises in the art of interception. The OCU also trained experienced pilots to qualify as IWCs and Instrument Rating Examiners.

With similar capabilities and performance to the F.1 and F.1A, the T.4 was certainly an experience for anyone taking their first Lightning flight, as Flt Lt Brian Clifford of No. 226 OCU and No. 11 Squadron recalls:

> Having completed basic and advanced flying training on the Jet Provost, Gnat and the Hunter, I was one of ten pilots at RAF Coltishall in Norfolk on the six-month conversion course to the Lightning aircraft before being posted to our various operational squadrons. We were in ground school, learning all the systems and controls before starting the flying training. But to put the learning in context and to give an appreciation of the aircraft's capabilities and its role, we were programmed for an early familiarisation flight that basically involved being a passenger with an instructor doing most of the flying while we observed.
>
> It was 26 January 1967, a cold winter's day with little cloud, a blue sky and a glorious sunset. My sortie was scheduled for a late afternoon take-off at about 4pm. My instructor and I were in XM997, and we were to be the Number 2 in a 'pairs' sortie. We briefed, taxied out and lined up in echelon as a pair at the threshold of runway 24 for a 10-second stream take-off with the sun on the horizon in our eyes. I was tense as I knew what was coming.

> The lead aircraft released his brakes. The reheats lit, and he shot off down the runway. After the 10-second delay, we started our take-off roll, and as our reheats lit and we accelerated at what seemed an unbelievable rate, the lead aircraft suddenly went into plan view and rose vertically. As I rotated my head back to follow him, my instructor said 'tense'. I just had time to note that we had achieved 280 knots, and almost instantly, we rotated 90 degrees, 'stood on our tail' and I was pulled into the seat with 4g. In just a few seconds, the aircraft rolled, and we were levelling at over 4,000 feet. I was thrilled to experience the famous Lightning rotation take-off on my very first sortie.
>
> What struck me almost at once was the wonderful quiet of the cockpit. The Lightning may make a lot of noise outside but in the cockpit, it really was amazingly quiet. We climbed to 20,000 or 30,000ft in no time and carried out radar attacks on each other. First, we were the target, then the attacker. The mysterious green glow from the radar screen and the various 'blips' on it were confusing (later to become very familiar). The quiet voice of the ground radar controller was captivating. I noted the side stick controller for the radar just behind the throttles. It was about 6 inches tall, rising vertically from the instrument panel to the right of my thigh and had a trigger for the index finger, two if not three wheels that could be rotated by the thumb and the whole thing could be pushed, pulled and rocked inboard and outboard. Any movement on any control had an effect on the radar. I remember wondering how one managed to control the aircraft, operate the throttles and also the radar. Lightning pilots had a high workload.
>
> In no time, we were descending for the return to Coltishall. With the clear weather, the sun was by now below the horizon, leaving a red glow to the west, and the lights from the ground, the coast and the airfield several miles inland were clearly visible. At lower levels, it was fully dark, and it would be a night landing. We arrived in the circuit, turned downwind, came around on the final approach over the runway lights and lined up. Whilst the glide path and approach were pretty 'normal', similar to the other aircraft I had flown, what was not was the speed at which we came over the runway threshold and touched down. Landing at about 165 knots or almost 190mph was a real eye-opener, much faster than anything previously attempted, and I remember wondering for a split second, 'Can I do this?' The tail parachute deployed, we slowed, and it was huge smiles all round. What a wonderful aircraft, and what a privilege it was to fly it later in squadron service.[21]

It had been a challenging time getting the Lightning into service, but through sheer hard work and determination from all involved, the aircraft now equipped three front-line squadrons and the OCU. However, this was just the beginning of the story as Britain's first truly supersonic fighter evolved to more impressive variants and higher levels of performance.

4

Interception Part Two: Lightning F.2, F.3 and T.5

'For a few days the planet seemed to face Armageddon. Then Russia's leader "blinked", and the world could breathe again.'[1]

The year 1962 was one in which the threat of a nuclear confrontation during the Cold War was at its highest. On 14 October a U-2 reconnaissance aircraft observed Soviet SS-4 Sandal medium-range ballistic missiles capable of reaching the USA on the island of Cuba. President Kennedy was alarmed at the presence of these munitions so close to the American mainland and vowed not to let the situation continue. He also implemented a naval blockade of the Caribbean island to prevent further missile or equipment delivery. There was a tense stand-off between the superpowers for nearly two weeks, with Strategic Air Command being placed on DEFCON (Defence Readiness Condition) 3 on 22 October and DEFCON 2 on the 24th. Thankfully, through diplomatic means an agreement was reached with Nikita Khrushchev that the missiles would be removed, with Kennedy agreeing never to invade Cuba. Nuclear war had been averted, but it had been a close-run thing. Britain's Thor missile sites were brought to operational readiness during the crisis, indicating the seriousness of the prevailing situation.

On a lighter note, the first episode of *Steptoe and Son* starring Harry H. Corbett and Wilfrid Brambell aired on the BBC in June. In August Marilyn Monroe was found dead in her home from an overdose, and Nelson Mandela, the leader of the African National Congress, was arrested for sabotage and received a life sentence. Ian Fleming's creation James Bond made his screen debut in October with the charismatic Scotsman Sean Connery playing 007 in *Dr No*. In the same month the Beatles released *Love Me Do*, which reached No. 17 on the charts. December saw the publication of Anthony Burgess's *A Clockwork Orange*, offering a dystopian view of the future and a tale of youth rebellion and riot. In the cinemas David Lean's (he of *Sound Barrier* fame) epic film *Lawrence of Arabia* opened.

The following year official thought was being given to the future plans for the Lightning Force. This led, after some debate and changes to the original proposals to the Air Council, to deciding upon nine squadrons and an OCU consisting of the following:

- One squadron for protecting the Cyprus Base Area in the Near East.
- One squadron for protecting interests in the Far East. It was originally planned for two, but the decision was taken that reinforcement from Britain could be implemented should the need arise.
- Five squadrons based in Britain.
- Two squadrons based in West Germany as part of Royal Air Force Germany (RAFG), consisting of the Lightning F.2, subsequently converted to F.2A standard.
- The OCU.

The Lightning joined the RAF in June 1960 and, as the decade progressed, improved versions of the supersonic interceptor were taken on charge. The following will detail each variant's specification, entry into service, the squadrons it served and a brief overview of some of the information held within the ORBs.

Lightning F.2

On the outside the F.2 was almost identical to the F.1A apart from the addition of a small inlet scoop mid-way along the spine providing cooling air for the standby generator, fitted for emergency use in the event of power failure. The aircraft was powered by a pair of Rolls-Royce Avon 210 axial-flow turbojets, producing 11,200lb of thrust at sea level and 14,400lb in fully variable reheat. Liquid oxygen equipment replaced the previous gaseous system and a partial (due to delays in development) OR946 instrument and control display system was fitted. Twin UHF sets provided radio communication, and provision for Identification, Friend or Foe (IFF) was provided. Limitations relating to g were (positive):

Speed	Ventral Empty	Fuel in Ventral	Single Missile
Up to M0.9	6g	5.5g	5g
M0.9 and above	5.5g	5g	3g
Negative: The maximum permissible negative acceleration is minus 3g. Negative g should not be applied for longer than 15 seconds.			

Referral to the Pilot's Notes will find the F.2's performance and armament were similar to the type's predecessors. However, there were some variations in limitations regarding the carriage of the Firestreak, which could now be launched between M0.6 to M1.7, manoeuvring to 3g up to 55,000ft. The minimum runway length for operation is detailed as 2,500 yards.

The F.2 was fitted with a Martin-Baker Type 4BSA Mk 2 ejection seat with the Pilot's Notes stating that the aircraft should not be flown above 60,000ft, which had more to do with the restrictions placed on the pilot by his oxygen regulator and personnel equipment than the aircraft's capabilities, as described below:

Personal Equipment	
P or Q mask	45,000ft
P and Q mask with sleeveless jerkin and anti g trousers	56,000ft

One man who has a long-term interest in the Lightning and pilot personnel equipment is Scott Bouchard, and he describes the masks below:

> The P/Q series of masks (and other derivatives such as the X-Type and AR-5) have been the mainstay of the RAF and RN and, alongside the H-Type, are one of the longest-serving types of oxygen mask. Most RAF/RN aircraft still fly with variants of the P and Q-Types. There are many variants of the masks to suit different aircraft and roles. These are distinguished with numerical suffixes and sometimes additional letters. The difference between the two types is purely size, P being the larger and Q the smaller.[2]

The first of the variant of the F.2 to fly was XN723 on 11 July 1961, piloted by Jimmy Dell. This aircraft spent its career in the test environment and was lost following an in-flight fire on 25 March 1964 with the pilot, Dennis Whitham, ejecting. Delays in equipment development ensured that it would take until 17 December 1962 for No. 19 Squadron to receive its first F.2.

Forty-four were constructed, running through serials XN723 to XN735 and XN767 to XN797, thirty-one of which were converted to F.2A configuration (to be discussed later). In addition, XN729, XN767, XN770, XN796 and XN797 became F.52s and were exported to Saudi Arabia. One F.2, XN785, was lost in RAF service following a double flame-out on 27 April 1964 while flying with No. 92 Squadron. The pilot, Fg Off. G. Davie, initiated ejection too late and was killed.

Two examples, XN725 and XN734, were used in F.3 development work and fitted between them with Avon 301 engines, Stage 3 fin, extended cable ducts and changes to internal equipment. The pair was also used to trial overwing fuel tanks and XN725, the cambered wing. XN734 later went on to take part in the development of the F.6 with the fitting of a large ventral tank. The last flight of an F.2 in RAF service took place on 22 May 1974 when XN794 of No. 19 Squadron piloted by Wg Cdr P. Vangucci landed at Gütersloh. The aircraft had flown 1,295 hours and was later used as a surface decoy.

No. 19 Squadron

In July 1962 No. 19 Squadron with Hunter F.6s based at Leconfield busied itself with air-to-air firing and a Kingpin Adex, an air defence exercise to test Britain's air defences. Along with the usual activities, preparations began for conversion to the Lightning F.2.

With a history going back to the Royal Flying Corps in the First World War, on 4 August 1938 the squadron became the first unit in the RAF to convert to the Spitfire I when K9789 was flown to Duxford. Shortly after receiving the new eight-gun fighter, the Second World War began. The unit was soon in the thick of the action during the Battle of France and Dunkirk. In the Battle of Britain its Spitfire Ibs were fitted with twin Hispano 20mm cannons in a trial to increase destructive power over the 0.303 Browning machine guns, prevalent at the time in RAF fighters. The fitment was not successful as the cannons experienced a high level of stoppages.

The squadron went on to fly more advanced marks of the Spitfire, converting to North American Mustang IVs in April 1945 and later the de Havilland Hornet in October of the following year. The jet age was ushered in when conversion to the Meteor F.4 came in January 1951, the F.8 in April of the same year and the Hunter F.6 in October 1956.

The local inhabitants of Leconfield would no doubt have been far from delighted when, in July 1962, the squadron began the Interim Lightning Syllabus, entailing night-flying between 22:30 hours and dawn. Although creating a disturbance, this was essential training to take the unit from day to all-weather day/night interceptor status. As pilots passed through and completed the course, they then attended Aviation Medicine Training at Upwood, followed by a visit to the LCS at Middleton-St-George in October to complete the transition to their new mounts.

The first Lightning to be received wasn't an F.2 but T.4, XM988, on 11 October. The ORB notes an element of sadness as four of the squadron's Hunters were flown away on the last day of the month to Binbrook for use by the AFDS. Delays in delivering the F.2s raised comment from the OC Sqn Ldr R.M. Raw AFC:

> We hope to receive our Mk 2s soon. English Electric have promised us 12 before Christmas. With the rest of the pilots returning from Middleton-St-George at the end of November, this delay in the Mk 2 programme could have been disastrous, but fortunately, the squadron has been given the task of accepting and flying the T.4s delivered from Warton to Fighter Command. This will enable aircrew and groundcrew to remain current on type.[3]

With the year closing, the squadron received an early Christmas present when the first F.2, XN775, arrived on 17 December, followed by a steady stream of deliveries through to May 1963. The aircraft were adorned with the unit's dolphin badge on the tail and blue and white chequers on the nose surrounding the roundel. The reason for the aquatic reference came from when No. 19 was equipped with the Sopwith Dolphin towards the end of the First World War.

The Phoenix Dynamo Manufacturing Co. Ltd from Bradford was one of the companies that went on to become part of the English Electric Co. Ltd after the end of the First World War. During the conflict it was involved in the subcontract manufacture of Short Type 184 seaplanes, one of which was N1631. (*Ken Ellis Collection*)

Dick, Kerr & Co. Ltd of Preston was subcontracted during the First World War to construct Felixstowe flying boats. Pictured here is a Short-built example, F.5 N4838. Dick, Kerr would later join Phoenix Dynamo as one of the founders of the English Electric Co. Ltd. (*Ken Ellis Collection*)

In November 1917 Phoenix was awarded a contract for two experimental twin-engine flying boats designated P.5 and named the Cork. The machine first took to the skies on 4 August 1918, with N86 pictured at Brough. Although it flew well, the aircraft did not go into production. (*Richard Hall Collection*)

English Electric's first in-house design was the M.1 Ayr, a single-engine biplane flying boat for fleet spotting and gunnery. Only one was constructed, serialled N148, but it refused to take off from the water when on trials at Lytham, which led to any further development being cancelled. (*Ken Ellis Collection*)

From the drawing board of William Oke Manning, the Wren was English Electric's first design to fly on 8 April 1923. Powered by a 3 hp 398cc ABC twin-cylinder motorcycle engine, one of the diminutive ultra-lights survives at the Shuttleworth Collection, Old Warden and is seen here making a brief flight in May 2023. (*Richard Hall*)

English Electric's second design was the twin Napier Lion IIb-powered P.5 Kingston flying boat. In total six, including prototype N168, were built between mid-May 1924 and early 1925, but production did not continue and none entered service. Following this, the company ceased aircraft production. (*Richard Hall Collection*)

With the threat of war looming in the 1930s, English Electric offered its services to the British government to supply war materials and was chosen to build subcontract Handley Page Hampden medium bombers. In total the company built 770 aircraft, one of which, AE436, is under long-term restoration at the Lincolnshire Aviation Heritage Centre, East Kirkby. (*Richard Hall*)

In addition to the Hampden, English Electric also manufactured subcontract Handley Page Halifax heavy bombers. By the end of production the company had built 2,150 examples, with very few of the type surviving into preservation. One that has is W1048 of No. 35 Squadron, which was lost on an operation to bomb the battleship *Tirpitz* on 27 April 1942. The aircraft was salvaged from Lake Hoklingen in Norway and is now displayed in unrestored condition at the RAFM Hendon. (*Richard Hall*)

English Electric entered the jet age in May 1944 when awarded a subcontract to manufacture the de Havilland Vampire. The company delivered 1,376 examples, one of which, F.1 VF301, is preserved at the Midland Air Museum Coventry. (*Richard Hall*)

The first jet-powered aircraft designed by Teddy Petter for English Electric was the A1, later to become the Canberra. The aircraft, serialled VN799, first flew at Warton with Roland Beamont at the controls on 13 May 1949. (*English Electric via Ken Ellis*)

The team that created the Canberra. Left to right: F.D. Crowe, chief draughtsman; D.L. Ellis, aerodynamicist; H.C. Harrison, production design; A.E. Ellison, assistant chief designer; W.E.W. Petter, chief engineer; R.P. Beamont, chief test pilot; D.B. Smith, administration; F.W. Page, assistant chief designer; H.S. Howat, Ministry of Supply technical officer. (*BAe via Ken Ellis*)

English Electric P.1A WG760, piloted by Roland Beamont, first flew from Boscombe Down on 4 August 1954. Seven days later it achieved M1.0 true and became Britain's first truly supersonic aircraft. Today the machine resides at the RAFM Cosford, with a very young-looking Beamont watching over proceedings. (*Richard Hall*)

The Short S.B.5 was designed to test different types of tail and wing sweep configurations to assist in the development of the P.1A, but its contribution has stirred varying debates. The aircraft WG768 is preserved at the RAFM Cosford. (*Richard Hall*)

Following the P.1A, English Electric constructed three P.1Bs to further develop the concept of what was to become the Lightning. The maiden flight of the first P.1B XA847 took place from Warton on 4 April 1957, the same day that the 1957 Defence White Paper was presented to Parliament, which predicted the end of the piloted interceptor. On 25 November 1958 it became the first British aircraft to achieve M2.0 and survives in a dismantled condition in private hands. The image shows the aircraft at the 1994 SBAC Air Show, Farnborough. (*Hugh Trevor*)

To ensure the development of the Lightning proceeded at pace, twenty F.1 Development Batch (also referred to as P.1B) aircraft were ordered and undertook a multitude of trials and tests. Three airframes and two cockpits survived into preservation; one, XG329, is pictured here at the Norfolk and Suffolk Aviation Museum, Flixton. (*Richard Hall*)

The Lightning F.1 was the first to enter operational service with the RAF in June 1960 with No. 74 Squadron at Leconfield. Just one survives in preservation, XM135, which resides at the Imperial War Museum, Duxford. Note the cannon fit and rounded fin that was a feature of the early Lightnings. (*Richard Hall*)

When introduced, the Lightning F.1A featured a UHF radio, external cable ducts, four-position reheat control and the ability to undertake inflight refuelling, which was vital to extending the aircraft's combat radius and ferry range. Four of the variant survive with XM172 seen here preserved by Lakes Lightnings at Spark Bridge. (*Richard Hall*)

To provide the capability to convert pilots onto the Lightning, the T.4 was a two-seat side-by-side trainer with similar performance to the F.1 and F.1A but with the cannons removed. The image shows XL629, the prototype designated P.11 and later T.4, preserved as a gate guard at Boscombe Down. (*Hugh Trevor*)

Externally the Lightning F.1A and F.2 were little different except for a small intake scoop on the spine that fed air to a standby electrical generator. The aircraft also featured a revised cockpit layout, partial OR946 instrumentation and fully variable reheat. The image depicts F.2, XN787'M' of No. 19 Squadron in the mid-1960s. (*Ken Ellis Collection*)

The Lightning F.3 entered RAF service with No. 74 Squadron at Leuchars in April 1964. The aircraft featured a larger Stage 3 square-topped fin, full OR946 instrumentation, uprated Avon 301 turbojets and the ability to launch the Red Top missile. However, its cannons had been removed. One of five complete F.3s preserved, XR713 is seen in the markings of No. 111 Squadron at the LPG Bruntingthorpe. (*Richard Hall*)

The first production flight of a Lightning T.5 took place on 17 July 1964. The aircraft was essentially an F.3 with a two-seat side-by-side cockpit grafted on. Its capabilities were similar to the single-seat variant, and it remained in service up until the end of Lightning operations in 1988. Eight complete airframes have been preserved with XS420 shown here at Farnborough Air Sciences Trust. (*Richard Hall*)

The Lightning F.6 introduced a large ventral tank, the cambered leading edge wing, the ability to carry overwing tanks and the reintroduction of twin 30mm ADEN cannons. Seventeen complete examples survive with XS925 seen here at RAFM Hendon in the configuration of the last variant to see RAF service. (*Richard Hall*)

Considered by some to be the best Lightning of them all, the F.2A spent its operational career in RAF Germany. The aircraft featured a large ventral tank and fin, a cambered leading edge wing and cannons, but was not able to launch the Red Top missile. Four complete airframes survive, with XN776 preserved at the National Museum of Flight, East Fortune. (*Hugh Trevor*)

Overseas sales of the Lightning never achieved their full potential, but contracts were signed to sell F.53s to the air forces of Saudi Arabia and Kuwait. In 1986 some F.53s were sold back to BAe and returned to Britain. One was 53-671 (ZF579), which is now preserved in ground-running condition at Gatwick Aviation Museum. (*Richard Hall*)

To provide training capability for the export Lightnings, T.55 and T.55Ks were sold to Saudi Arabia and Kuwait. Similar to the F.53s, some T.55s came back to Britain and survive as complete aircraft or cockpits. No. 55-713 (ZF598) is seen here at the Midland Air Museum, Coventry. (*Richard Hall*)

The Hawker Siddeley Dynamics Red Top was the first all-aspect missile to enter RAF and FAA service and equipped the Lightning and Sea Vixen. It possessed head-on capability, which alleviated the need to position for a stern shot, and remained in service until the Lightning's retirement in 1988. (*Richard Hall*)

Entering service in 1957, the de Havilland Propellers Firestreak was a first-generation air-to-air guided weapon and the first within the RAF's inventory. The missile equipped the Lightning, Javelin and Sea Vixen. Note the red 'Noddy Cap' used to protect the seeker head while on the ground. (*Richard Hall*)

The Rolls-Royce Avon axial flow turbojet powered all Lightning variants except the two P.1As which utilized the Armstrong-Whitworth Sapphire Sa.5. Engines within the Avon 200 and 300 Series were fitted, with a 301 shown here on display at the Gatwick Aviation Museum. (*Richard Hall*)

The Lightning's primary role was intercepting intruders into Britain's airspace, a duty it held until the final days of No. 11 Squadron in April 1988. On 16 September 1972 two Red Top-armed No. 29 Squadron F.3s are seen holding QRA at Wattisham during the station's Battle of Britain Day. (*A.J.F. Murray*)

Control of Britain's air defences was coordinated by radar stations such as Neatishead, which is now preserved as the Radar Museum. It was from here that the QRA Lightnings and Phantoms would be ordered to scramble to intercept hostile threats. (*Richard Hall*)

Interceptions could result in the meeting of East and West, often high over the North Sea. Typical prey was the Tupolev Tu-16 Badger and Tu-95 Bear, the latter seen here in the company of Lightning F.6 XR753 'A' of Leuchars-based No. 23 Squadron. This Lightning has been preserved at RAF Coningsby. (*No. 23 Squadron via Ken Ellis*)

After retirement, some Lightnings found further use in ground-based roles. One was F.3 XP748, which took up gate guardian duties at Binbrook in May 1977. It would remain here until May 1988 and end its days on the Pendine Range in 1997. (*Hugh Trevor*)

After the disbandment of the LTF in April 1987, two Lightning F.3s were retained by No. 5 Squadron for the year's aeros season. One was XP741 'AR', and upon completion of its air show duties the aircraft was flown to the fire-fighting school at Manston where it was seen in 1988. (*Richard Hall*)

Lightning F.3 XP694 'BO' of No. 11 Squadron comes in to land past Binbrook's QRA shed sometime in the early to mid-1980s. (*Taken by my late brother, Chris Hall*)

With the retirement of the Lightning in April 1988, it was fortunate that some airframes were preserved in a live condition. The LPG purchased two F.6s, XR728 'JS' and XS904 'BQ', the latter of which is pictured here with the No. 2 Avon in reheat during a twilight run. (*Richard Hall*)

In addition to preserving two F.6s, an F.3 and a T.5 cockpit, the LPG has also saved a piece of Cold War infrastructure by reassembling the former Wattisham QRA Shed at its Bruntingthorpe headquarters. (*Richard Hall*)

The preservation of a small number of live Lightnings allows some former pilots to relive their past experiences. Seen here at Cranfield, former LTF boss Sqn Ldr Dennis Brooks walks away from T.5 XS458 after a successful taxi run in 2013. (*Richard Hall*)

In addition to preserving complete airframes, many Lightnings live on as cockpits long after the rest of the aircraft has been scrapped. F.6 XS932 is owned by Richard Scarborough and is seen here at Cockpit-Fest held annually at the Newark Air Museum. (*Richard Hall*)

The QRA Shed, an echo of the Cold War, still exists at Binbrook, but it has been subject to vandalism in recent years. Seen here in 2012, imagine the drama when the klaxon sounded and the flurry of activity to scramble a Lightning out over the cold North Sea to meet an incoming intruder. Today all is quiet save for the sound of the skylark. (*Richard Hall*)

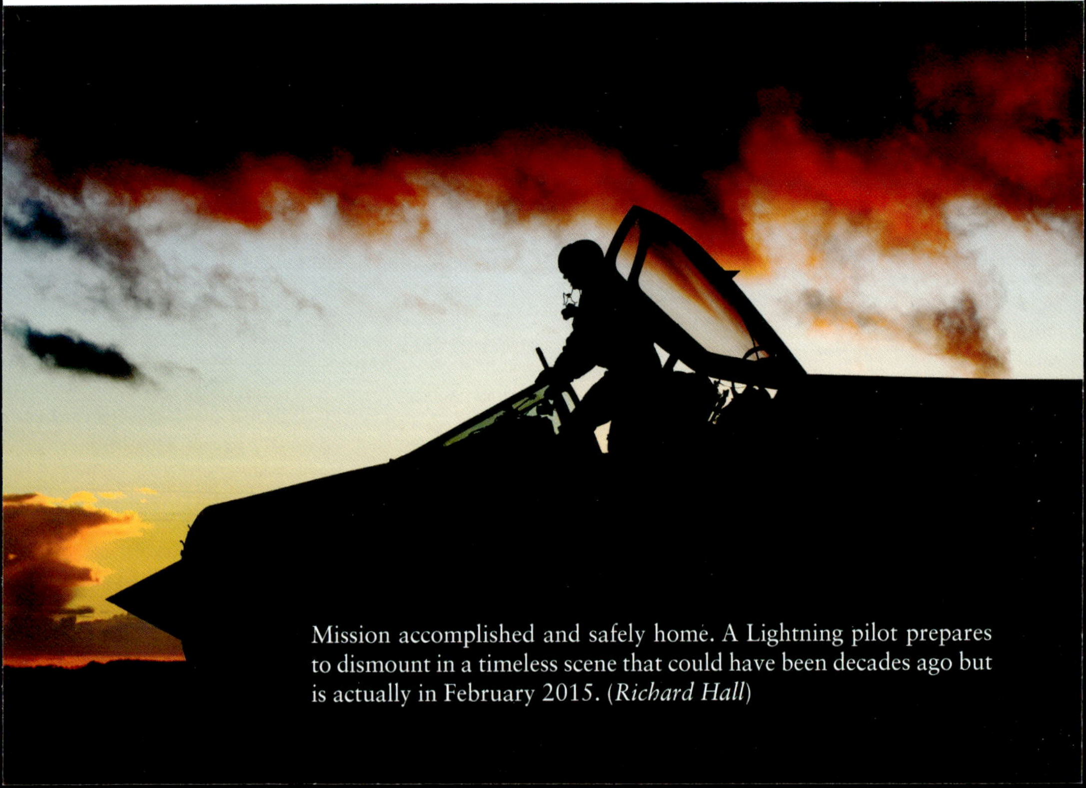

Mission accomplished and safely home. A Lightning pilot prepares to dismount in a timeless scene that could have been decades ago but is actually in February 2015. (*Richard Hall*)

Poor weather conditions in January severely curtailed flying, and just three hours each was logged on the T.4 and F.2. On the 10th XN775 flew for the first time with the unit, but a fault was found in the reheat system. A second F.2, XN788, arrived, but on its second air test, a No. 1 engine fire indication was noted, necessitating a diversion to Finningley with the aircraft returning to the squadron the following month. Meanwhile pilot conversion was almost complete, with operational status commencing in March 1963. By the middle of the month twelve F.2s were on strength with one T.4.

In April the Lightning Acceptance programme was completed, and a modification to the reheat system allowed pilots to slam-select reheat without monitoring engine instruments to ensure correct light-up. This was considered a great tactical improvement. As the month progressed, airborne interception set problems resulted in only one available aircraft with nineteen unserviceable. The cause of this was determined to be a lack of trained personnel and specialized equipment. The OC commented as follows: 'Hard work and careful planning are improving the situation. Efforts are being made to bring trained personnel and equipment up to strength, and when these are successful, the squadron should quickly become operational again.'[4]

It can be seen that No. 19 Squadron was experiencing similar issues in their early days of Lightning operation to those who had already converted to the type. However, the situation slowly improved over the coming months. In July Sqn Ldr W.F. Page took command, and the squadron experienced above-average aircraft availability and improved radar serviceability. This led to its being declared operational on 1 August 1963. In September No. 19 took up QRA, with four scrambles undertaken between the 2nd and 25th. On 15 October Flt Lt David Jones exercised some skilful flying when XN774's nose wheel failed to deploy. Allowing speed to decay gradually, Jones carefully lowered the Lightning's nose onto the runway, with the aircraft sustaining little damage.

The squadron settled into the usual routine of training, exercises and operational commitments. Unlike other Lightning units, No. 19 (along with No. 92) also began to train to use its aircraft in the ground-attack role to give additional capability.

Training in IFR commenced in February 1964 with an MPC attended at Valley in May. Cyprus was now a popular deployment with No. 19 making its first visit in June under Exercise Forthright V. Following arrival at Akrotiri on the 24th, three Lightnings flew to Bahrain in an operation known as Choctaw. This was the furthest east the type had operated so far. The flight was led by Page with Flt Lts Want and Farrer, who stayed in Bahrain after their OC returned to Cyprus on the 28th. The two remaining Lightnings were XN730 and XN778 which had all markings removed, with the former flown and displayed to dignitaries at Riyadh, Saudi Arabia on 4 July by Wg Cdr Jimmy Dell. In all likelihood it was this display that helped pave the way towards future export deals for the Lightning with the Arabian kingdom.

While deployed in Cyprus there was time for a little rest and recreation, resulting in the following being recorded in the ORB:

> One day during the middle of a detachment, the QRA force consisting of Fg Off. Ingham, swimming and Flt Lt Jones, on his sailing surfboard, were scrambled to rescue the Station Commander, Group Captain Horsley, whose mini-sail had turned over and could not be righted successfully. After twenty minutes or so, the rescue was completed, and artificial respiration was found to be unnecessary.[5]

Life returned to normal with the squadron back at Leconfield following its deployment to Cyprus. Of note, a detachment with the French Air Force took place to Reims on 17 August for three days, with Sqn Ldr Page leading four Lightnings. Once again there was time for a little fun:

> A very bedraggled champagne-soaked body of men returned, but they assured us they had enjoyed it. The following week, four Vautour aircraft of 3/30 Squadron at Rheims reciprocated the visit. We entertained them as best we could. Whitbread cannot compete with Moet and Chandon, but we sent them home a little green around the gills.[6]

September was a busy month for the squadron, with participation in Exercise Profit (involving electronic countermeasures-equipped Canberras as targets), IFR Continuation Training and Bomber Affiliation (with some very sporting gentlemen flying Vulcans). The static displays at Battle of Britain events at Finningley and Waddington were enhanced by the appearance of an F.2 at each, while towards the end of the month two aircraft were prepared and detached to Leuchars for QRA duties in October.

During the coming months PIs, QRA and IFR were the order of the day, resulting in the scribe of the ORB making the following comment in December 1964:

> Tanking this month consisted of thirteen sorties only before the Valiants were all grounded for further structural inspections. The final sortie provided much food for thought, not least for the writer. The drogue came off the hose as I made a connection, and fuel from the broken hose found its way into the intake and put out both fires, with typical RR reliability, they both relit without hesitation while I drove smartly home plus a basket and minus a little dignity.[7]

Even the most valiant of Lightning pilots could be fazed by the weather when, later in the month, a freak line-squall-cum-tornado gave Wratton, Jones, Cutting and Grainger a very bad shaking. The former pair diverted to Binbrook; all four were very white-faced afterwards.

January 1965 saw the squadron participate in the flypast for Winston Churchill's funeral. The T.4 was well utilized, with the OC checking out most pilots on lights-out Visidents and tactical handling. Time was also put in with the Taylor helmets carrying out supersonics with targets at 55,000ft and M1.1. The pilots stated this was a very satisfying manoeuvre.

February was busy, with noise and missile trials conducted at Coningsby and Valley respectively, together with low-level and supersonic PIs. The following month achieved something of a record when the squadron put more Lightnings into the air more often than at any other time since conversion. On the 24th the unit undertook its first IFR sortie with a Victor tanker. The RAF had permanently grounded its Valiants in January 1965 after discovering fatigue in its wing spars.

At the end of March the award of the Dacre Trophy came, recognizing the unit as the most proficient fighter squadron in the RAF for the previous year with the following inscription: 'This Trophy is awarded to the Regular Squadron in Fighter Command which is declared to be the most proficient in weapons training'. The criteria for this award changed with the creation of Strike Command in April 1968 and were given to the 11 Group squadron, judged to be the most proficient in all aspects of fighter operations.

For No. 19 Squadron the trophy was presented by Air Commodore G.B. Dacre, CBE, DSO, DL and his wife in memory of their son, Fg Off. Kenneth Fraser Dacre DFC. Dacre (junior) who was killed while flying Mosquito VI HJ790 'UP-R' with No. 605 Squadron from Castle Camps, Cambridgeshire on 22 September 1943. He failed to return from an intruder operation to Ardorf and his navigator, Sgt S.R. Didsbury, died with him.

During April and May two stints of QRA were held, with three live scrambles in the latter month when a Fairchild C-119 Flying Boxcar, which was chased but not caught, an Avro Shackleton and a Douglas Dakota were intercepted. At the end of May four Lightnings flew to Cyprus to relieve No. 92 Squadron of their QRA commitment.

Previously in December 1963 the Air Council decided that two F.2 squadrons (Nos. 19 and 92) would be sent to West Germany to serve with the 2nd Allied Tactical Air Force. The role entailed maintaining a Battle Flight to protect the zonal border between East and West Germany. Incursions by any aircraft over the border or into the Air Defence Identification Zone (ADIZ) were to be intercepted, while further to the west a buffer zone was set up to guide errant aviators if they were straying too close to the border. It was also decreed that the F.2 would be upgraded to F.2A standard.

Over the coming months preparations began for the squadron to relocate to Gütersloh, with Wg Cdr Cox taking over as OC. The move came on 23 September 1965 and was described in the ORB:

> Briefing for the flight took place with many representatives of the Press present. At 10:15 hours, amidst a barrage of photographers and well-wishers, Wg Cdr Cox led the pilots to the aircraft. On the line were thirteen aircraft, which included the Lightning T.4 and the Hunter T.7. Wg Cdr Cox was to fly the T.4 accompanied

> by a BBC Air Correspondent – Colin Riach. All aircraft started simultaneously, and all pilots checked in on R/T as being serviceable. At 10:30 hours, the twelve Lightnings took off in three boxes of four, followed by the Hunter.[8]

A Pathé newsreel from the time named *Lightnings to Germany* shows a group of smiling No. 19 Squadron pilots at a misty Leconfield shortly before their departure, with Wg Cdr Jones, Grp Capt Wootten and cheering ground crew seeing them off. A pairs take-off is seen with the commentator stating that the 420-mile trip took forty minutes to achieve. The arrival at Gütersloh details a four-ship formation flypast with white Firestreaks starkly outlined against the aircraft's bare aluminium finish and an impressive landing with plenty of vortex-creating tyre smoke, air brakes deployed and the brake 'chute streaming. The pilots were welcomed by Air Marshal Sir R.B. Lees DFC*, Commander-in-Chief (C-in-C) of RAF Germany, who had flown with No. 72 Squadron in the Battle of Britain. Further narration follows describing the role of the RAF fighter force in Germany as the investigation of unidentified aircraft in a 30-mile-wide defence zone. The aircraft's four 30mm ADEN cannon fit is evident when observed on the ground, with the clip concluding by stating that the Lightning increases Britain's contribution to peace in the West.

Upon their arrival at Gütersloh No. 19 Squadron ceased to be under the command of C-in-C Fighter Command and transferred to C-in-C RAF Germany. On 6 October the unit was declared operational and took over Battle Flight on the 18th, although the alert hangar had yet to be built. The duty entailed keeping two fully armed aircraft at readiness, with one pilot at five minutes and a second at thirty minutes. The alert would last for fourteen days and, during its first stint, one Lightning was scrambled to investigate an unidentified track, which turned out to be a light aircraft flying at 90 knots at 4,000ft.

The squadron would continue with its F.2s in West Germany, performing a vital role on NATO's front line. However, on 15 January 1968 replacement with the Lightning F.2A began, and the unit would equip with the variant that many pilots considered to be the best.

No. 92 Squadron

On 1 September 1917 Britain had been at war with Germany for just over three years, and on this day No. 92 Squadron formed at London Colney. It worked up on the Sopwith Pup, SPAD S.7 and Royal Aircraft Factory S.E.5a. By the war's end, thirty-seven enemy aircraft had been claimed as destroyed. Following the cessation of hostilities it disbanded, reforming at Tangmere on 10 October 1939, initially with the fighter variant of the Blenheim and later Spitfire Is. Very soon the unit was fighting in the Battles of France and Britain; it later went on the offensive with fighter sweeps across occupied Europe. In October 1941 No. 92 left for Egypt to participate in the desert and later Italian campaigns. On 30 December 1946 it disbanded at Zeltweg with a claimed score of 317 enemy aircraft destroyed.

The squadron reformed at Acklington on 31 January 1947, equipping with Meteor F.3s before converting to the F.4 and later the F.8. Between January 1954 and April 1956 it had a stint flying Sabre F.4s based at Linton-on-Ouse. Conversion to the Hunter F.4 came in April 1954 and the F.6 in February 1957. In 1961 it became the RAF's official display team, performing to much acclaim as the 'Blue Diamonds'.

The following year No. 92 Squadron, based at Leconfield with No. 19, received word that it was to convert to the Lightning, and on 23 January 1963 the first F.2 was received when XN727 arrived piloted by J.K. Isherwood.

Sqn Ldr P.B. Hine commanded the unit, and on 26 March 1963 he collected T.4 XM971 from the LCS and F.2 XN783 from Warton. As with the other Lightning squadrons, No. 92's aircraft were soon adorned with its badge of a reared-up cobra entwined with maple leaves on the fin and red and orange arrows cutting through the roundel. In later years the arrows would give way to squares.

On 23 June the squadron received its last F.2, XN792, but to date conversion had been slow, eliciting comment from the OC:

> A rather disappointing start has been made to our radar conversion. The serviceability of AI has been fair, but output of the bullets from the electronics centre remains too slow for current requirements. A great deal of trouble has been experienced with general aircraft serviceability, and at the moment, practically every sortie is flown at a considerable cost in terms of the manpower effort. No night flying has been carried out since this would have affected the radar conversion programme. Our aim is to recover as many aircraft as possible during the night, and so start the day with the maximum number of fully serviceable aircraft.[9]

The ground crews often commented that keeping the Lightning in the air took considerable effort and dedication. From the statement above, it appears that long hours, both day and night, gave some credence to this.

As autumn approached the squadron busied itself with the Battle of Britain 'At Home' display season and also assisted in a curiously named Fire Brigade trial. The latter was a new system controlled by an Elliot 920C Interception Computer installed at Patrington that was proposed to be used with the Lightning F.3 when it came into service. It was designed to allow a controller to guide an interceptor in all-weather to high-flying targets by sending height, speed and heading instructions by voice to the aircraft, with the ability to amend these as the situation progressed. From the available evidence, the system became operational at Neatishead and Boulmer.

The squadron became operational on 1 October 1963 and undertook its first QRA duties on 2 November, followed by the usual routines, including an MPC at Valley in January of the following year. However, similar to other Lightning units at the time, there were concerns over poor serviceability rates.

In April 1964 IFR training started, but on the 27th of the month XN785 crashed at Hutton Cranswick with the loss of Fg Off. G. Davie following a refuelling sortie. The pilot had experienced problems taking on fuel and elected to return to Leconfield, but an electrical failure of the alternating current system occurred. In such a situation the direct current pumps in the wings should have taken over supplying fuel to the engines, but these were prone to icing if subjected to the cold at altitude, which could have been the case following tanking from the Valiant. With its engines starved of fuel the aircraft crashed at an angle of 35 to 45 degrees, the pilot initiating ejection too late to survive. It had been a sad month for the squadron as on the 14th Flt Lt C.M. Cameron was killed while practising an aerobatic display in Hunter T.7 XL594.

In the early days of Lightning operations the aircraft was afflicted with spurious fire warnings and No. 92 Squadron was no exception. On one occasion in June 1964, Sqn Ldr Hine was leading a four-ship rehearsal for the Queen's birthday flypast piloting XN792. His attention was drawn to the illumination of the No. 2 engine fire warning panel. He felt it best to beat a hasty retreat as he was within 2 miles of Buckingham Palace. Having done so, it transpired that the warning was false.

Fire warnings were not the only spurious event experienced by the unit in June. On the 26th, while holding QRA, a Lightning was scrambled to intercept an unknown supersonic target off the north-east coast of Scotland. Excitement grew as the target headed east to west before heading down the Irish Sea, but this was quelled when it was discovered that the contact resulted from a radar fault.

In July display flying was undertaken at Lyneham, Culdrose and Brawdy, with Sqn Ldr Hine flying the sequences at the last two venues. A display by the Lightning was always a noisy, impressive affair, and it can only be imagined how many marvelled at witnessing the sleek machine in bare aluminium finish with blue fin and spine being put through its paces. Many years later, when speaking to those who attended air shows in the 1960s, they often reminisce about how the Lightning stood on its tail and hurtled almost vertically skyward. It was an aircraft creating lasting memories that persist to this day.

Problems with Lightning fins were nothing new, and one manifestation of this was noted upon arrival at Culdrose when the rudder of XN789 became detached, the cause being a defective stabilizer that set up vibrations leading to failure. It was showtime again in September when the squadron was tasked to provide six aircraft for the 1964 SBAC show at Farnborough.

In October command changed with Sqn Ldr L.J. Hargreaves taking over the reins, with stints of QRA and an MPC undertaken leading up to Christmas. In the New Year a detachment to Cyprus took place, with No. 56 relieved of its QRA commitment on the island. The unit returned to Leconfield in June, with No. 19 Squadron taking over at Akrotiri. A further change of command came in September with Wg Cdr Gilbert assuming the helm.

Like their No. 19 Squadron counterparts, No. 92 was destined to move to Germany and proceeded to do so, departing to Geilenkirchen on 29 December. At this time tensions within the Cold War remained high, but had passed the time of the Cuban Missile Crisis of 1962 when it looked as though the Third World War could well have broken out. However, the skies around East German airspace remained dangerous, and the Soviets thought nothing of downing any Allied aircraft straying away from designated areas. One such incident occurred on 10 March 1964 when Douglas RB-66 Destroyer 54-451 of the USAF's 10th Tactical Reconnaissance Unit operating from Toul-Rosières departed its intended track, possibly due to a faulty compass. Unfortunately the aircraft had flown over a Soviet army exercise, and a quick interception was made using MiG-19 Farmers that were conducting a defensive air patrol and QRA. The RB-66 failed to heed a warning to follow the fighters, turned west and was subsequently fired on, resulting in it being shot down and the crew captured. It can be seen that any small miscalculation could have serious consequences which in turn could lead to even more dire situations arising and a potential escalation of events.

The two German-based Lightning squadrons played a pivotal role in defending the airspace between East and West. The aircraft's ability to react quickly using its phenomenal performance and rate of climb made it ideally suited to the task at hand. There was always the chance that the Soviets could try to blockade Berlin as they had previously in 1948 by closing air and land routes. The Allies used three air corridors to maintain their right of access to the city, and should hostile action be encountered, it would have been the task of Nos. 19 and 92 Squadrons to ensure friendly aircraft using the routes could go about their business unmolested.

The unit would continue to fly the F.2, moving in January 1968 to join No. 19 at Gütersloh. Conversion to the F.2A began in June of the same year when XN773 was taken on charge following modification works at Warton. In its original state as an F.2 the aircraft had previously been used by Rolls-Royce for Avon 210/211 trials.

Lightning F.3

The fourth development of the single-seat Lightning to enter service was the F.3, which differed externally from its predecessors in featuring a square-topped fin with an increase in surface area of 15 per cent. This was required to aid longitudinal stability when carrying the Red Top missile at high speed. One other small change was the extension of the fuselage cable ducts. A full Phase 2 OR946 Instrument and Control Display system and an upgraded AI 23B radar were fitted together with a missile pack designed to allow Firestreak or Red Top carriage. The traditional airspeed indicator dial was replaced with a futuristic-looking strip speed indicator (SSI). Those of a certain vintage will remember that some cars of the era such as the Morris 1100 were also fitted with an SSI.

One aspect of the F.3's development could be construed as rather short-sighted: the removal of the cannons. This decision was taken in 1957 by the AM to create space for additional equipment in the upgraded version of the aircraft. There also appeared at the time in officialdom to be a blind faith in the ability of missiles, brought into sharp focus in the Vietnam War when the USAF had many problems with its Sparrows and Sidewinders. The McDonnell Douglas F-4 Phantom used by the USAF and US Navy (USN) was, for a time, not fitted with a cannon and could find itself in a close-in dogfight with Vietnamese fighters and was at a disadvantage in being unable to take a shot. The oversight was remedied in time as the Phantom was retrofitted with a centreline cannon pack. Given the nature of the Lightning's mission, it needed to be able to give any intruder a warning shot instead of blowing it out of the sky with a missile. Therefore thoughts returned to fitting cannons, which later reappeared on the F.6.

The F.3 was initially powered by a pair of Rolls-Royce Avon 301 (later uprated to 302) axial-flow turbojets, producing 12,600lb of thrust at sea level and 16,300lb in fully variable reheat with the latter engine fitted. It had a wingspan of 34ft 10in, a length of 55ft 3in, a height of 19ft 7in and a tailplane span of 14ft 6in. Maximum take-off weight was 36,000lb with a maximum landing of 34,500lb (except in an emergency).

Airspeed limitations, either clean or with missiles and ventral tank, were M2.0/650 knots depending on which was reached first, or M1.8/650 knots with a single missile and 625 knots with an IFR probe fitted. The minimum speed detailed was 180 knots with flaps and undercarriage up or 140 knots with both down. The Aircrew Manual states although the machine was cleared to 60,000ft, it should not be flown higher than 50,000ft due to the limits imposed by the oxygen system and the pilot's personnel equipment. The aircraft was fitted with a Martin-Baker Type 4BSC Mk 2 ejection seat.

Limitations relating to g were (positive):

Speed	Ventral Empty	Fuel in Ventral	Single Missile
Up to M0.9	6g	6g	4g
M0.9 to M1.8	6g	5.5g	4g
Above M1.8	4g	4g	-
Note 1: When winged Red Top missiles are carried, the limit is +4g except in operational necessity.			
Note: Above M1.8 with two wingless Red Top missiles fitted, the limit is +3g.			
Negative: The maximum permissible negative acceleration is minus 3g. Negative g should not be applied for longer than 15 seconds. The Lightning T.5 g limitations were as above.			

A new fueldraulic system was provided with fuel carried in integral wing tanks, flaps and jettisonable ventral, giving a usable supply of 966 gallons (or 957 gallons depending on which version of the Pilot's Notes is read). Although a more advanced machine than the preceding variants, the F.3 was still afflicted by a lack of fuel and, in some ways, capability with the removal of the cannons. However, plans had been afoot for some years to explore ways to extend the range of the F.3.

In September 1962 the AM issued a requirement to increase the ferry range up to 2,000 miles with one IFR and the operational endurance of the Lightning, together with improvements to radio and navigation aids. This tied in with a decision by the Defence Committee dating back to 1960 for Fighter Command to move from the defence of the deterrent to a role of deterring hostile reconnaissance, interception of unknown aircraft, prevention of jamming of Britain's radar systems and the reinforcement of overseas bases. The plans in time would see the Lightning fitted with a larger ventral tank, provision for overwing tanks and installation of the previously dismissed cambered wing.

The first F.3 to fly was XP693 on 16 June 1962 in the hands of Jimmy Dell. This aircraft was destined to develop the extended range version that would become the F.6 together with XP697. Development problems entailed a delay to the variants in service release, and it was not until 1 January 1964 that XP695 would be delivered to the AFDS at Binbrook.

In total sixty F.3s entered RAF service commencing in June 1964, and it was the most numerous of the type to do so. Serials ran from XP694 to XP696, XP698 to XP708, XP735 to XP765, XR711 to XR721 and XR748 to XR751. Eight further examples were constructed, XP693, XR723 to XR728 and XR747, but after their first flights they were sent to Warton for conversion to F.6 standard. It was planned to convert XR748 to XR750 to F.6 status, but this was cancelled and the aircraft remained in their original configuration. A further sixteen airframes, XR752 to XR767, were taken from the F.3 production line and modified to F.6 Interim standard. The F.3 was to suffer a high loss rate in service with twenty-three written off in accidents. Following its conversion to Saudi F.53 53-666, XR722 was also lost when a 30mm shell exploded in the starboard cannon bay on 6 February 1972.

Although the variant handed over the air defence role in the first instance to the F.6 and later the Phantom, it was to remain within the RAF inventory, almost to the end of the Lightning's service career. Like the F.1 and F.1A, examples found their way to the Wattisham's and Leuchar's TFFs and No. 226 OCU, where they joined No. 21 Squadron. Others continued to be utilized by Nos. 5 and 11 Squadrons and the Lightning Training Flight (LTF) at the time, all based at Binbrook in Lincolnshire. When asked, Sqn Ldr Dennis Brooks gave the following details as to why the F.3 continued to be used in service and its role:

> The F.3s were fully operational but obviously had less fuel than the F.6s and also had no guns. The F.6s were running out of airframe fatigue life, and this had to be eked out by restricting the amount of 'g' used on training sorties. The F.3s still had plenty of fatigue life left, so it could be used on high 'g' sorties such as air combat training.[10]

With the disbandment of the LTF in April 1987 two F.3s, XP741 'AR' and XR716 'AQ', were retained by No. 5 Squadron for display flying during the year's air show season. Following this the former was flown to Manston on 30 September 1987 for use by the fire-fighting school based there. It had succumbed by August 1995. Allocated to similar duties at Cottesmore, XR716 arrived by air on the same day that XP741 flew to Manston. This F.3 became the target of souvenir hunters and preservationists with many items, including the fin, removed. By June 1994 XR716 was no more, meeting its fate at the hands of the scrap man, G. Johnson Metals of Wolverhampton. The two flights marked the end of the F.3's service career in the air.

Hawker Siddeley Dynamics Red Top

Until the introduction of the Lightning F.3 the early marks relied upon the Firestreak, a missile of first-generation technology restricted to pursuit interceptions. The AM wanted an improved version capable of use from all aspects and specified a weapon that could be used from heights between sea level and 65,000ft. It was also required to be effective against aircraft flying at speeds from M0.7 to M2.0. Initially known as the Firestreak IV, de Havilland (later Hawker Siddeley Dynamics) developed the missile, which differed from the original to the extent that it was renamed. The upgraded weapon featured a Linnet solid propellant (cordite) rocket motor providing higher thrust at 6,510lb and a larger 67lb expanding rod warhead which, according to the notes, acted like a buzz saw when it hit the target. A new seeker head provided greater look angles, limited all-around capability and greater snap-up performance. It had a length of 128.85in and a weight of 375lb with range improved to around 7 miles. It could reach a speed of approximately M1.7 over launch at motor burn-out, which was 2.33 seconds. The Red Top featured transistorized electronics, removing the need for cooling by ammonia, although the seeker head required cooling by filtered pure air. However, heating was needed for the missile control unit, gyroscope and accelerometer group, proximity fuze and guidance electronics.

When fitted to the Lightning F.3, F.6 and T.5, a pair was carried on a fuselage-mounted pack below the cockpit. It could be conveyed throughout the flight envelope with a minimum launch speed of M0.5 to M1.8, manoeuvring to 4g between heights of 300 and 55,000ft. One drawback of the weapon, in common with the Firestreak, was that it couldn't be used in cloud. Fuzing was either proximity, contact or self-destruct.

The Red Top was the first all-aspect missile to enter RAF and FAA service, equipping the Lightning and the Sea Vixen. With a head-on capability, the need to position for a stern shot was alleviated and it remained in service until the Lightning's retirement in 1988.

Fire Integrity Programme

It has previously been noted in an earlier chapter that the Lightning's engine layout was unorthodox. To recap, the No. 1 Avon was mounted low to the front of the fuselage, while the No. 2 was mounted above and to the rear. With No. 2 directly above No. 1's long jet pipe, any fuel or hydraulic leaks from the latter engine would likely find their way into the Fire Zone No. 3 area through which the No. 1 jet pipe ran. If there was inadequate sealing under the No. 2 powerplant, the chances of fire increased as escaped liquids came into contact with hot surfaces below.

From the early years of operation, fires accounted for the highest number of accidents and write-offs within the Lightning fleet. The F.3 was the most likely variant to be affected by the issue, followed by the F.1, F.1A and F.6.

To reduce the risk Lightnings were passed on a rolling basis in the late 1960s to early 1970s through the Fire Integrity Programme (FIP), where a fuel and oil-resistant synthetic rubber material known as Viton® was applied to the floor of the No. 2 engine bay. However, the problem of fire was not eradicated and losses continued. Colin Murray of Wattisham TFF, Nos. 29 and 19 Squadrons recalls:

> I didn't have much, if anything, to do with the development of the Fire Integrity Programme, and what follows would have been only a small part of it. It was being carried out in 2 Hangar at Wattisham, the home of TFF and ASF [Aircraft Servicing Flight]. The work was undertaken by a Contractor Working Party (CWP) team with probably a few RAF techies under the charge of the engineering Officer, Flt Lt Tim Henington, and was certainly going on in the early 70s. RAF techies could have been either seconded from the Squadrons or part of the CWP team. The only basic details I can recall were at least one F.3 having the mid-fuselage below the level of the top engine hatch painted with matt white paint, possibly distemper, and red dyed liquid was then released into No.2 ECU bay, I believe on the ground and in the air. Any leakage could then be seen on the paint. Areas would be investigated to see where the fluid was getting through, and preventative measures would be put together to block/cure the leaks for fleet-wide implementation. The only part that I vaguely remember being visible externally were two modded panels, possibly 55p and 56s. They had a large extended drainpipe fitted with a wind deflector at the end. These were to drain and move leaked fuel to the outside of the No.2 ECU bay. I think I'm correct on this, but memory fades after fifty-plus years. I nearly forgot another bane of one's life: Viton® tape wrapping the hydraulic pressure line couplings to prevent oil spray/mist in the event of leakage.[11]

Dave Rowberry, who served with the Wattisham TFF, Aircraft Storage and Support Flight, Aircraft Servicing Flight and No. 5 Squadron, adds:

> The modded panels were designed to create a negative pressure within the engine bay, so sucking volatile vapours away, the end plates were cunningly designed to cause maximum pain if (when) you walked into them. Leaked fluids were allowed or encouraged to escape outboard and not onto a hot No.1 engine and jet pipe. Also, they learned that unions prone to leakage (i.e. hydraulics) were wrapped in Viton® tape, so you got a drip rather than an atomised spray. Fire integrity was an ongoing thing, so anytime an engine was taken out, full fire integrity checks were carried out and signed for before the engine could go back in. The fuel gallery had metal canisters that clipped around the Flight Refuelling System (FRS) couplings for the same reason. The X-raying of FRS couplings to check the various pipe ends were correctly aligned was introduced as part of fire integrity.[12]

Of note, only one T.4 was lost through fire, while no F.2s and '2As or T.5s (while in RAF service) succumbed to the element. It is possible that the F.2's lower risk of loss was due to the cooler running of its Avon 200 series engines and a different fuel system to the F.3 and F.6. These latter variants featured a high-pressure fueldraulic system which, if it leaked, sprayed highly flammable fuel around the hot engine bays. It seems strange that the T.5 fitted with the same engines as the F.3 and F.6 had no loss through fire in RAF service, and there appears to be no real explanation as to why the variant had a more reliable record in this respect.

As previously stated, the FIP did not completely remove the risk to the F.3 and F.6 and the differences between the Avon 200 and 300 were investigated. The latter engine had the fueldraulic system, higher operating temperatures, which increased those in the bays and a Hot-Streak reheat ignition, all considered factors in increased fire risk.

In time further measures were implemented to take care of weaknesses in the fueldraulic system, as described by Dave Rowberry:

> As for the fueldraulics, there was a problem with the four studs that attached the flex pipe to the body pulling out of the aluminium casting, so we had a mod to add helicoil inserts, and I think that was later superseded by steel inserts at the manufacturers. There was also a problem with the sealing of the same junction. Initially, it was a blue fibre gasket and Hylomar®, but we had to replace that with a steel and bonded rubber gasket. I think there was also the danger of people using the pink transportation gasket, which was even less up to the job. I'm not certain, but I think it was the gasket first in the early 70's and then the studs. Fueldraulics was F.3, F.6 and T.5, anything with the 300 series engines. There would have been various Preliminary Warning Instructions (PWI) and then Special Technical Instructions, Servicing Instructions and MODs for each of the snags. The PWIs normally arrived on a Friday morning, entailing weekend working.[13]

The FIP evolved over time and went on to include changes to gaskets, checking for cracks in the jet pipe leading to the replacement of the intermediate section, outlet guide vanes and cyclic fatigue testing of the Hot-Streak system. With regard to the last item listed, Dave Rowberry explains its operation:

> The Hot Streak was a jet of fuel injected into the engine exhaust just aft of the turbine. This ignited and travelled down the interpipe to light the fuel being sprayed into the reheat pipe to give reheat. The hot streak only lasted for a couple of seconds; once lit, the flame was retained on the reheat burners by the flame gutters. Initiation was automatic on selecting reheat, the fuel being contained in an accumulator atop the engine.[14]

To ensure that fire integrity remained uppermost in people's minds, technicians new to the Lightning were given the best possible training regarding this to ensure that the lessons learned were passed on. Thankfully the instances of fires reduced (but did not cease) as had they not, the Lightning may have been withdrawn from service earlier than envisaged. Such a situation would have seriously affected Britain's defence capabilities as the Lightning's planned replacement, the Phantom, was not yet fully in service.

At the time of implementing the FIP and other measures to contain fire, the Lightning Force was at its peak, with nine front-line squadrons and the OCU. The personnel, not least the ground crews, involved in the operation of the F.3 and later the F.6, certainly in the late 1960s and early 1970s, had much to contend with. Within the ORBs from the time there are numerous references to serviceability issues due to modifications, the FIP and spares. Yet QRA and Battle Flight were maintained, a true credit to all those involved.

Lightning F.3 versus Spitfire XIX

In 1963 British Commonwealth Forces and Indonesia were engaged in a period known as 'The Confrontation' that lasted until 1966. The cause of the dispute is outside the scope of this book, but it is fair to say there was an interest in the RAF of how its present-day supersonic interceptor would deal with the Indonesian Air Force's North American P-51D Mustang piston-engine machines if combat were joined.

Wg Cdr John Nicholls DFC AFC (later Air Vice Marshal and Sir) was in charge of the AFDS at Binbrook and, in February 1964, arranged a short battle trial with Spitfire XIX PS853 – the designation used prior to changes in early 1948 from Roman to Arabic numerals – and a Lightning F.3. The Second World War vintage fighter was on charge at the airfield and was originally destined to become a gate guardian but was kept in an airworthy condition, which was useful as it had a similar performance to the Mustang. The Spitfire was flown by Nicholls and the F.3 by Sqn Ldr R. Lees.

There was no doubt that the Lightning could easily outpace the Spitfire, but it presented a poor target for infrared missiles. A dogfight with an F.3 would be out of the question as it lacked cannons. However, if in combat with an F.1A or F.2 and the ADENs came into play, the Lightning would have to slow down. This is where the piston-engine fighter's manoeuvrability would come into play and the supersonic machine could well lose. If the Spitfire pilot had sufficient warning of an attack he could meet the Lightning head-on, presenting the most difficult of targets.

So how best to deal with the situation? A tactic was devised to utilize the Spitfire's blind spot, necessitating a climbing attack from below and behind, giving the best chance of achieving a heat source for the missiles. With an advantage in sheer power-to-weight ratio, if the attack was unsuccessful the Lightning could climb out of harm's way where the Spitfire had no chance of pursuing and then try again. It was considered that a competent Lightning pilot using such tactics could always defeat the Spitfire or Mustang. However, it was never put to the test in anger.

Lightning F.3 in Service

As the 1960s progressed, Britain's air defence system continued to be tested by the intrusion of Soviet reconnaissance aircraft, typically the Tupolev Tu-16 Badger and Tu-95 Bear, attempting to gather electronic intelligence and test reaction times. The F.1 and F.1A had been withdrawn from the front line by 1966, but with the assistance of Victor tankers, Lightning F.3s intercepted and shadowed the unwelcome visitors over the North Sea. The encounters often led to some iconic photographs of the Lightning flying alongside the intruders.

During the F.3's career a change occurred within the RAF's structure. On 30 April 1968 Fighter and Bomber Command merged to form Strike Command, which absorbed Signals and Coastal Command the year after.

The following details the variant's entry into service and provides an overview of the squadrons and units with which the variant served.

No. 74 Squadron

Following the move to Leuchars in April 1964, the squadron settled into a routine of supersonic and subsonic PIs and Visidents. The first Lightning F.3 to enter RAF service, XP700, joined No. 74 on 14 April, followed by XP751 fifteen days later. The latter was the first built to full-production standard. The unit had brought the F.1 into service in June 1960 and was now to do the same with the F.3 under the command of Sqn Ldr Peter Botterill who made the following comment:

> The age and hard usage of the Mk 1 Lightning is beginning to be very noticeable in terms of serviceability. Many faults occur with monotonous regularity in all aircraft systems there being no general trend. Despite many hours of rectifications put in by the long-suffering ground crew, the flying hours achieved continue to be very low. With the introduction of the Mk 3 aircraft the squadron looks forward hopefully to more reliability, performance and flying. No 74 was the first to be equipped with the Lightning Mk 1 and is again first with the Mk 3.[15]

The F.1 continued flying with the squadron until mid-June 1964, and by the end of the month nine F.3s were on strength. August was marred by the loss of Flt Lt G.M. Owen on the 28th while practising aerobatics over the airfield for the Battle of Britain display. He was piloting XP704 when the aircraft entered a spin at the top of a loop and was too low to recover. Owen was buried with full military honours at St Michael's Cemetery, Leuchars. At age 31 he was a seasoned aviator and had survived two ejections, from Canadair Sabre F.4 XD758 on 22 July 1954 and from XD772 on 29 November in the same year.

After a period of working up on the F.3, the squadron became operational again on 1 December 1964 with QRA held and command handed over to Sqn Ldr W.B. Maish in the same month.

Upon entering service its aircraft were adorned with the Tiger's Head badge, and a large national flash was applied to the fin which was painted black along with the spine. The roundel on the nose was bordered on either side by black and orange triangles. This colour scheme was quite conservative compared with what was to come from Nos. 56 and 111 Squadrons, but it was not long before those in higher office decided that the days of the flamboyant fins were numbered and it was decreed that all such adornments would cease from 14 February 1965. After this date it was instructed that badges should be within an 18in diameter circle and nose markings would conform to a strict geometrical pattern. The days of the outlandish colour scheme were over, but at least for now the Lightning retained its bare aluminium finish.

During March an interesting exercise was undertaken with Maish flying to Upper Heyford to trial IFR with a USAF Boeing KC-135 Stratotanker, which was deemed a success, with the comment that the American crew's issuing of Green Shield stamps was much appreciated. Further tanking would take place with the KC-135s in April under the name of Operation Billy Boy.

In August four F.3s detached to Akrotiri with IFR provided by Victors, which was to be the tanker's and the latest Lightning variant's first visit overseas. Of note, four aircraft were deployed to Teheran for the Iranian Air Force Day in October. How times have changed, as such an event would be unthinkable in today's world.

The squadron continued to hold QRA and in December 1965 undertook three practice scrambles and one operational launch to investigate a contact that turned away before it could be intercepted. However, on 4 July 1966 four Lightnings were scrambled and three Myasishchev M-4 Bisons that came within 140 miles of Leuchars were shadowed. This was the first time the unit had met Soviet aircraft over the North Sea, with the intruders becoming regular prey for the Lightnings.

August was an interesting month for the unit, with the arrival of the first full production standard F.6, XR768, and further North Sea interceptions against Soviet aircraft while holding Northern QRA, leading to the following comment from Maish:

> QRA interceptions against Russian aircraft over the high seas ensured that all personnel viewed QRA with more interest and enthusiasm. The Mk 6 Lightning will improve our ability to intercept at longer ranges, but though we have one such aircraft in the hangar due to technical reasons it has not flown this month.[16]

In October Wg Cdr Ken Goodwin took command, with the pilots continuing to fly the F.3 until the end of December 1966. Conversion to the F.6 came in January 1967, and the next chapter in the unit's career began.

No. 23 Squadron

The second unit to equip with the F.3, No. 23 Squadron, began conversion to the type at the end of August 1964. Like other Lightning operators, it could trace its lineage back to the days of the RFC and, between the wars, flew biplanes including the Gloster Gamecock, Bristol Bulldog and the fighter version of the Hawker Hart. One notable squadron member in the interwar years was Douglas Bader, who lost his legs in a flying accident at Woodley on 14 December 1931 while performing aerobatics in Bulldog IIA K1676. He went on to achieve fame by returning to flying with artificial legs just before the outbreak of the Second World War. He took part in the Battle of France and Britain flying with Nos. 222 and 242 Squadrons, but ended the war in German captivity after his Spitfire Va, W3185, came down in France on 9 August 1941 with differing theories as to how the loss occurred.

At the outbreak of the Second World War the unit was equipped with the Blenheim If in the night fighter role and progressed to intrude over Luftwaffe bomber bases. In March 1941 it converted to the Douglas Havoc I and later the Boston III. It continued in the intruder role with further conversion to the Mosquito II in January 1942. While operating the Mosquito in 1944, the squadron had been part of 100 (Bomber Support) Group whose role was to defend Bomber Command against Luftwaffe night fighters by intruding over its airfields or interception in the bomber stream. It disbanded in September 1945, but reformed a year later as a night fighter unit equipped with the Mosquito NF.30. The jet age was entered with conversion to the Vampire NF.10 in October 1952, the Venom NF.2 in June 1954 and Javelin in March 1957, equipping with the FAW.4, '7 and '9 variants.

In March 1963 No. 23 moved from Coltishall to Leuchars, where in April 1964 it was joined by the Lightning F.3s of No. 74 Squadron. Time was split between preparing to retire the unit's Javelin FAW.9s and accepting its first F.3s XP707, XP708 and XP756, which arrived the following month. The aircraft soon received a striking white tail and spine livery, with a large national flash and red eagle adorning the fin. Blue and red vertical bars bordered the roundel under the cockpit. As with other Lightning operators, the scheme would be toned down in time to a bare aluminium finish and smaller markings.

The Javelins remained on QRA until this ended in September. Command transferred to Sqn Ldr J. McLeod, with status as a Lightning squadron becoming effective on 1 October. With the exception of the CO and one other pilot, No. 23 was made up of experienced Lightning pilots selected from other units. A full complement of F.3s and one T.4 (XM973) had been received by November 1964, and by then all Javelin flying had ceased. At the end of the month the CO commented:

> November was a satisfying month which saw the squadron practically complete its conversion to the Mk 3 Lightning. All but two of our aircraft finished

> acceptance tests, and the pilots flew, on average twice every three working days. Night flying started gently in view of the groundcrew's albeit fast-disappearing inexperience and we are leading up to the fully operational exercises such as visual identification and scramble procedures.[17]

The unit was declared operational in December, with the first QRA held in February 1965. To improve the ever-constant problem of range, the fitting of IFR probes began and in April tanking began under Exercise Billy Boy with USAF KC-135s, leading to the following comment from the CO in May:

> The reintroduction in a new form this month of in-flight refuelling has proved a welcome stimulus to our training task. Since 75% of our pilots have experience of in-flight refuelling and we had initially the lion's share of the KC-135, the squadron is now in the position of being the most experienced one on in-flight refuelling the Mk 3 Lightning. However, we have also broken the largest number of probes. This weakness will be eliminated by a current modification. The delivery of a Hunter T.7A, incorporating display OR946, is a most welcome addition.[18]

In June QRA was again held with seven scrambles, three resulting in interceptions and shadowing of Soviet Tu-16 Badgers some 200 miles out over the North Sea. This was the first month that the squadron used the new purpose-built hangar constructed at Leuchars. During August the unit had its first MPC at Valley and began tanking from the Victor, while a deployment to Cyprus came in October. In the final month of 1965 No. 23 received T.5 XS417, but it was not to fly until January 1966 due to numerous minor snags.

On 16 May Wg Cdr K. Williamson took the helm in a change decreed by the Air Force Board that entailed the rank of wing commander taking over as squadron commanders and squadron leaders as flight commanders. Encounters with Soviet aircraft continued and in the same month, on the 26th, Flt Lt Bob Driscoll, piloting XP708 and accompanied by his flight commander, intercepted a pair of Tu-95 Bears at 40,000ft.

Flying the Lightning was not without its risks, as Flt Lt A. Turley found on 24 August 1966. He had taken off in XP760 for a practice interception with four Hunters at 35,000ft. He shut down one engine to conserve fuel, but upon relight he was presented with dual reheat fire warnings. The aircraft pitched up violently to 70 degrees and, with speed decaying, entered an incipient spin. Turley then noticed the hydraulic warning light had illuminated. Despite his efforts Turley could not regain control and ejected at 5,000ft over the North Sea. He was quickly rescued by helicopter. After this incident the shutting down of one engine was banned.

In March 1967 a statistical summary for the previous year showed that No. 23 Squadron had flown more training sorties than any other unit in Fighter Command. This led to the award of the Dacre Trophy in a ceremony at Leuchars in May.

The days of F.3 operation were beginning to end, as on 8 May 1967 the first F.6 Interim XR761 arrived for the squadron and conversion had been completed by the end of October the same year.

No. 111 Squadron

The Lightning F.3 began to reequip No. 111 Squadron in December 1964, with XP738 the first example to arrive at Wattisham and XP742 the last of twelve in February the following year. At this time Sqn Ldr G. Black was still in command and oversaw the full conversion to the new variant, which was achieved on 12 March 1965. The last F.1A had flown with the unit the previous month.

Squadron markings were applied to the F.3s with a black lightning flash outlined in yellow cutting through the roundel on the nose and an ornate squadron badge of two swords in saltire charged with three seaxes on the fin, which was painted yellow upon a black background. The spine was also coloured black, with a small yellow flash extending back to just above the wing root.

In April IFR began again with the USAF's KC-135s following the grounding of the RAF's Valiants in January. Sqn Ldr Black made the following comment:

> Flight refuelling sorties were flown with KC-135s from SAC 919 Squadron. Each refuelling sortie of approximately 1 hour on refuelling practice terminated in normal interception practice, Lightning v Lightning. Initial contacts on the 'boomed' KC 135s proved relatively easy compared to the Valiant; however, the kinking and distortion of the KC-135's hose and drogue (9ft) has proved strenuous on probe rivets and remaining in contact for prolonged periods of up to 5 minutes, more exacting and tiring than the Valiant.[19]

A first public outing to the Bentwaters Armed Forces Day came on 22 May, where Flt Lt Doyle flew a five-minute solo display for 30,000 spectators. Two days later four Lightnings overflew St Paul's London in commemoration of the twentieth anniversary of VE Day. Practice had also begun for a nine-ship formation proposed to be flown at the Paris Air Show in conjunction with the Folland Gnats of the 'Red Arrows', which arrived at Wattisham at the end of the month. In due course nine Lightnings and seven Gnats flew at the event on 20 June.

After his debut at Bentwaters, the squadron's regular display pilot Flt Lt T. Doyle flew to St Mawgan on 26 June to position for a performance at the Exeter Air Show. Completing his routine, spectators noticed smoke and flame streaming from the rear of F.3 XR712. The pilot headed back to St Mawgan, but upon trying to land he experienced control issues and initiated an ejection, which was accomplished safely. The Lightning came down around 3 miles off the coast. The wreckage was not recovered, but it was concluded that the likely cause was an explosion in the No. 1 engine followed by a fire. The aircraft had flown for a total of 145 hours at the time of loss, and it was the first write-off of an F.3 sustained by the unit. Not to be beaten, Doyle was back on the display circuit the following month, performing at Scampton, Wattisham, Culdrose and Plymouth.

August was a month for training as the unit picked up pace after its display commitments. The list included night flying, supersonic and high-level interceptions, Visidents, bomber affiliation, Exercise Profit (jamming) and a survival scramble. Also practised for the first time were low-level interceptions, but this achieved only moderate success.

On 6 September the squadron received Lightning T.5 XS450 to replace T.4 XM992, which had suffered a brake failure accident on 14 July. During the same month a diamond nine was flown at Biggin Hill in what was to be the last display by a whole Lightning squadron.

In October the unit undertook its first IFR from the Victor and six Lightnings with eight pilots deployed to Valley for an MPC. The following gives details of the type of activities that took place:

> The squadron successfully launched five Firestreaks. One missile was launched at low level with the target at 100 feet at 250 knots. The fighter was at 1,200 feet at 380 knots and started his attack at 3,000 yards diving towards the target. Two missiles were launched with the target at 45,000 feet at M0.7. The fighter carried out a parallel head-on attack displaced 10 miles, accelerating to M1.2 in the turn onto the target's heading and following the Head Down Display. The two further missiles were launched with the target at 50,000 feet at M0.7, with the fighter accelerating from M0.95 at 15 miles line astern to M1.3 and starting the 'Snap Up' attack from 6 miles. This was also flown on the Head Down Display.[20]

The New Year of 1966 saw No. 111 Squadron detached to Cyprus, and in June a Red Top missile pack was fitted to one aircraft with encouraging results. However, the additional weight and fuel consumption were noticeable.

A change of command came in August 1966, with Black handing over to Wg Cdr D.P. Hall AFC. Problems with the unit's Lightnings came in June 1967 as fuel leaks were further compounded by a lack of spare parts including canopies and the Maxaret braking system, yet QRA and training were still required to be undertaken. Of note, on 20 December, while piloting T.5 XS450 on a training flight, Wg Cdr Hall and Fg Off. Phillips intercepted an unidentified aircraft, which turned out to be a Bréguet Atlantic of the German navy.

A well-known saying in the RAF is 'If you can't take a joke, you shouldn't have joined up.' For Christmas 1967 the squadron was none too pleased as it was placed on QRA over the festive season:

> Southern QRA was taken over from 29 Squadron on the 22nd of December, just in time for 111 to make it four Christmases in a row. Although all members can see the need to put a good squadron on QRA over the holiday period, the 100% feeling is that some other unit should be given a chance to prove themselves next year.[21]

Not content with disrupting Christmas, it was decided to call Exercise Ricochet at 05:45 hours on the 28th. With memories of the festivities rapidly fading, the ground crews managed to generate seven F.3s and the T.5, which between them flew eight sorties.

It would appear that the spares situation had not improved to any great extent if the CO's comments in the ORB for January 1968 are anything to go by:

> Overall, the squadron has not made a bad start to 1968. All sections of the squadron are pulling their weight and standing up well to the continual pressures and the amount of overtime being worked. In fact, at the beginning of the month, a whole shift volunteered to a man to work extra overtime to clear the backlog of unserviceabilities. The spares situation is still a disgrace, and those responsible for the inept provisioning arrangements bear a great responsibility. The tremendous efforts put in by the ground crew are invariably needed because of the shortcomings of the provisioning system.[22]

There were more problems during March with numerous hydraulic issues coming to light. Although of a minor nature, repairing often entailed removing engines or jet pipes, a time-consuming and difficult operation.

In May 1968 Wg Cdr L. Swart assumed command, and in the same month the unit took over Southern QRA from No. 29 Squadron for three weeks before handing it over to No. 5 Squadron. During this time two operational scrambles of airliners were undertaken, with an unmarked Boeing 707 intercepted and a Douglas DC 6 identified before contact was made. Also during the month, PIs were undertaken up to 56,000ft at M1.2. Comment was made that operations of this type were considered near the limits of the F.3's capability.

Over the coming months the squadron settled into the usual routines of training, PIs, weapon training, QRA, MPCs and IFR (including at night). In November 1968 the unit's aircraft began appearing on the line with Red Tops fitted, raising comment that this was the first time they had been used for serious weapons training, although some squadrons had been using them for some time. However, the lack of packs and the weather hampered conversion to the Red Top as the CO describes:

> A depressing end to the year. The poor flying weather almost prevented our conversion to the Red Top missile in time for our next period of QRA duty. The New Year finds the squadron short of flying practice, short of aircraft and with a diminishing experience level among the groundcrew due to a rush of postings. Great efforts will be required in the New Year to establish a regular flying programme, increase the flying hours achieved and meet the many commitments in view.[23]

The weather impacted the first month of 1969, but QRA was held throughout, with the first Red Top fired at the range in Cardigan Bay. On the last day of January the alert was handed to No. 5 Squadron, but again the climate had other plans. Within three days the alert was back with No. 111 Squadron as heavy snowfall blanketed Binbrook and the Lincolnshire Wolds.

As the year progressed and the weather improved, the squadron took part in the Queen's Birthday Flypast on 14 June over London. Interestingly, the second prototype Concorde followed the Lightning at one mile astern.

On 14 July 1969 the squadron detached to Binbrook and deployed ten Lightnings within the week. The unit was soon participating in QRA from the airfield's hangar, which was stated as being more comfortable than the one at Wattisham. The pilots and ground crew were most appreciative of the do-it-yourself cooking facilities, and there were few complaints during the twenty-four-hour stints of duty. Also two major exercises, High Noon and Recant, were undertaken in the month.

High Noon was a three-day, no-notice exercise involving all the forces of Strike Command. The unit was held in a heightened state of readiness with a survival scramble on the third day. Recant lasted for one day, with the east coast simulating the south coast of Cyprus in a deteriorating Middle East situation, with the area defended against high and low-level attacks.

In September 1969 the squadron moved again, this time to Coltishall, and the following month returned to Cyprus for an air defence exercise. In December a return to Wattisham was made and a familiar tradition was handed down from on high, the holding of QRA over Christmas, which would make it five years in a row. Remember the old RAF saying from earlier in the chapter? Well it was very apt now.

The year 1970 followed a familiar course for the squadron, but it is of note that in May the Queen's Birthday flypast generated the following comment in the ORB:

> A practice for the Queen's Birthday was held on 13 May. In the past, this has been a preserve of the Lightnings, but now more units from Strike Command have edged their way in, and the result will be a composite formation from Vulcans, Phantoms, Lightnings and a Nimrod.[24]

The McDonnell Douglas Phantom, in time, would begin to eat away at the Lightning's hold of Britain's air interception duties, which will be explored in more detail later. The squadron continued with the F.3 until September 1974 when its air defence role was handed over to the Phantom FGR.2. The unit had flown the Lightning for more than thirteen years, both in its early and improved form. It had had its fair share of problems, but the memories and friendships created would endure way off into the future.

No. 56 Squadron

To show that it was not all work and no play, on 13 March 1965 squadron members and their wives and some from No. 111 Squadron travelled to Ipswich and participated in ten-pin bowling followed by a Chinese meal. On 24 March a games night was held in the Officers' Mess, where the sergeants were thrashed (according to the ORB). Aside from all the fun, March was an important month for more serious reasons as conversion to the Lightning F.3 began, with XR719 arriving on the 16th followed by XP743 and XR717 within two weeks. A squadron strength of twelve was not achieved until early August of the same year, which was considered to be somewhat slow.

As per other Lightning units, it was not long before No. 56's aircraft were adorned with one of the most striking colour schemes yet applied. While the fuselage remained bare polished aluminium, the fin was painted with red and white chequers with the former colour extending along the spine. Two overlapping chevrons continued the squadron colours ahead of the roundel on the nose, with its motif mounted within a white circle at the head of the chevron. Individual aircraft codes were applied in red to the air brakes.

The squadron was declared non-operational in April to allow for conversion to the new variant and the continued disposal of the F.1As, although the latter's usage had not ceased. During the month Flt Lt John Ward had an unfortunate incident with F.1A XM174 during a practice interception with a Meteor NF.14. After a hard turn at high altitude, he was caught in the slipstream of the preceding aircraft and his machine flicked, which in turn bent the pitot tube around the radome. Not only was he deprived of the ability to monitor airspeed, but the altimeter was also gyrating to the extent of being unusable. Letting down through cloud without either speed or altitude information required careful thought, therefore John set up an orbit to assess his options. Thankfully he was soon joined by Flt Lt Chris Rowe, who flew on his wing and guided him back to Wattisham. With the introduction of the F.3 a secondary pitot was fitted within the intake, which fed information to an additional airspeed indicator in the cockpit, thus providing back-up in the event of main pitot failure.

Flt Lt Ward was not the only pilot with No. 56 to experience problems in April. On the 23rd Flt Lt P. Wild was flying X719 when he experienced lateral control restrictions but was able to return to Wattisham. It was subsequently found that a loose bolt was fouling the aileron control rods, which had probably been there since manufacture. Five days later Flt Lt P. Clee experienced a similar problem while piloting T.4 XM989. He found he could not turn to port but, with skilful flying, managed to land safely. An investigation found a half-inch spanner jamming the aileron controls, in all likelihood left there during servicing works.

On 7 May 1965 a notable aviator came to the squadron and was flown in the resident twin-seater XM989 by Sqn Ldr Martin. Air Commodore Al Deere, DSO, OBE and DFC* was a former Battle of Britain pilot who flew Spitfires with No. 54

Squadron and finished the war with twenty-two confirmed 'kills', ten 'probables' and eighteen damaged. At the time of his visit he was Air Officer Commanding (AOC) of No. 12 Sector, and on this day the unit flew a wing survival and battle scramble as part of his inspection.

In June the USAF 'Thunderbirds' aerobatic team with its F-100 Super Sabres came to Wattisham as part of a European tour and, upon arrival, gave an impressive display, after which the squadron provided lunch. Later in the day, six Sabres and four Lightnings launched and flew in formation; the event is recorded in the ORB with a black and white photo.

The squadron endeavoured to get to grips with its new mount and, for the remainder of 1965, continued with the usual activities associated with operating the Lightning as described previously. A change of command came in December with Wg Cdr C.H. Bidie AFC taking over the reins.

From the available evidence, in its service career with the RAF (including those serving with the AFDS), seventy-nine Lightnings (including two of the DB) were lost due to accidents or damage either in the air or on the ground, leading to the aircraft not flying again or being a write-off. Two more of the DB, one F.1A, one F.2, one P.11 and one prototype T.5 can be added to this total (excludes RSAF aircraft), all of which were not on active service at the time of loss or write-off. One particularly tragic incident occurred on 5 January 1966. On this day Fg Off. Derek Law was undertaking routine training, and while on approach to Bentwaters for a practice crash diversion the No. 1 engine seized. The pilot elected to return to Wattisham, but could not maintain height on the remaining Avon and stated he would eject. His aircraft, F.3 XR721, came down 11 miles east of Wattisham with Law found dead around 25 yards away.

An investigation found that the No. 1 engine starter had not disengaged and disintegrated during the flight, with parts being sent into the intake and then ingested by both engines. The ejection failed when the starboard canopy shoot bolt did not operate as intended, which left the canopy in place and stopped the seat from firing. Law had made an incredible job of crash-landing the Lightning, but the jolting dislodged the canopy and he was ejected at ground level which was unsurvivable. It was a very sad state of affairs as if the canopy had remained in place he would have walked away.

The squadron often held Southern QRA, and during a talk by John Ward at Farnborough in September 2013, which the author attended, a story relating to the asinine decision to remove the F.3's cannons was related. One Saturday in 1966, a captive balloon used by the army for parachute training decided it was a nice day to break its moorings and take a sightseeing trip across the Home Counties carried along by the prevailing wind. This presented a hazard to commercial air traffic, which urgently needed to be halted. Bawdsey brought Wattisham's QRA to readiness in anticipation of bringing the wayward blimp to earth, but the response from the alert crew of which John was part was not what the controller expected. It was explained as the F.3 had no cannons, little could be done to shoot the balloon down. However, Pete Clee, who was also with John as a QRA pilot, did helpfully suggest he was happy to go and 'frighten' it. So the errant inflatable merrily continued unmolested on its way and drifted out to sea off the Essex coast where it presumably met a watery grave.

With squadron life following a predictable course for the remainder of 1966, in February 1967 news came that the unit would take over the all-weather fighter commitment held by the Javelins of No. 29 Squadron for the Near East Air Force (NEAF) at Akrotiri. The duty was officially handed over on 11 May of the same year with a review conducted by Air Marshal E. Gordon-Jones, CB, CBE, DSO, DFC, C-in-C NEAF.

Following this a Battle Flight was maintained with one pilot at ten minutes readiness, another at thirty and two at ninety. On 24 May, due to religious/political disputes between the Arabs and Israelis, the readiness state was upgraded to 04:00 to 06:30, two pilots at five minutes readiness, 06:30 to 19:30, one pilot at five minutes, one at thirty, 19:30 to 04:00 one pilot at fifteen minutes readiness. All aircraft reverted to the Firestreak role, having previously worked up on Red Top in April.

Very soon scrambles were being ordered, and contacts were made with Israeli Air Force Nord Noratlas transports on 1 June and the 11th, by Sqn Ldr Graydon flying XR717 and XP748, and on 5 June by Fg Off. R. Somerville piloting XR720. Battle scrambles continued to be flown as the year progressed, including the interesting use of T.5 XS456 on 7 October when Wg Cdr Bidie AFC led four other Lightnings to intercept and photograph two Soviet Antonov An-12 Cub transports. Interceptions continued in November, but the prey this time was Turkish Republic F-84 Thunderjets and F-84F Thunderstreaks, North American F-100 Super Sabres and Lockheed T-33s, with a single Soviet Antonov An-24 Coke transport.

Tensions between Greek Cypriots and Turkish Cypriots and the threat of Turkey invading the island had caused the increased air activity, which in turn led to higher interception rates by the No. 56 Squadron Lightnings. In Stewart Scott's book *The Lightning Force*, John Ward made the following comment:

> Turkish Air Force fighter-recce aircraft made many incursions, and we intercepted most, usually at low level somewhere over the island. I recall sliding alongside an F-84 who was orbiting Nicosia at around 3,000 feet and smiling at the marked twitch and double-take from the cockpit when he suddenly realised I was there and made a swift departure to the north. They were slow and easy targets and probably led to the appearance on later recce/flag-waving sorties for the Turkish supporters on the ground of F-100 and F-104 fighters. They were faster and, as we later surmised, seemed to have a way of knowing that we were on our way. Hence, the later adoption of silent scrambles. But at the time, we were trying everything we could to get amongst them.[25]

Due to runway resurfacing works at Akrotiri in April 1968, three Lightnings detached to Nicosia to continue with the Battle Flight. From here, on 13 April

Fg Off. R. Colebrook (XR748), Flt Lt J. Ward (XR749) and Flt Lt M. Wraight (XP759) were scrambled and intercepted nine Tu-16 Badgers and an An-12 Cub transiting from Damascus to the Soviet Union.

In July 1968 the unit was notified that a Target Facilities Flight would join it at Akrotiri, utilizing not Lightnings but two EE Canberras adorned with the squadron's red and white chequers on the nose with a centrally placed 'Firebird' badge. The flight would provide high, medium and low-level targets by both day and night.

During September 1968 the squadron began to try to intercept United Arab Republic (UAR – Egyptian/Syrian co-operation) Tu-16 Badgers approaching the Cyprus Sovereign Base Area (SBA). It was considered that these aircraft were Soviet Air Force machines and often turned away through early warning of the interceptor's presence. The lack of endurance of the F.3 precluded any kind of chase. Therefore new tactics were devised to limit radio and airborne transmissions, which paid off on 19 October when Flt Lt S. Boston intercepted and identified a pair of Badgers SSW of Akrotiri, with further encounters over the coming months.

The short legs of the F.3 led to Air Marshal Gordon-Jones' request to the CAS for the F.6 to be deployed to the NEAF. However, the plea was not successful as it was felt that the Soviet threat was greater to the UK than in the Eastern Mediterranean.

The year ended with the following remarks from Wg Cdr W.E. Kelly, who had taken over command the previous October:

> The last month of the year epitomised 1968 for the Squadron. Aircraft availability was poor, not due to a lack of effort but external factors; the pilots made the most of the flying they were able to get, and the Squadron kept its collective sense of humour. We all look forward to 1969 when our new accommodation and hangar at Akrotiri should at last allow the Squadron's efforts to be rewarded with formal tasks fully achieved, lots of good flying, and a pleasant atmosphere in which to work.[26]

With squadron life continuing routinely in 1969, it would appear that not all interceptions were military in nature, as the ORB in March attests:

> An unscheduled radar return, 70 miles to the southwest of Akrotiri at 7,000 feet turned out to be on investigation by Fg Off. Colebrook a Piper Twin Comanche. The pilot of the aircraft was so preoccupied in talking to a young lady sitting next to him that he was quite unaware of our intrepid aviator sitting on his wing taking his registration. He was American registered on his way to Beirut. The curtains in the rear window were drawn; we wonder why.[27]

March was notable in the Lightning world when a fault was discovered in the Avon 300 series ignition unit, which on the 22nd grounded the squadron's aircraft except for operational flying until modifications to the fuel system could be made. To assist with Battle Flight, four Lightnings from Leuchars were deployed to cover the shortfall.

With the summer temperatures rising in Cyprus, problems were experienced with the Lightning's AVPIN starting system. As is well-known, aluminium is a superb conductor of heat, so much so the temperature within the starter bay reached higher than the boiling point of AVPIN, potentially leading to vaporization and contributing to non-starting. The solution was to paint the spine covers over the area white which lent itself to improving starting reliability, a simple solution enabling the Lightning to carry on with its operational commitments. In the coming months further engineering problems were encountered with engine defects and the requirement to strengthen the airframe around the No. 1 engine area, factors contributing to poor serviceability rates.

As the year progressed, UAR (or Soviet) Badgers were still making their presence felt. The lack of cannons again returned to haunt Flt Lt John Ward while piloting XP702 on 26 May. An interception of two Tu-16s led to one infringing the SBA and a low-level chase ensued. John was ordered to instruct the Badger to land, but despite all his best efforts of hand signals and wing-waggling, he was ignored and the aircraft continued on its way. If he had had cannons warning shots could have been fired, but alas this was not to be. The ORB makes the following comment:

> The Battle Flight is to maintain the integrity of the SBA airspace, and as this is not an isolated instance of infringement, we can only speculate on our effectiveness of deterrence. Perhaps if we had cannons and could fire a shot across their bows, more notice would be taken of our instructions.[28]

There could be little doubt if the boot had been on the other foot, a Soviet cannon-armed fighter pilot wouldn't have thought twice about dispatching a NATO aircraft failing to heed its instructions.

An interesting interception occurred on 5 September 1969 when a scramble by Fg Off. Somerville piloting XR719 identified four Israeli F-4 Phantoms with four Mirages flying top cover at 25,000ft. The encounter occurred when the Israelis were carrying out 'flying artillery' raids utilizing the Phantom against Egyptian positions in the region of the Suez Canal.

During the same month the squadron's display team re-emerged with four Lightnings flying as the 'Firebird Four' for the Battle of Britain Air Fete held at Akrotiri. The participating pilots were Sqn Ldr B. Weedon and Flt Lts R. Palin, J. May and D. Hampton. Fg Off. R. Somerville flew a solo aerobatic sequence.

Notable interceptions continued with Fg Off. Childs piloting XP753 identifying four USN F.4E Phantoms 60 miles south-east of the island on 15 November. On 18 December Sqn Ldr B. Weedon (XP702) and Flt Lt A. Markell (XP747) found two Soviet Beriev Be-12 Mail amphibians flying 500ft above the sea.

January 1970 opened poorly for the squadron as serviceability restricted flying hours. The cause was engineers holding aircraft to get ahead of progressive servicing for an upcoming MPC. As the year progressed so did the scrambles and interceptions with many varied targets encountered, some friendly and others not. The Form 541s – details of flights and launchings annex within the ORB – make for some interesting reading.

In March four aircraft from Leuchars arrived to reinforce the unit as tensions rose on the island and between Greece and Turkey. The year continued with the usual mix of Battle Flight, training and exercises, including a Tactical Evaluation (TACEVAL) in May with targets including Argosy, Canberra, Phantom and Vulcan.

In January 1971 Wg Cdr Brian Farrer assumed command of the squadron, and the interceptions continued along with the usual routines. May brought further serviceability issues which gave cause for concern, further compounded by the loss of XP744 on the 10th. The pilot, Flt Lt Cole, ejected 7 miles south of Akrotiri following an in-flight fire. A Lockheed Hercules from No.242 OCU was in the area and circled the downed pilot until he was rescued by an RAF SAR helicopter. This was the first major accident for the unit since 1967; not a bad track record.

The following September six Lightning F.6s arrived and conversion began. By February 1972 just one F.3, XP702, remained. On 17 August of the same year, this was flown by Wg Cdr Farrer, leading three F.6s to mark its imminent departure. On the next day the F.3 was dispatched to No. 60 MU. However, this was not the end of the unit's involvement with the variant.

In January 1975 the squadron returned home to Wattisham and became a mixed fleet of nine F.6s, three F.3s and two T.5s. Of note one of the first F.3s to arrive, XP702, had been the last to leave in August 1972 when conversion to the F.6 came.

From the available evidence, No. 56 Squadron used four F.3s during 1975: XP694, XP701, XP702 and XR716 (which became one of the last two F.3s to fly on 30 September 1987). By 25 July of the same year all four had been returned to Wattisham's Storage Flight, ending an association with the F.3 lasting just over a decade.

No. 29 Squadron

In March 1967 No. 29 Squadron's OC, Wg Cdr R. Neil, wrote the following comment in the unit's ORB:

> There is very little to say about the month of March 1967 except for the excellent serviceability of our 'old' Javelin aircraft; it has been a most satisfying month with a total of 303 hours and 40 minutes being flown. This is particularly gratifying as it is the last month when the Squadron will be at full operational strength at Akrotiri before the redeployment to the UK to reequip with Lightning aircraft.[29]

On 7 November 1915 No. 29 Squadron formed at Gosport equipped with the strange-looking Airco DH.2 single-seat pusher biplane. The unit was soon in action in France and took part in the Battle of the Somme from June to September 1916. Conversion to the Nieuport 17 came in March 1917, and in April the following year the Royal Aircraft Factory S.E.5A. The squadron disbanded at the end of 1919, but reformed on 1 April 1924 with Sopwith Snipes followed in January 1925 by Gloster Grebes.

In March 1935 it flew the Hawker Demon and took part in the Abyssinian crisis in October of the same year. A change to bombers came in March 1936 with conversion to the Fairey Gordon and later a return to the turret-armed Demon.

With the approach of war, the unit received the Blenheim If in December 1938 and in June 1940 it began to take on Luftwaffe bombers by day and night flying from Digby in Lincolnshire. The following September, conversion to the Beaufighter If came and in November a pilot joined who would become one of the most famous in RAF history, Guy Penrose Gibson.

Gibson had already completed a tour of thirty operations flying Handley Page Hampdens with No. 83 Squadron of Bomber Command when he was posted to No. 29. He went on to lead Operation Chastise on 16/17 May 1943, the attack on the German dams that sealed his name into the history books, as well as being awarded the Victoria Cross. However, it could all have ended for Gibson when flying with the squadron from Wellingore on 8 April 1941.

At 21:57 hours Flt Lt Gibson with Sgt Bell took off on an uneventful patrol. Landing back at Wellingore at 23:48 hours, his Beaufighter If, R2250, was attacked by a Luftwaffe intruder (most likely a Junkers Ju 88) loitering to try to catch RAF night fighters and bombers when they were at their most vulnerable. On approach with his navigation lights lit and around 50ft off the ground, the intruder opened fire, wounding Bell in the leg with a 20mm cannon shell. The Beaufighter overshot and ended up in the trees at the end of the runway. Gibson walked away uninjured, but it had been a close call.

As the war progressed the unit converted to various marks of the Mosquito in the night-fighting role and entered the jet age with the Meteor NF.11 in 1950. Conversion to the all-weather Javelin FAW.6 came in December 1957 and then the FAW.9 in 1961. On 10 May 1967 No. 29 Squadron left Akrotiri to return to Wattisham to convert to the Lightning F.3, with No. 56 Squadron taking over the island's air defence.

Under the command of Sqn Ldr L.A. Boyer, the squadron's conversion was implemented with a nucleus of four pilots from No. 56 Squadron and two from No. 111. The first Lightning F.3 was received on 10 May 1967, after which followed a stream of hand-me-downs from Nos. 23, 56 and 111 Squadrons. The aircraft were in a bare aluminium finish with a badge of an eagle preying on a buzzard on the tail. On the nose the unit's XXX markings in red on a white background were applied on either side of the roundel. There are varying explanations as to why XXX was used as in Roman numerals; this represents 30, whereas 29 would be XXIX. For those with a curious mind, various theories as to why this occurred are available online and within the history books should further research be deemed necessary by the reader.

The squadron began getting to grips with its 'new' mount over the coming months, but the CO's frustration can be seen in his comments from July 1967:

> The squadron has got firmly into its stride as a frontline unit this month, and results have been very heartening. The excellent efforts, including overtime where necessary by our groundcrew, resulted in a utilisation rate of available aircraft that beats all other squadrons in the Lightning Force. This was achieved with cast-off F.3s that are continually unserviceable compared to the shiny new Mk 6s that four of the other six squadrons possess. The squadron is now nearly up to full strength with aircraft and pilots and this month marks the end of a successful work-up period.[30]

On 16 August 1967 the unit was deemed operational, with command now under Wg Cdr L.W. Phipps AFC. The usual routines of training, exercises, IFR and MPCs continued, and in the following month Southern QRA was held. This was not without its problems, as a shortage of pilots and serviceable aircraft was an ongoing issue, further compounded by No. 111 Squadron's move to Leuchars which added further pressure on resourcing QRA. At the end of December 1967, Phipps concluded:

> A miserable month for flying hours but a happier one in other respects. The Squadron Entertainment Committee arranged several well-supported high-class social events, as befitted the season, and we were not on QRA at Christmas [author's note: remember 111 Squadron's views on Christmas QRA from earlier in the chapter]. The grant was a long one and welcomed by all personnel. At the end of our first year (or part year) as a Lightning squadron, everyone is in good heart, and we are happy with our lot. We look forward to 1968 with interest and enthusiasm.[31]

In August 1968 the squadron undertook a ten-day exchange with five Lightnings and six aircrew joining the F-104 Starfighters of the Italian Air Force base at Grosseto. Several of the RAF pilots were fortunate to be given a chance to fly the twin-seat variant. In return, four F-104s came to Wattisham and participated in exercises as described in the ORB:

> At home the F-104s took part in fighter v fighter exercises with Lightnings and this was the first opportunity for most pilots of the squadron to fight against a different type of fighter. In fact the tactics of coming in low and very fast against manoeuvrable opposition proved to be very successful; invariably the attackers were never seen until too late. The whole two-way detachment was a complete success which is very gratifying as this was the first such visit which had been undertaken by the Italian Air Force.[32]

A detachment to Cyprus came in September 1968, and with major runway resurfacing works taking place at Wattisham, the squadron deployed to Coltishall in July 1969. The following month the unit was hit with a series of Cat.3 issues, mostly relating to fuel leaks that grounded six out of thirteen aircraft. A further move to Binbrook came in September, from where it took over QRA from No. 5 Squadron in the latter part of the month. The ORB quotes:

> On September 24th, the squadron took over QRA at Binbrook, which, apart from exercising the culinary skills of those marooned in the QRA 'shack' was a salutary reminder of the facts of a Lightning squadron's existence. At the moment we have three pilots who are non-combat-ready which increases the load upon those who are and also upon the organisation. Add to this the fact that QRA at Binbrook involves two pilots in the alert shed all the time and it may be seen that the squadron could run out of available bodies.[33]

In October command changed with Wg Cdr B. Carroll taking over the helm, at which time sixteen pilots were available to the squadron. During the same month a notable visitor came to Binbrook, the actor Kenneth More who had starred in the 1956 Lewis Gilbert-directed film *Reach for the Sky* in which he portrayed Douglas Bader and, in 1969, Grp Capt. Barker in the Harry Saltzman/S. Benjamin Fisz-produced epic *Battle of Britain*. During his visit to No. 29 Squadron, More was taken for a flight in T.5 XV328, which he pronounced as being thoroughly enjoyable. Later he was to write an article for a national newspaper detailing the life and activities of a Lightning squadron and described the pilots as supermen.

In mid-December, despite the best efforts of the weather, the squadron returned to Wattisham, a move broadly welcomed by all personnel. The cold British weather was left behind in February 1970 as the unit flew ten Lightnings to Akrotiri to provide air defence of the SBA, while No. 56 Squadron attended an MPC at Valley. Scrambles were few; however, on 4 March some fun was had when three Lightnings claimed four out of five HS Harriers in a 'bounce' as they homed on Akrotiri.

A return home began in mid-March, but shortly after all F.3s, F.6s and T.5s were grounded following an incident with a No. 111 Squadron machine. The problem lay with the Hot Streak system of the Avon 302 when it transpired that over-torquing caused the stripping of threads in the body of the units. The remedy was to drop the No. 1 engine and hatch lifts of No. 2 to enable repairs to be made. Once again the poor hard-worked ground crews bore the brunt of the problem by working through Easter to get the Lightnings back in the air.

As previously discussed, fires were no stranger to the F.3. On 25 January 1971 pilot Capt. B. Povilus USAF was forced to eject – successfully – from XP756 off the coast of East Anglia during a night interception sortie. The wreckage was not located, but the subsequent Board of Inquiry, upon hearing the pilot's evidence, deduced that a fire was the likely reason for the loss caused either by leaking hydraulic fluid or the failure of a fuel transfer pipe passing through the Fire Zone.

On 18 May an exchange visit was made with four Lightnings and eight pilots deploying to the base of No. 322 Squadron Starfighters, Royal Netherlands Air Force (RNAF) at Leeuwarden. Six RNAF F-104s came to Wattisham and exercised with the Lightnings. There was also time for a little social activity:

> While at Wattisham the Dutch pilots were able to fly sorties against ECM aircraft and witness Lightnings air-to-air refuelling. Combat between the two types was also organised and it was found that though the F-104 had a tactical advantage in superior endurance and in being very difficult to pick up visually, the Lightning's excellent turning and climbing performance gave our pilots the upper hand. The arrival of the Dutch detachment signalled the start of an almost gruelling social programme. On the first two nights local pubs were visited prior to some serious drinking in the mess bar. On the afternoon of the 21st the visitors held a barbecue with Amstel beer to drink and grilled kebabs with peanut sauce to eat which people found enjoyable. Saturday 22nd was the night of a party in the Squadron Commander's house. A squadron party took place at the Cedars Hotel, Stowmarket on Monday the 24th. Pilots exchanged gifts for certain ordeals and the occasion was a great success. Final farewells were said in the bar on the 26th at the end of a highly successful detachment.[34]

During the exchange fire issues continued. On 21 May Flt Lt G. Clarke, piloting XP708, experienced a Fire 1 warning shortly after take-off. The drill for such a scenario was to jettison the ventral tank, but the pilot was unsure of his position due to cloud. However, GCI assured him that it would be safe to discard the tank, which was duly undertaken. Upon pulling the lever in the cockpit the tank went on its way, continued to fly for some distance and came to earth in a farmer's garden near Stowmarket. XP708 survived to fly another day.

As the year progressed, QRA was renamed Interceptor Alert Force (IAF). Another F.3, XP705, succumbed to an in-flight fire on 8 July 1971 while the squadron was detached to Cyprus. Flt Lt G. Clarke, the subject of the previous paragraph, successfully ejected at 13,400ft after receiving two reheat fire warnings and an imminent loss of control in pitch. He came down in the sea and was rescued by a Westland Whirlwind HAR.10 of No. 1563 Flight. The aircraft crashed in 6,500ft of water, making recovery impossible.

The subsequent Board of Inquiry could not positively identify the cause of the loss, but it was likely to have been a fuel leak from the main refuelling and transfer gallery pooling in the area of Fire Zone 3. The application of negative g could have caused the fuel to be brought into contact with a hot surface leading to a fire in the No. 1 jet pipe, which spread to the No. 2 engine and, in turn, triggered the Reheat 2 warning. It was concluded that the inadequate drainage of leaked fuel within the fuselage contributed to the loss.

From 12 July the unit, like others operating the Lightning, began to receive a series of instructions resulting from investigations into earlier fires. This severely restricted flying and led to the grounding of all aircraft apart from those required for operational reasons. A period of frantic activity ensued for the ground crews as they acted upon the information received, and it was not until the 26th of the month that flying began again.

On 30 July Wg Cdr P. Carter took command, and on the following day No. 29 Squadron returned to Wattisham after No. 56 Squadron resumed the air defence of the SBA. Due to problems with the Italian Military Air Corridor, the nine Lightnings all had to return on one day and required the support of seventeen tankers. One F.3, XP751, piloted by Flt Lt A. Martin and accompanied by Flt Lt G. Clarke in XP708, had a Reheat 1 fire warning necessitating a diversion for the pair to Orange in France. This machine returned to Wattisham on 4 August, by which time it had been 'zapped' on the fin with the emblem of No. 15 Fighter Squadron of the French Air Force. Five days later XP751 finally made it back to Suffolk after it was concluded that the fire warning was spurious.

In August a new policy was introduced to allow the Wattisham Wing to gain more experience of intercepting Soviet aircraft. The first chance came on the 11th when Flt Lt P. Copper was scrambled with a tanker to a point 500 miles north of Leuchars, but he returned disappointed as nothing was seen.

A tragic event occurred on 22 September 1971 with the loss of XP736 and its pilot, Fg Off. P. Mottershead. The accident occurred over the North Sea during a practice supersonic interception, during which a Mayday call was made. The target Lightning attempted to get visual contact with the stricken Lightning, but only saw a condensation trail disappearing into cloud at 32,000ft. Following this XP736 vanished from radar screens, and nothing further was heard via radio transmissions. The Board of Inquiry concluded with some difficulty from the small amount of wreckage recovered that the cause of the accident must remain unknown, but could have been attributable to either control malfunction, inertia cross-coupling or a mishandled emergency situation. Sadly the body of Phil Mottershead was not found, although his dinghy was recovered by a USAF SAR helicopter an hour after the loss and his Mk 2A helmet twenty-two days later.

As squadron life continued, Flt Lt G. Clarke was congratulated on 3 February 1972 by Wg Cdr Carter when he achieved 1,000 hours on Lightnings. This was overshadowed on 16 February when two of the unit's F.3s collided over the North Sea. Following a night practice interception, Flt Lts P. Reynolds piloting XP698 and P. Cooper in XP747 were recovering to Wattisham when the collision occurred. The former managed to eject following a loss of control and came down in the sea; he was rescued by a Dutch fishing boat. Flt Lt Cooper was never found, and no wreckage from the Lightnings was recovered. The accident highlighted the difficulty of forming up with another aircraft at night and the dangers it presented.

A further loss occurred on 7 August when XP700, piloted by Flt Lt G. Fenton, was one of five aircraft briefed to take off in reheat with the flaps retracted. After raising the undercarriage, the F.3 sank back onto the runway, which ruptured the ventral tank. The jet efflux ignited leaking fuel, causing a bright orange flame to be emitted. Climbing to around 3,000ft, the pilot received a Reheat 2 warning and stiffening of the controls, leaving him with no option but to eject; he landed safely but sustained back injuries. The Lightning crashed at Newton, a small village near Sudbury. This would be the unit's sixth F.3 loss in two years, but not the last.

In July 1973 Wg Cdr J. Hawtin assumed command and the exercises continued. During the month the unit took part in Exercise Blackmail (an operational ECM exercise), Joint Venture (refuelling involving USAF KC-135s), Coffee (a night ECM exercise), MACEX (a joint naval exercise) and Priory (a No. 11 Group sponsored air defence exercise).

As summer faded into autumn in October 1973, the Organization of Petroleum Exporting Countries (OPEC) imposed an oil embargo on nations supporting Israel during the Yom Kippur War. Britain was one of the nations that suffered fuel restrictions, which curtailed the unit's training programme along with others in No. 11 Group. It would be May 1974 before the situation returned to something considered normal.

Further air defence exercises, exchanges, IAF, TACEVAL, MPC and deployment to Cyprus kept the squadron busy, and another F.3 loss was experienced. On 13 February 1974 Flt Lt T. Butcher was piloting XR715 and participating in low-level PIs when he was alerted to a Reheat 2 warning, which cleared only to be followed by a Reheat 1 warning, which again went out. Climbing to a safer height, the pilot began to experience fore and aft control restrictions. The options were now limited so he decided to eject. However, XR715 had other ideas and circled for around ten minutes until it crashed at Blyford Green.

In June Operation Springfield was conducted with the squadron deploying nine F.3s to Akrotiri where concentrated fighter combat was undertaken, together with low-level airborne early warning (AEW) work with the assistance of two No. 8 Squadron Avro Shackleton AEW.2s. Often described as 40,000 rivets flying in formation, the vintage Avro airframe was a relative of the Lancaster, the AEW.2 a conversion of the MR.2 fitted with an AN/APS-20 radar salvaged from redundant FAA Fairey Gannet AEW.3s. It entered service in early 1972 to plug a deficiency in the RAF's capability to detect low-flying aircraft in the Faroes-Iceland Gap. The AEW.2 remained operational until mid-1991 when it was replaced by the Boeing E-3D Sentry AEW.1. Continuing with No. 29 Squadron, Battle Flight was held between 10 and 17 June, with an interception made on the 16th by Flt Lts J. Jarron and C. Stevens against a Soviet An-12 Cub.

On 19 July Wg Cdr Hawtin was presented with the Dacre Trophy by Mrs E.F. Dacre MBE in recognition of No. 29 being judged the most efficient squadron for the previous year within No. 11 Group. The unit's time with the F.3 was nearing its end, but exercises continued and IAF held, although there were no scrambles.

The final day for the squadron and the F.3 came on the morning of 31 December 1974 when six Lightnings flew a formation to Coningsby, where they were joined by five Phantom FGR.2s from No. 29 Squadron Designate. A handover parade of the unit's standard was held in the afternoon, commanded by Wg Cdr Hawtin, concluding seven years of Lightning operations.

Lightning T.5

The Lightning T.5 was essentially an F.3 with a twin-seat side-by-side cockpit grafted on. It was initially powered by a pair of Rolls-Royce Avon 301 (later uprated to 302) axial-flow turbojets producing 12,600lb of thrust at sea level and 16,300lb (in the later variant) in fully variable reheat. Apart from a small increase in the frontal area, fuel capacity, avionics, radar and weapons fit, dimensions, limitations and combat capabilities were broadly similar to the F.3. However, the Aircrew Manual states that although the aircraft was cleared to 60,000ft, it should not be flown higher than 43,000ft due to the limits imposed by the oxygen system and the pilot's personnel equipment. The T.5 was fitted with a pair of Martin-Baker Type 4BSB Mk 2 ejection seats.

In the cockpit the instructor's throttles and radar hand controller moved to the starboard consul. Like the T.4 before, changes to the frontal area produced a very elegant-looking design with the brutish lines of the single-seater softened.

The first T.5 to fly, XM967, took to the skies on 29 March 1962 in the hands of Jimmy Dell. It was initially constructed as a T.4, but before completion was sent to Bristol at Filton for conversion to the upgraded variant. The aircraft was displayed at the SBAC Air Show, Farnborough in September 1962 with 'ENGLISH ELECTRIC LIGHTNING MK.5' emblazoned on the nose. It was to spend its career in the test environment and later took part in Stage 3 fin-loading stress evaluation following the loss of XM966 as described below. Its days were to end on the fire dump at Kemble circa 1979. Notably XM967 featured an electric start for the Avons over the more typical AVPIN system. In later years, T.5 XS458, preserved at Cranfield in a ground running condition, was also converted to electric start as AVPIN became more challenging to obtain.

A second T.4, XM966, was also converted at Filton to T.5 standard, having first flown on 15 July 1960 piloted by Roland Beamont and as the later variant with Jimmy Dell on 1 December 1962. Handling and performance trials were completed by the latter part of 1964 allowing the T.5 to enter RAF service, but there was a problem.

Fin failure caused the loss of prototype T.4 XL628, and a similar accident befell XM966 on 22 July 1965. Piloted by Dell with flight test observer Graham Elkington on board, the T.5 was carrying out an extreme rolling manoeuvre with the 2in rocket pack extended when control was lost, forcing a successful ejection by the two crew. The cause of the accident was again fin failure through roll/yaw coupling, and measures were put in place to strengthen the Stage 3 fins of the other T.5s coming into service.

The first production flight of a T.5 took place on 17 July 1964 when XS417 was flown by Dell. Twenty were initially constructed through the serial ranges of XS416 to XS423 and XS449 to XS460, with the cockpit sections manufactured at Filton as Samlesbury was working to capacity at the time. Once completed, each nose section was transported to Lancashire for attachment to a waiting fuselage.

All but one T.5 constructed entered RAF service; the exception was XS460, which became prototype Saudi T.55 55-710. This machine would have a short career of fifteen hours as when landing at Warton on 7 March 1967 it encountered a violent crosswind and left the runway. Damage was severe, with the Lightning breaking its back and leading to a write-off. Thankfully the pilot Jimmy Dell and his passenger, Mr P. Williams of Airwork Services, survived. A further order for two aircraft, XV328 and XV329, was placed in 1965 with both making their first flights in December 1966.

Unlike the T.4, the T.5s were not heavily involved in the test environment and served predominantly with No. 226 OCU: the first XS419 arrived at Coltishall on 20 April 1965. Others went on squadron strength with No. 111, the first to receive a T.5, XS450, on 6 September of the same year.

With the reduction in the F.3 squadrons in the mid-1970s the number of T.5s also reduced, but the variant would serve the RAF until the very end of Lightning operations. One, XS422 of the Empire Test Pilot School, found a degree of fame by featuring in the 1986 BBC mini-series *Test Pilot*. Redundant airframes found their way to Binbrook's decoy line or went into storage, with one XS421 sent to the Proof and Experimental Establishment at Foulness Island for foreign object damage (FOD) trials.

The final flights of the T.5 in RAF squadron service were made on 21 June 1988 by XS452 and, three days later, XV328 and XS458. However, the variant graced UK skies for one last time on 29 June when all three were flown to Cranfield for preservation after purchase by Arnold Glass (to be discussed in a later chapter).

Twenty-two T.5s (excluding the prototypes) were built, with three written off due to accidents: XS453 and XS455 while in RAF service and XS460 as noted above.

Want to Fly a Lightning?

It was a cold winter's morning with rain hammering on the window when 10-year-old Brian emerged from under his bed sheets to contemplate another depressing paper round and the thought of school. 'Time to get up,' says his father as he enters the room and hands the young lad a copy of *The Boy's Own Paper*, dated January 1959, priced at one shilling. The front cover states 'Lightnings In Action' with an artist's impression of two of the supersonic interceptors. Within its pages a detailed article penned by Ian Bruce describes the Lightning and whether it will be the RAF's last interceptor, together with details of its capabilities. With his curiosity aroused, Brian flicks through the pages, noting adverts for the Miller Dynamo Set, Keil Kraft model boats and the Stanley Gibbons Fanfare Stamp Album. He decrees he will read all about the Lightning upon his return from school.

Settled in front of a roaring coal fire after a hearty tea of sausage and mash and with the cold winter's night shut out by the heavy curtains, Brian reads the article's opening lines as CAS, Marshal of the RAF Sir Dermot Boyle, CGB, KCVO, KBE, DFC proudly proclaims, 'I am confident that in the aircraft we see before us, sleek, powerful and aggressive, the Royal Air Force has a winner.' The young boy reads on, and by the end of the prose he has made a decision: 'I want to fly a Lightning.' Although a fictitious tale, how many other young lads were so allured by the Lightning's obvious appeal that they decided to try to make a career out of piloting the machine?

One was Steve Gyles, who flew the F.1A, 2A, 4, 5 and 6. He describes below what it took to realize a young boy's dream of piloting the iconic interceptor:

> Back in the Spring of 1965, I knew I wanted an aviation career. However, all my teenage years had been with the scouting movement in which I was by then a Queen Scout. My only flying-related experience was my hobby of model aircraft control line flying. Also, my family summer holidays had always been to the south coast at Eartham near Goodwood, where I had frequently watched the Fleet Air Arm aircraft flying out of Ford dive bombing and rocketing off the West Wittering coast. I was in the 6th Form at Enfield Grammar School in north London and shortly to take my A-Levels. During my studies, I had given a formal talk to the rest of the 6th form on the Battle of Britain. I had flying in my blood and had gathered various brochures for both military and civilian aviation careers, but as winter departed, I had done nothing about it. Future careers had been a talking point with us 6th formers, and I had frequently told them I could not contemplate an office job. I intended to be a pilot flying fighters in the RAF. One of the brochures showed the latest RAF frontline fighter, the Mach 2 capable Lightning. In front of the aircraft were three first-tour pilots, each barely twenty-one years old. This captivated me. Yes, that was what I wanted to do.
>
> One morning in the upper 6th form library, a spotty-faced fellow student with National Health spectacles announced he had applied for an RAF Cranwell engineering cadetship. I was furious with my inactivity, and I had been beaten to an application by this upstart colleague. His announcement spurred me immediately into action. Forms flowed back and forth and included an interview with the headmaster. A few weeks later, with Easter fast approaching, my schoolmate and I attended the same five-day selection course at RAF Biggin Hill, along with fifty-eight other hopefuls. By the end of day one, which included medicals and aptitude tests, he and some twenty other candidates had departed. I have to admit I guiltily felt a degree of smug satisfaction at his demise but was grateful for the kick up the backside his earlier action had given me. Over the next four days, various tests and leadership tasks slowly whittled the group down until just six of us survived for the interview phase on the fifth day.

Two weeks later, I received my letter of offer from the RAF, not to Cranwell but for a Direct Entry Commission for pilot training starting on 1 September 1965 at RAF South Cerney in Gloucestershire. What followed were sixteen weeks of square bashing, military studies and physical fitness, which were demanding, but my academic, sporting and scouting background put me in good stead.

Early January 1966 saw me back at South Cerney and graduate with the next course, followed by an immediate transfer to the flightline for my 30 hours of primary pilot assessment and training in the piston engine Chipmunk (first flight 27 January 1966, T.10 WZ878). I recall nothing of the preliminaries, including aircraft systems lectures. However, I remember we all did a practice ejection on a training rig that fired each of us about 15 feet up a pair of rails. I took to flying quite well as I was solo in 8 hours, and I do not recall any issues. A couple of the chaps failed to make it. The usual procedure for them was a transfer to navigator training or a ground role such as air traffic controller. Occasionally, they would opt to exit the service.

The 'Wings' course was to be ten months long. It would involve 190 hours flying the Jet Provost T.3 (first flight, 30 March 1966, XM409 and T.4, 16 August 1966, XP669). On completion, we would receive the coveted 'Wings' brevet to wear proudly on our uniforms. But the actual flying was just one element of an intensive training programme. Every aspect of airmanship had to be taught, including navigation, meteorology, pressure instruments, radio aids, Morse code, air law, etc. The list was almost endless, and of course, we had to pass exams in each subject. On top of that, we had to learn everything about the Jet Provost, plus its checklists, operating limitations and emergencies.

The course went well for me, so I have no intention of lingering on the details. I was not the best, as university air squadron pilots were on the course with many more flying hours than myself, but I was probably well up in the top echelon, as my later posting would suggest.

At this stage, we were streamed fast jet, multi-engine, or helicopter. I and about five others were posted to the advanced fast jet course at RAF Valley to fly the Gnat. One of our course members who went the multi-engine route was Martin Withers. Later, he piloted the Vulcan that bombed Port Stanley in the Falklands War.

On 12 February 1967, our twenty-strong No.31 Gnat Course assembled at RAF Valley. A handful of students came from our Syerston course, but the rest were from the other basic flying training schools dotted up the A1 from Lincolnshire northwards. The Gnat was an amazing aircraft to fly (first flight 4 March 1967, T.1 XR539) but had issues and an alarming accident rate. Many of the previous courses had accidents, and expectations were we would likely have one. The Gnat was like sitting in a Formula One race car with its very low seating position, and legs stretched forward into the nose. The main instrumentation was modern, being the same as the Lightning. I loved flying it with one exception: landing in a strong crosswind. With its narrow undercarriage, it was a handful until you got a few hours under your belt.

My prime instructor was an excellent chap, Porky Munroe. He had just completed a tour with the Tripartite Kestrel (Harrier) evaluation squadron. I learned a lot from Porky and passed the course without difficulty, and with about two weeks to go of the six months, we received our postings to our operational aircraft. It was a day of great trepidation. The options in those days were Hunter, Lightning, Canberra or back into the training system to become a flying instructor. At about the same time, the V Force was complaining it was not getting any high-calibre pilots from the streaming system. Therefore, it was determined from on high that one of the top pilots from each Gnat course would go to the Vulcan or Victor. Now, how do you engineer your progress through the course to not be one of those top two? Luck was with me that day. I was absolutely delighted to be one of three to get the Lightning. How we celebrated that night.

My time with Training Command was now finished. I had learned to fly, although, of course, you never truly stop learning, but the formal pure flying teaching was over. My next stop was Fighter Command, where I would learn how to operate an aircraft as a weapons platform. That is the demanding part of military flying. Anyone can fly an aircraft, but operating it as an efficient war machine is another matter. Unfortunately, there was now a six-month log jam in the training system before I could continue my next phase of flying. It would be at RAF Chivenor in North Devon learning to operate the Hunter (first flight 29 December 1968, XL578) in tactical formations, both low and high level, combined with simulated combat and weapons firing.

On 17 June 1968, I arrived at RAF Coltishall in Norfolk to commence what turned out to be six years of flying the mighty Lightning. It had been my inspirational aircraft for the past three and a half years, and now here I was. I was going to fly it. The first time I saw one for real was in 1966 at RAF Syerston during my basic flying training. The ATC tannoy had boomed out the message that a Lightning F.6 was on the approach. We dropped everything, interrupting briefings and lectures to rush outside to watch. What a machine, awesome in its polished metal skin finish. And now here I was. Mach 2, here we come.[35]

Steve achieved his dream of flying the Lightning and first flew T.4 XM990 with instructor Flt Lt Morgan on 17 June 1968. He then undertook his first solo when he piloted T.4 XM973 with No. 226 OCU on 9 July 1968. Three days later he flew F.1A XM215 and, after completing basic conversion, transferred to the T.5. The first dual sortie came with the 'Tub' (as the two-seater was known) on 27 September 1968 aboard XS454, and on 11 October solo piloting XS422. With training complete, he began his operational career with No. 11 Squadron, where he flew F.6 XS932 for the first time on 12 December 1968. A stint as a simulator instructor came with No. 92 Squadron, during which an association began with the F.2A when Steve took XN780 aloft on 8 March 1972. He then joined No. 19 Squadron and flew his first sortie with XN781 on 7 November of the same year.

Steve flew his last Lightning sortie on 14 August 1974 while helping out No. 92 Squadron with Battle Flight due to a shortage of pilots. His mount for the day was T.2A XN781, and he was launched on an operational scramble to intercept a Beech 18 illegally taking photos in the border area. Although the Lightning days ended, operational flying for Steve continued, with the Phantom until 1980 and after that the Panavia Tornado F.3.

No. 226 Operational Conversion Unit and the Lightning Training Flight

By mid-1965 the T.5 had joined No. 226 OCU's ranks and resided at Coltishall with its T.4s and F.1As. All aircraft were resplendent in a bare aluminium finish and wearing the markings of No. 145 Squadron, a scarlet cross drawn upon a white disc cut through by a sword, while the roundel on either side of the nose was edged with the Cross of St George. The three digits of the aircraft's serial number were applied to the tail in large, bold black characters. Three squadrons operated within the OCU at the time: No. 1 flew the Lightning F.1A, No. 2 the T.4 and No. 3 the T.5. Also residing at Coltishall were the Westland Whirlwind HAR.10 helicopters of 'D' Flight No. 202 Squadron which performed SAR duties, along with the Historic Aircraft Flight with Hurricane IIc LF363 and Spitfire XIX PM631 which were joined by Spitfire Vb AB910 in September 1965.

On 8 June 1967 the OCU prepared to receive a special visitor when Her Royal Highness The Duchess of Gloucester visited Coltishall. Within the ORB, documents show the lengths the RAF went to in ensuring that the visit went smoothly, and an account of the day follows as it makes for a fascinating historical insight into the world of the base and the Lightning.

The visit began at noon with the arrival of the Duchess by air onboard RAF Queen's Flight HS Andover CC.2 XS790. (The cockpit of XS790 has been preserved by the Boscombe Down Aviation Collection, Old Sarum.) After an inspection of some of the unit's representative aircraft, for the first hour she toured the Officers' Mess, the WRAF's domestic accommodation, the Social Club, the Junior Ranks' Mess and the Bowling Alley. All of this was timed to the minute. At 12:58 hours, the royal visitor retired to the Officers' Mess to prepare for luncheon shown on the schedule as starting at 13:08 hours in the presence of Air Marshal Sir Frederick Rosier, CBE, DSO (later GCB), AOC Fighter Command, Lady Rosier, Grp Capt. Hobson, OC RAF Coltishall, and his wife together with many of the station's senior personnel. On the menu this day were the following:

- Chilled Consommé Brunoise with Crescent Rolls
- Fresh Salmon Mayonnaise, New Potatoes, Salad in Season
- Fresh Fruit Salad, Fresh Cream
- Coffee
- Liebfraumilch – Crown of Crowns

No doubt replete after such fine fare, the Duchess retired for a brief ten-minute rest at 14:25 hours and then resumed her official duty of signing the visitor's book and the presentation of a bouquet. At 14:43 hours the visits continued, taking in the Station Medical Centre, Gymnasium and Swimming Pool, Brake Parachute Section and the Supply Squadron. At 15:15 hours she arrived at Hangar No. 2 to see the aircraft servicing work undertaken by WRAF personnel, followed by a visit to ATC in the tower. Matters had concluded by 15:45 hours, with the Duchess emplaning ten minutes later and flying out to her homeward destination. It had been a busy day for the station with everyone on their best behaviour, so maybe now there would be time to relax a little.

The following year in February, four Lightning T.55s of the Royal Saudi Air Force arrived to join the OCU's No. 3 Squadron. The unit's role now included training the kingdom's pilots to fly its latest acquisition, the F.53 (discussed in a later chapter).

As will be recalled from the previous chapter with the T.4, joining the 1,000 Miles Per Hour Club was a popular achievement and this continued with the arrival of the T.5. A notable occurrence of this took place on 3 April 1969 when the OCU's CO, Wg Cdr G. Black, marked 1,000 hours on Lightnings by taking his son Stuart on a supersonic flight in XS420 and thus making him the club's youngest member. The accolade had previously been held by Plt Off. Vivienne Whyer, an ATC officer based at Coltishall, who on 29 February 1968 became the 1,000th member. The CO liked XS420 as it was reputed to have a particularly accurate navigation system and was often used to head up formation flypasts where the need for precise timings and positioning was paramount.

A change at the OCU in 1971 saw the resident F.1As and T.4s break away to form No. 65 (Shadow) Squadron, with the unit's F.3s and T.5s taking on the identity of No. 2T Squadron. The reason for this can be traced back to a report written on 10 November 1969 and contained within No. 226's ORB, its Introduction stating as follows:

> With the presently limited numbers of operational aircraft available to Strike Command, it is essential to consider the most effective organisation of 226 OCU to achieve the primary training task in peace whilst ensuring maximum contribution in war. With more than the capability of two squadrons in terms of operational aircraft and highly experienced fighter pilot instructors, RAF Coltishall has the resources to provide a stronger and more flexible operational contribution. Moreover, the fact that this is necessary has already been evidenced by the demands beyond its current reserve squadron commitments, which have been placed on the OCU during recent alerts. The present OCU structure, however, has its main emphasis on the primary training task, and it follows that an enhanced operational role requires the introduction of a more compatible organisation to support both the primary peacetime and war tasks. The aim of this paper is to propose the OCU organisation to achieve its primary peacetime role whilst ensuring the maximum contribution in war.[36]

With the new structure implemented, the previous No. 145 Squadron markings of the No. 2T aircraft were replaced with a blue chevron on either side of the nose roundel and the unit's crest on the tail. The F.1As and T.4s acquired the markings of No. 65 Squadron consisting of a badge on the fin defined as: 'In front of fifteen swords in pile, the hilts in base, a lion passant.' The roundels on the nose were bordered by white bars with four red chevrons. In the same year No. 65 Squadron was declared to the Supreme Commander Europe (SACEUR) and, in doing so, became an operational unit in its own right. Therefore it could be called upon if required to undertake interceptions.

Like other Lightning squadrons, No. 65 had a long history stretching back to the days of the RFC and was an early recipient of the Spitfire I, which it operated during the Battles of France and Britain. As the war progressed it flew further variants of the Spitfire, Mustang IIIs and the twin-engine Hornet F.1 and 3. In April 1951 conversion to the Meteor F.8 came, followed by the Hunter F.6 in March 1957. The squadron disbanded on 31 March 1961 with resurrection as a shadow unit, as stated above.

As could be expected, No. 226 OCU had some very experienced Lightning pilots within its ranks acting in the training and assessment role. One was John Ward, a Senior Qualified Weapons Instructor who, after amassing 2,000 hours on the Lightning, relates the following:

> Over its twenty-eight-year service life, numerous Lightnings were lost because of a variety of problems. Crash locations are dotted around the UK countryside and North Sea, the Mediterranean, Saudi Arabia, Singapore and the China Sea. There are several pilots with more take-offs than landings in their logbooks, and too many had just that one final landing. Of the 'variety of problems', the records list 'loss of control' sometimes with caveats in a significant number of cases. The tale I'm about to recount has an element of introspection, which engenders dark thoughts that are best locked away and certainly not brought to mind when trying to sleep.
>
> The date was 8 August 1973 and involved T.5 XS454. Earlier, in June, I had become the very first pilot to achieve 2,000 hours Lightning, and BAe had invited me to Warton for a Director's Lunch to mark the occasion. I think it's worth mentioning here that most of that time had been achieved on the short-range models, F.1, F.1A, F.3, T.4 and T.5, with often very short flight times, sometimes as little as twenty minutes. So, it probably involved at least 3,000 strap-ins. Well worth a lunch on BAC. Those were the days when you felt deprived if you didn't get at least three trips a day.
>
> So, Andy Griffin and I launched from Coltishall to Warton, and he was to fly us back after lunch, which would allow me to have a taste of the Director's Finest Reserve. Present at the lunch, in addition to the 'suits', were some well-known faces from Flight Ops, such as Jimmy Dell. They were very busy with the Jaguar programme; I recall John Cockburn, famous for his Lightning spinning trials,

talking about how wonderful it was to fly the Jaguar because by simply marking the fuel gauges in kilograms, 'you always had twice as much as you thought!' Bea [Beamont] presented me with a magnificent, engraved silver Lightning; I was almost as much impressed by the superbly crafted wood case made for it by the apprentices.

It was time to leave, and the silver Lightning, snug in its tailor-made felt-lined case, was duly secured in the right-hand elephant ear. I was comfortably relaxed in the right-hand seat as Andy taxied us to the eastern end of the runway, ready for a nice, easy ride back to Norfolk. We hadn't discussed the flight; it was a nice day; he was just my taxi driver. I don't even remember him selecting max reheat. So, it was the most tremendous shock when, very quickly after the nosewheel thumped home, he snatched back the stick into a vicious 'rotation'.

Now, the purists will understand that the reason a Typhoon cannot do a classical 'rotation' take-off is because its canards simply lift the nose skywards into an energy climb. In a Lightning 'rotation', the tailplane pushes the back end rapidly *down*, like a skidding manoeuvre, washing off a bunch of energy. It caught me totally by surprise, jolting me, in a flash, out of my relaxed posture. I recall vividly the thoughts that flashed instantly through my mind: 'That was too aggressive,' 'My model will burn,' and 'Why didn't he warn me?' Two thousand hours told me we were not in a good place. The aircraft was 'fishtailing', a sure sign of imminent departure. I shouted, 'Unload', and watched intently as those two glorious Avons slowly blew us out of the hole beside the runway that I had imagined us in.

What the spectators on the ground thought doesn't bear thinking about. I certainly think about it every time I look at that beautiful model and reflect on how fortunate I am that I can still admire it. We were so close to becoming another statistic. Sadly, XS454 eventually finished up on the fire dump anyway. I've had a number of amazing close calls in various aircraft over the years, and I hesitate to think how many of my allocated 'Nine' I've used up. But I certainly used one that day.[37]

In days gone by there can be few displays during Britain's air show season that left such a lasting impression as those flown by the Lightning. Coltishall's final year with the jet came in 1974 and Flt Lt P. Chapman, an instructor with the OCU, was the season's display pilot. His preferred mount was F.3 XP696 of No. 2T Squadron, which sported a bare aluminium finish with the spine and fin painted white and blue chevrons adorning the nose. A small Union Jack was applied just below the unit's badge on the tail. The scheme was striking and a fitting way to end Coltishall's time with the Lightning in the public arena. One who remembers the displays was Clive Hammond of No. 2T Squadron:

One very clear memory was the visit to Woodford Aerodrome, which was, I believe, owned by Hawker Siddeley. My ex-father-in-law was an inspector in the paint shop, so we always got tickets whenever there was an open day. During my time on 2T (1972-1974), Flt Lt Pete Chapman was the Lightning solo display pilot and, on one such occasion, was displaying at Woodford.

> His normal display was always exciting and involved copious amounts of noise and reheat.
>
> He had completed his display, landed, refuelled, etc. (it was said because of the use of reheat, he was limited to a maximum display time of about seven and a half minutes due to fuel). During the latter parts of the air display, he was set for departure from Woodford to return to RAF Coltishall. All went well with a full burner take-off and climb, which was quite normal. However, due to the shortish runway as he rotated, and it being the height of summer, the grass at the end of the runway caught fire, which needed the fire service attendance to extinguish it.
>
> The second incident I remember was probably the last detachment to Finningley for the Battle of Britain Air Display. Wednesday was the 'Press Day', where local TV and media would assemble to witness and record various displays as planned for the big day. This would have been towards the end of the 2T era, as it was shortly before I was posted to Finningley. All went well with the normal display, and the final manoeuvre was a high-speed/low-level run down the runway's centre line. We ground crew were at the end of the runway on the ORP and witnessed one very low and very fast F.3 Lightning (probably no more than 10 feet). As he pulled up to complete his display, the sound of breaking glass could be heard in the new housing estate being built nearby. Shortly after landing, the Finningley Station Commander's Austin 1800 staff car drew up, and a young LAC MT driver conveyed the Boss's invitation to Flt Lt Chapman to join him in the Control Tower. Sometime later, the chastened pilot returned red-faced, muttering something about 'bloody Flying Training Command'. The actual weekend display was probably a little more sedate but still mightily impressive with the roar of two Rolls-Royce Avon engines in full re-heat at very close quarters!![38]

The disbandment of No. 226 OCU came in September 1974 with the commitment for Lightning training moving to Binbrook, with No. 11 Squadron, where 'C' Flight was formed. However, the Lightning's presence at Coltishall continued as on 24 September of the same year, F.1A XM172 was placed on gate guardian duties in the colours of No. 145 Squadron. In 1989 the aircraft was repainted to represent a No. 226 OCU machine until its removal shortly after, although it has survived into preservation and now resides with Lakes Lightnings in Cumbria.

From April 1964 to September 1974 No. 226 OCU trained 810 students to fly the Lightning. The unit would reform at Lossiemouth the day after disbandment; its role was to train SEPECAT Jaguar pilots.

With the move to Binbrook, the training role for 'C' Flight was described in the ORB: 'Their prime job is Lightning Standardisation, but they are also established to train ex-Lightning pilots, renew Instrument Rating Examiners qualifications and to upgrade QFIs on the Lightning.'[39]

On 1 October 1975 'C' Flight was disbanded and the Lightning Training Flight (LTF) was formed and became semi-autonomous within the Operations Wing. However, due to an initial lack of hangarage, it operated from the former No. 85 Squadron dispersal. The Flight was allocated three F.3s and three T.5s manned by six staff instructors, one administrative SNCO and fifty-two technical personnel. The unit's aircraft were bare aluminium with the Binbrook Lion in blue applied to the fin with LTF written above. In time, the colour schemes would change to include dark green, camouflage and grey.

From 22 April to 27 October 1976 Binbrook closed to allow for runway and aircraft servicing areas resurfacing and reinforcement works. Under the name of Exercise Bolthole, Nos. 5 and 11 Squadrons deployed to Leconfield and the LTF to Coningsby. Upon return to Binbrook in October and under the command of Sqn Ldr D. Brooks, the LTF took up residence in No. 1 hangar.

During 1983 Flt Lt Mike Thompson was the Lightning display pilot for the year and flew some notable routines during the air show season, winning the best solo at the International Air Tattoo, Greenham Common in July. On 26 August Thompson was tasked to position F.3 XP753 from Binbrook to Teeside Airport for a display the next day. He had received a request to undertake a flypast of an RAF recruiting event at Scarborough on the way, and although officially he was not cleared to do so, he agreed. Arriving at the seaside town, the pilot made a couple of passes and was then observed to be approaching Castle Cliff flying at low airspeed with a high angle of attack. The F.3 was then seen with a nose-up attitude and banking to starboard as it headed across the coastline towards the sea, where the angle of bank reduced but with the nose above the horizon. Observers then stated that XP753 appeared to hang in the air before the nose dropped, the aircraft rolled to starboard and hit the sea 200 to 300 yards from the shore. Thompson did not survive the resultant impact. From the available evidence, it appears that the pilot misjudged his proximity to Castle Cliff and had stalled the aircraft while trying to avoid it. This was the first fatal Lightning loss in more than eight years.

The LTF continued to perform its role until disbandment on 30 April 1987; its final OC was Sqn Ldr C. Rowley, and the last pilot to complete training was Flt Lt I. Black.

One who served with the LTF was Sgt Ian Brett, and he has a striking memory of a loss:

> Early on the morning of 19 March 1987, I was in the LTF line hut as the line desk sergeant, sorting out the Form 700s (Tech Logs) for our Lightnings for the day's flying. We had an early practice scheduled for the new aeros pilot for the year, Flt Lt B. Lennon of No. 5 Squadron. He had taken over from Flt Lt J. Aldington, who had flown the 1986 aeros for the full season, and I had been a ground crew supervisor for the team. Several years later, I worked with John Aldington again when we were both employed by KLM, him as a Fokker 50 Captain and me as a Licensed Engineer.
>
> Flt Lt Lennon was due to do a higher altitude (5,000ft min) practice in the 'sporty' F.3 with dummy Firestreak missiles fitted rather than the heavier F.6 he usually flew. The dummy Firestreaks, I was told, with wings acted like canards and improved the turn rate. As he worked on the routine, the altitude would be reduced. This was all happening before the regular flying programme started,

so he was in to sign the aircraft out at about 07:30 hours. I had plenty to do, and he went off to XP707, fleet code DB, with the starter crew Lineys (line engineers).

I got a call from the hangar Sumpies (propulsion engineers) asking to borrow the line tug to tow a Lightning for ground runs on the detuner (big silencer to reduce the noise) on the far side of the airfield. The hangar tug was dead, so ours was the only one we had at the time. I almost let them take it but remembered the aeros flight was just going up, and we had to have a tractor available when we were operating in case we needed a tow off the runway. I told them they would have to wait twenty minutes until the aeros practice was down. They were not happy with the delay. With its smaller ventral tank, the F.3 was pretty empty after a few minutes of reheat, in which it flew for most of the display routine. The display aircraft was usually down about fifteen minutes after take-off.

With all the distractions of a busy line hut, phones, squawk boxes, etc. I hadn't really noticed the aeros Lightning depart from the line, but my attention was grabbed when one of the Lineys outside banged on the large window and shouted, 'He's got out!' I replied, 'What do you mean he's got out, he's gone,' looking at the gap in the line of Lightnings where DB had been. He pointed up at the Lightning, sat on its tail and gently sliding backwards. I am not sure now, it could have been in reheat, but it certainly had some power on.

The canopy had gone, and the ejection seat rail was extended like a harpoon stuck in it. I then noticed the pilot hanging on his chute, but my eyes were fixed on the stricken Lightning, now sliding into a vertical dive and accelerating rapidly. Strangely, I hoped it would pull out of the dive and land on the runway below. It didn't but instead hit the ground and disappeared in a flash of yellow flames and black smoke on the far side of the airfield, not too far from the detuner. That was the same detuner the Sumpies would have been positioning the ground run Lightning on if they had got the tug they had cursed me for not letting them have.

The fire section bell had obviously gone off, and the fire engine charged out of the shed near the Control Tower in seconds, heading at maximum speed for a real live fire! Meanwhile, Flt Lt Lennon was slowly descending for what seemed like ages on his chute. From our angle, it looked like the fire engine, now going as fast as it could over the grass, would arrive at his landing point just in time to run him over! Luckily, he didn't get run over and was picked up and brought back to the line hut in good order. He asked if I wanted him to write anything in Form 700. It was probably best not to, as it had gone by then anyway. I asked him if he knew what happened, as we were all more than a bit anxious. He said it had been serviceable when he left it, a relief to many of us. He then went off to get checked over at the sick quarters.

As always, the F700 was impounded within a few minutes, and I just had time to check again that everything was signed as it should have been. The evening before, I had been working in the hangar on DB and had signed off some jobs, so my signature was 'all over it'.

> When the board of enquiry sat, I was notified I would be called. Even though I was sure everything was correct, some sleepless nights followed. In the end, I wasn't asked anything, and the initial reason we heard was that it was a handling error. Later, when the report was published, the blame was put on a slow-feeding ventral tank, putting the C of G out of limits. It could have been, but usually, all the ventral tank fuel in an F.3 is gone first, soon after take-off, and there wasn't much fuel in the fire when it crashed; the fireball wasn't massive. XP707 was reduced to lots of small bits and a big hole in the ground, so nothing of use to the investigation was recovered to confirm or deny the theory of a slow-feeding ventral tank being the reason. Flt Lt Lennon didn't continue with the Lightning aeros, with one of the LTF instructors, Flt Lt Fynes, taking over the role for the final Lightning displays.[40]

As for Coltishall, it became home to the Jaguars of Nos. 54 and 6 Squadrons in August and November 1974, and later Nos. 41 and 16 Squadrons in April 1977 and July 2000 respectively. The Defence White Paper of 2003 set in motion the events that sealed Coltishall's ultimate fate. In July 2004 Defence Secretary Geoff Hoon stood up in the House of Commons and announced the base's closure as part of large-scale defence spending cuts. On 30 November 2006 Coltishall was formally closed with a flypast from four No. 6 Squadron Jaguars and a Hurricane from the Historic Aircraft Company, Duxford, ending 66 years of service. Today the excellent RAF Coltishall Heritage Centre and its volunteers keep the history and memories of the base alive.

The Story So Far

From the Lightning's entry into service in 1960, it was clear that the RAF had a potent interceptor within its ranks. However, it was limited in range and weaponry and initially suffered from poor serviceability and spares resourcing.

The F.1A and F.2 were helped by the availability of IFR, which extended range and allowed overseas deployments. However, the squadrons relied on the Valiant and Victor tankers to facilitate the completion of their operational roles.

With the introduction of the F.3 and the Red Top capability was enhanced, but the range issue had not been addressed. The decision to remove the cannons was wrong and led to situations that the F.3 could not satisfactorily resolve. Fire issues were a major problem within the Lightning units that disrupted squadron activities. Although measures were implemented to reduce the risk, it was never completely eradicated.

Between 1965 and 1971 the Lightning Force reached its peak, after which it began to decline as the Phantom started to eat into its ranks. However, the introduction of the F.6 Interim brought extended range and with the definitive F.6, the reintroduction of the cannons. The next chapter will examine the final variants of the Lightning through to retirement and the exports.

5

Interception Part Three: Lightning F.6 Interim, F.6, F.2A and Exports

'They think it's all over! It is now!'

If 1966 is remembered for one thing, it will be the immortal words above of Kenneth Wolstenholme, DFC*, a former RAFVR bomber pilot with Nos. 105 and 107 Squadrons, as he commented on England's FIFA World Cup 4-2 win against West Germany. Aside from football, the miniskirt came into vogue while The Monkees and Beach Boys rode high in the music charts, with the first episode of *Star Trek* hitting the small screen. It was the year in which John Lennon proclaimed that the Beatles were more popular than Jesus, inciting quite a negative reaction in America's 'Bible Belt'. Henry Cooper floored Muhammad Ali in a boxing match at Wembley, only to be beaten in the fifth round. War raged in Vietnam, while in Britain the first credit card was launched together with the introduction of colour television. In space, on 3 February the Soviet Union softly landed its Luna 9 unmanned spacecraft on the Moon, making it the first country to achieve such a feat. Just under a month later, it also impacted Venus with the entry probe of the Venera 3 spacecraft, again the first earth-launched vehicle to impact another planet. As its Surveyor 1 probe soft-landed on the Moon on 2 June, the Americans were not far behind in the space race.

While the Americans and the Soviet Union continued their proxy war in South-East Asia, the Cold War in Europe was far from abating as the Western and Eastern powers faced off. There was also a problem within NATO as France decided to leave the organization. The country was unwilling to allow the integration of its nuclear deterrent with other North Atlantic powers or accept any form of collective control over its forces. To this end, America was expelled from all its bases with a deadline set for April 1969. However, the USA decided to leave by April 1967 and Operation FRELOC (French Relocation) was implemented. Some USAF units went to West Germany; others came to Alconbury, Lakenheath and Mildenhall in Britain. This sudden influx of aircraft and personnel put an added strain on resources, and it was announced in January 1967 that Chelveston, Greenham Common and Sculthorpe would be brought back into use.

This was also the year of a Defence White Paper penned by the Wilson Labour government that cancelled the Royal Navy's proposed CVA-01 aircraft carrier and all but one (HMS *Bristol*) of the Type 82 destroyers. It was considered that by the time the ships came into service the nation's defence commitments would have been reduced to the extent that they wouldn't be needed. The paper envisaged investment in the Hawker P.1127 (became the Harrier), a BAC/Dassault project known as the Anglo-French Variable Geometry (AFVG, a supersonic multi-role combat aircraft) and the American General Dynamics F.111A (designation for RAF service was F-111K) as a replacement for the Canberra and the cancelled TSR.2. Only the first of these projects would evolve to see the light of day.

The AFVG collaboration folded when France decided to leave the project on the grounds of cost. The Blackburn/BAC Buccaneer took on the Canberra's role after the F-111A procurement was cancelled, again due to concerns over cost and protracted delivery times.

The year would also see the first flight in the USA of McDonnell Douglas YF-4K Phantom XT595 on 27 June at St. Louis in the hands of test pilot Joe Dobronski. The Rolls-Royce Spey-powered F-4K Phantom would eventually enter service with the Royal Navy and the RAF as the F-4M. Why is this important? Well the F-4, in time, would take over a large proportion of the Lightning's air defence role. In September 1966 plans for the interceptor's future were being discussed within the senior ranks, including modifications, one of which was the reintroduction of the cannon armament. It was envisaged that the Phantom would begin to take over the air defence role from 1972/73 as the aircraft was considered more capable due to its longer range, armament and radar system. However, for now the Lightning would continue as the nation's front-line interceptor.

The F-4 Phantom in the British Military

In the early 1960s thoughts were given to manufacturing a Vertical Take-off and Landing (VTOL) fighter and attack aircraft for the Royal Navy and the RAF. It was considered that the design, known as the Hawker P.1154, would replace the FAA's Sea Vixens in the interceptor role and the Hunter for ground attack with the RAF. Expecting the two services to work on a mutual project was bound to be fraught with difficulties, and the FAA began to question whether the P.1154 was suitable for its needs.

Approaches by McDonnell Douglas with a proposal for a derivative of the Phantom suitable for the Navy's carriers were not ignored and over time, discussions continued. The P.1154, with its VTOL capabilities, could operate from smaller ships, and the Admiralty could probably see that the writing was potentially on the wall for its carriers such as HMS *Ark Royal*, *Eagle* and *Hermes*. With the economic difficulties prevailing in Britain at the time, reducing costs was a topic always high on the agenda. Therefore, with the option of the Phantom on the table, if the Navy could get the aircraft procured it could keep its carriers, and unsurprisingly, interest in the P.1154 waned from the nautical perspective, with questions raised about capability and the effect on ship's decks of downward directed exhaust gases. It was clear that the Navy was favouring the Phantom, and in July 1964 the service got its way when two prototype F-4Ks were ordered, leaving the RAF to pursue the P.1154 alone.

The proposed fleet of Phantoms for the Navy required adaption to enable the aircraft to operate from the smaller decks of the carriers. Therefore it was agreed that the more powerful and fuel-efficient Rolls-Royce Spey turbofans would be fitted to the machine in place of the General Electric J79s. There was also a political element to the thinking as using a British powerplant and other components gave credence to the design being partially home-grown and providing domestic jobs. However, there was a problem fitting the Spey due to its larger size, which led to a radical redesign of the fuselage with the negative effect of increasing drag negating much of the benefit of the engine's enhanced performance.

In October 1964 a Labour government came to power. It was not long before Defence Minister Denis Healey began looking at ways to cut costs, which saw the cancellation of the TSR.2 and the P.1154 soon came into his sights. He favoured the Navy's position of buying off the shelf and concluded this was also probably the best route for the RAF. How often have we seen this happen since, for instance, Nimrod AEW.3 and MRA.4 to Boeing E-3A Sentry and P-8 Poseidon respectively. Therefore the question was raised about whether the P.1154 should be abandoned and the Phantom procured to replace the Hunter in the ground attack role for the RAF. The answer on both counts was yes, although the RAF were not content with the Spey engine option, which was overruled as it was considered that having a fleet of aircraft with the same powerplant would reduce costs and logistics.

Procuring the Phantom did not stop the Navy's carriers from coming under threat, and due to a shrinking commitment in the Middle and Far East, in time just one remained: HMS *Ark Royal*. Fifty F-4Ks were ultimately ordered for the FAA, but fourteen of these were sent to the RAF for air defence.

On 29 June 1968 the first three Phantom FG.1s arrived at Yeovilton, and the following day No. 700P Naval Air Squadron (NAS) was formed. After acceptance trials were complete, No. 767 NAS was designated to provide training on the Phantom to the crews of No. 892 NAS based at Yeovilton and No. 43 Squadron of the RAF. In time, the RAF would be responsible for training its and NAS F-4 crews.

The RAF's prototype YF-4M, XT852, first flew on 17 February 1967 with the initial unit No. 43 Squadron, 'The Fighting Cocks', forming at Leuchars on 1 September 1969. Here its FG.1s joined the Lightnings of Nos. 11 and 23 Squadrons, where it undertook long-range interceptions within the Eastern and Northern UK Air Defence Region. The machine's longer range, more effective radar and increased weapon fit (four Sidewinders, four Sparrows and centreline SUU-23 20mm gun pod) made it ideal for countering Soviet Air Force and naval aviation bombers and reconnaissance aircraft far out over the North Sea and North Atlantic. The type would initially operate in two variants with the RAF, the FG.1 in the air defence role and the ground attack and tactical reconnaissance FGR.2. Later in 1984 a third was introduced when fifteen F-4J(UK) Phantoms were procured following the Falklands War.

On 27 November 1978 Phantom FG.1 XT870 was catapulted off the deck of HMS *Ark Royal*, making it the last aircraft from a British carrier to perform such an action. The ship was decommissioned in February 1979, but the FAA F-4s were not retired and later found further use in RAF service. Of note, XT870 appeared in the static display at the 'Last Lightning Show' held at Binbrook on 22 August 1987 at which time it was serving with No. 111 Squadron. Fifteen RAF squadrons and a single OCU equipped with the F-4, seven of which - Nos. 19, 23, 29, 56, 74, 92 and 111 - had previously flown the Lightning.

With the entry into service of the Jaguar for ground attack in 1974, Phantoms FGR.2s reverted to a pure interceptor role. It began to replace the Lightning during the mid-1970s, leaving just Nos. 5 and 11 Squadrons to continue with the type until April 1988 when its duties were taken over by the Panavia Tornado F.3.

At the time of the first flight of an F-4 Phantom destined for the British military, the Lightning Force was enhancing its capability within the RAF. The following chapter will explore the design changes taken to extend the type's range, the return of the cannons and a look at squadron life.

Lightning F.3 Extended Range (F.6 Interim)

A common theme throughout this work's narrative thus far is the Lightning's lack of range. Although a more advanced machine than the variants preceding it, the F.3 was still afflicted by a shortage of fuel and, in some ways, capability with the removal of the cannons. It was envisaged that this Lightning variant would be the last of the line so development plans had not initially advanced, although EE had a plethora of ideas to bring to the table. However, official thinking continually evolved, and it was decided by the Defence Committee in 1960 that Fighter Command's role was to move from the defence of the deterrent to a position of deterring hostile reconnaissance, interception of unknown aircraft, prevention of jamming of Britain's radar systems and the reinforcement of overseas bases.

In September 1962 the AM issued a requirement to increase the Lightning's ferry range up to 2,000 miles with one IFR, together with improvements to radio and navigation aids. So the goalposts moved and the Lightning found itself as the guardian of British airspace and the nation's interests in West Germany, the Near East and the Far East. The original concept of a stopgap until SAGWs came into full operation was gone.

The F.1 was ruled out from further development, but thought was given to extending the range of the F.1A and F.2, which again did not come to fruition.

However, a radical rework of the latter would result in the F.2A, which will be described later.

For the F.3 fuel load was increased by redesigning the ventral tank to a larger size and allowing provision for overwing tanks, adding 560 (later 600) and 540 gallons respectively. It will be remembered that the Cambered Leading Edge (CLE) wing flown originally by P.1A WG760 in the mid-1950s was dismissed as an option for the earlier marks of the Lightning. However, the concept was revisited with a view to improving subsonic cruising efficiency. Earlier concerns about the CLE's negative effect on supersonic performance were allayed as the F.3's Avon 301s (later 302) had increased thrust to overcome the previous deficiency. The changes to the design led to the Lightning F.3 Extended Range (ER), later known as the F.6 Interim.

Sixteen airframes serialled through XR752 to XR767 were taken from the F.3 production line and were modified to the Interim configuration. However, the aircraft were not equipped to convey the overwing tanks, but would do so once converted to full F.6 standard.

The first to fly was XR752 on 16 June 1965 piloted by de Villiers, followed seven days later by XR753 with Beamont at the helm. The latter was flown to the AFDS on 16 November of the same year, while squadron deliveries commenced in December. Conversion to full F.6 standard began in 1967 and was completed the following year. All but one of the sixteen Interims were converted. The exception was XR766 of No. 23 Squadron, which crashed into the North Sea on 7 September 1967 with pilot Sqn Ldr R. Blackburn initiating a successful ejection.

Lightning F.6

The Lightning F.6 advanced the type's design with a larger ventral tank, the CLE wing, provision for overwing tanks and an airfield arrestor hook (used to engage rotary hydraulic arrestor gear in the event of brake failure). The enlarged ventral tank allowed the twin 30mm ADEN cannons to be reintroduced as a pack installed within its forward area, although this reduced fuel capacity but only marginally. Radar improvements led to the fitting of the AI 23C/D.

A pair of Rolls-Royce Avon 301 (later uprated to 302) axial-flow turbojets powered the aircraft, producing 12,600lb of thrust at sea level and 16,300lb in fully variable reheat with the latter engine fitted. A fueldraulic system was provided with fuel carried in integral wing tanks, flaps and non-jettisonable ventral, giving a usable supply of 1,326 gallons (ventral tank 610 gallons, reduced to 535 with the cannons fitted), a 27 per cent increase over the F.3. The addition of the overwing tanks added a further 520 gallons (as per the Aircrew Manual).

Dimensions were the same as the F.3 except for wing area, which increased from 458.5 sq ft to 474.5 sq ft. Maximum take-off weight was 45,700lb, landing 34,500lb and emergency 40,500lb. Airspeed limitations, either clean or with missiles and ventral tank, were M2.0/650 knots depending on which was reached first. With overwing tanks, limitations were M0.98/525 knots, M0.90/525 knots with a single missile, an IFR probe fitted, 625 knots and Red Top below 10,000ft in peacetime, 525 knots. The minimum speed is detailed as 180 knots with flaps and undercarriage up or 140 knots with both down. The Aircrew Manual states although the aircraft was cleared to 60,000ft, it should not be flown higher than 50,000ft due to the limits imposed by the oxygen system and the pilot's personnel equipment. As per the F.3, a Martin-Baker Type 4BSC Mk 2 ejection seat was fitted.

Limitations relating to g were without overwing tanks (positive):

Speed	Ventral Empty	Ventral Tank Fuel			Single Missile
		Up to 1,000lb	1,000lb to 3,500lb	More than 3,500lb	
Up to M0.9	6g	6g	5.5g	5g	4g
M0.9 to M1.8	6g	5.5g	5g	4.5g	4g
Above M1.8	4g	4g	4g	4g	4g
Note 1: When winged Red Top missiles are carried, the limit is +4g except in operational necessity.					
Note: Above M1.8 with two wingless Red Top missiles fitted, the limit is +3g.					
Negative: The maximum permissible negative acceleration is minus 3g. Negative g should not be applied for longer than 15 seconds.					

With overwing tanks:

Speed (Knots)	Overwing Tanks		Single Missile
	With Fuel	Empty	
Below 475	3.5g	4g	2g
Above 475	3g	3.5g	2g

The Aircrew Manual gives details regarding the overwing tanks and states: 'Jettisoning should not be attempted above 500 knots. Empty tanks may be jettisoned between 200 and 250 knots and up to M0.75 at heights up to 40,000 feet in straight and level flight. Overwing tanks containing fuel should not be jettisoned.'[1]

Initially starting out as an F.3 in June 1962, XP693 went on to become a trials aircraft for the Extended Range F.3. It was then converted to F.6 configuration for trials with overwing tanks and an arrester hook in 1965/66. Eleven further F.3s were earmarked for conversion to F.6 following their first flights running through serials XR747 to XR751 and XR723 to XR728. From the first batch only XR747 was converted, with the others remaining in F.3 configuration.

In the hands of Beamont the first full-production F.6 to fly was XR768 on 24 November 1965. In total forty-six entered RAF service (including seven converted from F.3s), bolstered by a further fifteen once the F.6 Interim had completed conversion. The F.6 serials ran through as stated above and from XR768 to XR773, XS893 to XS904 and XS918 to XS938.

The RAF now had a more versatile Lightning within its ranks with enhanced range but not necessarily armament. A lack of investment and vision within the Air Staff had hampered the aircraft's true potential, but at least at a later date the cannons would be reintroduced.

Like its predecessors the F.6 was prone to the same issues with fire and went through the Fire Integrity Programme in the late 1960s to early 1970s, impacting the squadrons' day-to-day operations. As with the F.3, the work helped but did not eradicate the issue, which would be a constant risk right up to the final days of Lightning flying. The F.6 (including Interim) was to lose twenty-six of its number to accidents and write-offs. Of note, all became casualties between the serials of XR760 to XR769.

The following will chronologically explore the F.6 Interim and F.6 from the first unit to retire the variant, No. 74 Squadron in 1971, to No. 56 Squadron in June 1976. The last two F.6 squadrons, Nos. 5 and 11, will be discussed in the following chapter. It is not the intention to go into full histories of the units that operated the F.6 as the typical types of training, operations, MPCs, etc. undertaken by the Lightning squadrons have been written about in previous chapters.

No. 74 Squadron

The first full production standard F.6, XR768, arrived with No. 74 Squadron at Leuchars on 1 August 1966. At the time the unit was holding Northern QRA and two days later Fg Off. 'Heinz' Frick was scrambled, piloting an F.3 against two Bisons. The interception was not without incident as when he joined the intruders his airbrakes remained extended and refused to retract, necessitating a PAN call (a term to describe a situation where assistance is required that does not represent an immediate threat to life). Returning to Kinloss, it was discovered that just five minutes of fuel endurance remained in the tanks.

October of the same year was also a busy month for QRA, and on the 25th a Bison was intercepted by two of the squadron's F.3s accompanied by an F.6 flown by Fg Off. A. Markell. He photographed his two colleagues flying with the Soviet aircraft, the images making it into the national press a few days later, unfortunately credited to No. 56 Squadron.

In the same month the well-liked and respected Wg Cdr K. Goodwin AFC took over command and working up on the F.6 began, including a deployment by four to Akrotiri on 13 December where Battle Flight was held. This left few Lightnings at Leuchars as the F.3s were readied for redeployment to other squadrons; however, by the 21st of the month twelve F.6s were on strength. The machines were in bare aluminium finish with the roundel on the nose bordered by orange and black triangles. The fin was adorned with the Tiger's Head on a white disc. In time the F.6s would gain black tails similar to those worn by its F.1s and F.3s earlier in the decade.

In March 1967 IFR training was high on the agenda, including trials with the overwing tanks and fuel taken from Victor tankers. With the art perfected, the squadron transited to Tengah, Singapore over three days from 4 June to form an element of the Far East Air Force (FEAF). Deployed under the name of Operation Hydraulic, this would be the furthest east the Lightning Force would operate. In the same year the Labour government decreed the withdrawal of British Forces to the East of Suez, a decision that would, in time, impact No. 74 Squadron.

A sad event occurred on 12 September 1968 resulting in the squadron's first fatality since the loss of Flt Lt G. Owen while piloting F.3 XP704 at Leuchars in August 1964. On the day Fg Off. P. Thompson was flying F.6 XS896 when Reheat Fire 1 and 2 captions illuminated as he was preparing to land. The aircraft was observed rolling through nearly 360 degrees and entering a flat upright spin. An ejection was initiated, but the pilot did not survive. From the evidence presented it appeared that fire had caused the disconnection of the rear section of the push/pull tubing operating the powered flying control unit to the tailplane.

Over the years many myths have prevailed over the speed and heights attained by the Lightning. In October 1968, while based at Tengah with No. 74 Squadron, Fg Off. D.C. Roome climbed to an altitude that must qualify as one of the highest attained by the interceptor. In the ORB for the month, a section entitled 'High Flyers' describes F.6s intercepting a Martin RB-57F, a high-altitude reconnaissance aircraft flown by the USAF, tracing its origins back to the Canberra.

The RB-57F was tasked to investigate high-altitude meteorological conditions and to test Singapore's new air defence system, where it would act as a target for the Lightnings. Trials began at 50,000ft and went through to 65,000ft; both heights met with successful interceptions by the F.6s. Then it was up to 80,000ft and a surprise for the RB-57F's pilot when an intercepting Lightning overtook him in the descent through his altitude. A further climb to 100,000ft put the aircraft out of reach. Roome had been involved in the intercepts and began thinking that with the tropopause being in the region of 55,000ft, the Lightning could probably climb above 85,000ft.

A few months later he gave it a go after filling his tanks from a Victor off the coast of Malaysia. Ascending to 50,000ft, he then accelerated to M2.0 and zoom-climbed to level off at 65,000ft. From here Roome allowed his speed to build to

M2.2 and pulled the stick back until he eventually contacted the backstops. Once this restriction was reached, he gently levelled out and noted that 87,800ft had been attained. At this height the intrepid pilot was rewarded with a scene few would have witnessed: above him a pitch-black sky with the Earth's curvature visible. With the performance of his F.6 at its limit Roome descended, advising ATC that he was passing flight level 720 on the way.

In February 1969 Sqn Ldr Carter took over temporary command of the squadron after Goodwin returned to Britain; the permanent replacement, Wg Cdr D. Caldwell, was in place by March. Exercise Leisure was undertaken in May, with the ORB giving an account of events:

> 74 Squadron's task was to mount an East-West CAP [Combat Air Patrol] at 1,500ft south of Mersing to intercept low-level targets attacking Singapore Island and also to act as a springboard for intercepting supersonic targets over the China Sea. Nine sorties were flown, and the squadron claimed six kills. These were three Mirages, two Canberras and a Meteor. Only two aircraft remained on CAP for the whole of their allocated period without seeing a target or being committed by CGI. Two aircraft were sent after supersonic targets but were accelerated too late and, consequently were unable to catch their target before the bomb release point. Another aircraft intercepted a target at M1.6 but, owing to unserviceability, was unable to launch a missile. The main lesson to come out of the exercise, as far as 74 Squadron was concerned, was the value of the Springboard CAP, which gave maximum aircraft utilisation and the need for a telebrief slave in our operations room. It is hoped to have this installed before the next exercise.[2]

A notable IFR deployment came on 16 June 1969 under the code name of Silver Swallow when four Lightnings flew in two waves to the Royal Australian Air Force (RAAF) base at Darwin. The F.6s were required to participate in Townhouse, an exercise to test the point defence of the airfield from both air and ground attack for seven days. The squadron mounted QRA for twenty-four hours a day, keeping one aircraft on two-minute alert with a pilot in the cockpit for the duration of the exercise. The Lightnings and Mirages (of the RAAF) were defending against Canberras and Vulcans of the RAF and Canberras of the RAAF and RNZAF. At the conclusion of the exercise, the unit had undertaken eighty scrambles with eighty-one 'kills' awarded, of which a small selection is shown below:

- 19 June: Flt Lt R. Davidson F.6 XR772 Vulcan
- 19 June: Flt Lt R. Lea F.6 XS897 Canberra (2)
- 22 June: Flt Lt I. McBride F.6 XR770 Canberra (2)
- 23 June: Fg Off. D. Roome F.6 XS893 Canberra (3)
- 24 June: Flt Lt D. Carden F.6 XR772 ECM Vulcan
- 25 June: Fg Off. S. Brown F.6 XR770 Canberra (2)[3]

The rest of 1969 was taken up with a multitude of exercises with some interesting names including High Swallow (deployment to Darwin), Synod Balloon (CAP exercise), Octennial (simulated attack against Butterworth), Fireflash (daylight and night firing of Firestreak missiles) and Lightrage (low-level CAP). Comment was made in the ORB relating to Lightrage:

> On 4 November, the squadron was tasked with mounting a low-level CAP for 3 hours. The exercise was highly successful as far as the squadron was concerned. A total of fourteen sorties were flown, with some aircraft and pilots doing three sorties. Eight out of ten Mirage targets were claimed. Four out of four medium/high levels were successfully intercepted, and four out of six low-level. Again, on this exercise, a single-engined Pioneer was used as a CAP coordinator with excellent results.[4]

During the first month of the New Year the squadron was tasked to participate in Exercise Janex mounted by Royal Navy and Commonwealth navies in the China Sea. In this instance, the Lightnings were assigned to act as Soviet SS-N-3 Shaddock and AS-5 Kelt missiles. The former was a simulated submarine launch at 80 nautical miles, while the latter was from a Vulcan at 60, with the F.6 accelerating to 600 knots to simulate the attack profiles of both weapons. The purpose of the exercise was for the navies to evaluate ECM tactics in the face of such an attack and would aid future training requirements.

In 1970 the Lightning Force was to lose one F.3, five F.6s and a T.4. Of the F.6s, three came from No. 74 Squadron. On 26 May Fg Off. J. Webster piloting XR767 flew into the sea at night during a practice interception with Fg Off. D. Roome. Very little of the Lightning was found except for a small part of one of the overwing tanks. From the available evidence, the pilot's body was not recovered.

Two months later on 27 July an accident occurred shortly after take-off when F.6 XS930, flown by Flt Lt F. Whitehouse, pulled into a steep reheat climb and entered into a spin at 600ft; the Lightning crashed into the jungle shortly after. The pilot tried to eject, but was too low and his parachute failed to deploy correctly. It was considered by those who witnessed the departure that too much g had been pulled in the rotation, but this was not the sole cause of the accident. During starting, taxiing and take-off, fuel was taken from the wing tanks, leaving a full ventral. This, in turn, led to a shift in the centre of gravity, resulting in decreased stability in pitch, especially when extreme manoeuvres were performed. The pilot was probably unaware that his actions would have such an outcome on the day.

A third loss came on 12 August 1970 when XS893 experienced an undercarriage malfunction, leaving the pilot, Fg Off. M. Rigg, with no other option but to eject. Thankfully this was successful, with an SAR Whirlwind helicopter picking him up from the sea.

With the coming of 1971 the squadron's time with the Lightning was nearing its end due to the decision for British Forces to be withdrawn from East of Suez. After eleven years of operating the supersonic fighter, preparations were made for the unit's disbandment. In July the last month of operations was commented on by Wg Cdr D. Caldwell:

> It was planned that in the best 74 tradition it would come off operational status with a nine-ship flypast over HQ FEAF on the last flying day. All engineering support was organised to this end and at the same time achieving the monthly flying task. Unfortunately, as so often in the past, the aircraft upset the schedule when a series of preliminary warnings were received which had to be completed before next flight. The result was that the aircraft were grounded for about a week, and neither target could be met. In defence of the Lightning it must be recorded that it is without doubt the finest flying machine in service today in its combat configuration and if the gun installation can be made to work it will become one of the best M2.0 air superiority fighters in the world. In spite of the problems associated with the aircraft, 74 Squadron has met all its operational requirements and 95 per cent of its flying tasks while in the Far East, and this has only been possible because of the very high standard of engineering, dedication to the job in hand, and long working hours of the ground support personnel.[5]

On 19 August 1971 ten F.6s with overwing tanks staged a flypast for Air Commander FEAF, Air Vice Marshal (AVM) Nigel Maynard. Six days later, on the evening of 25 August 1971, the Squadron Standard was paraded for the last time in the Far East, led by Wg Cdr Caldwell with three officers and thirty-seven other ranks. Support on the day also came from No. 63 Squadron, RAF Regiment. Four aircraft overflew the reviewing dais for the General Salute, and a lone Lightning appeared from behind and disappeared upwards in reheat as the Standard was marched off the parade.

Following this, the unit's former aircraft were handed over to No. 56 Squadron and flown to Akrotiri. The squadron was the first to bring the Lightning into service and would be the first to retire the type upon its disbandment.

No. 111 Squadron

The squadron's association with the Lightning F.6 was to be very brief as it was not until May 1974 that three, XR747, XR752 and XS895, were received at Wattisham while the unit was under the command of Wg Cdr R. Horsfield. Fatigue restrictions relating to the F.6 and the grounding of No. 23 Squadron's target F.1As had left it short of aircraft to use for combat training. Therefore three F.3s from No. 111 were sent to Leuchars, with the F.6s coming in return.

On 30 September of the same year, the squadron relinquished its air defence responsibilities to the Phantom FGR.2, the first of the Lightning units to do so.

No. 23 Squadron

On 8 May 1967 No. 23 Squadron took delivery of its first F.6 Interim XR761 at Leuchars and XR757 nine days later while it was holding Northern QRA. The aircraft were in bare aluminium finish with blue and red vertical bars on either side of the roundel on the nose and a small red eagle upon a white disc applied to the tail. The extended range of the variant was welcomed, as noted by Wg Cdr K.A. Williamson in the ORB:

> The arrival of our two Interim Mk VI aircraft together with a firm promise of four more to come has increased the squadron's operational potential at a propitious time. The training target should now be easier to achieve and interception on targets that have hitherto been outside our range can now be undertaken.[6]

In July 1967 the squadron received its final four F.6 Interims, XR752, XR753, XR766 and XR767. It was not long before the first loss occurred. On 7 September 1967 XR766, piloted by Sqn Ldr R. Blackburn, was undertaking a practice interception but entered an unrecoverable flat spin. Despite commendable efforts by the pilot, the aircraft rapidly lost height and at 8,000ft Blackburn ejected and was later fished out of the North Sea by a helicopter of 'C' Flight, No. 202 Squadron. The incident sparked an investigation into the spinning characteristics of the F.6 by BAC and the A&AEE. One of the recommendations was that Lightning pilots be given practice in spinning annually in the Jet Provost to ensure they were current in the art.

As the year progressed conversion to the full-standard F.6s came, with the Interims returning to Warton. On 28 August the final production F.6, XS938, was collected from the manufacturers and delivered to the squadron.

October saw an increase in QRA practice scrambles and a Fawn exercise to Sola in Norway, while at Leuchars the last two remaining F.3s were flown to Wattisham. In a precursor of what was to come over the following months and years, on 19 December a live scramble occurred when Flt Lt A. Craig piloting F.6 XS936 went after a target that turned away at extreme range before the interception could be completed.

Life settled into the usual routines of a typical Lightning unit, including more live interceptions. On 21 May 1968 the squadron launched seven QRA scrambles due to heightened Soviet activity. The pilots taking part were Sqn Ldrs E. Durham, N. McEwen, Fg Off. C. Robinson and Flt Lts J. Anders, J. Fawcett and A. Ellender. The ORB describes one interception: 'QRA Scramble. Russian Badger long-range reconnaissance aircraft intercepted approximately 250 miles north-east of base.

Badger photographed and escorted south to middle of North Sea before it turned eastwards and out of range.'[7]

Activity in June ratcheted up further as the Soviets continued to provide trade for the Leuchars-based squadron:

- 4 June: Sqn Ldr N. McEwen F.6 XS935 – Two Russian Bear Ds 300 miles from base.
- 4 June: Fg Off. D Hemmings F.6 XR727 – Two Russian aircraft escorted.
- 4 June: Fg Off. H. Oliver F.6 XR763 – One Russian Bear intercepted 260 miles from base.
- 5 June: Fg Off. M. Donaldson F.6 XS938 – Two targets intercepted, one identified as Bear D.
- 5 June: Fg Off. C. Robinson F.6 XS935 – Bear shadowed.
- 5 June: Major F. Pieri USMC F.6 XR727 – Bear D intercepted 130 miles north of base.
- Sqn Ldr N. McEwen and Fg Off. R. Pengelly T.5 XS417 – Bear shadowed 135 miles from base.
- 5 June: Flt Lt G. Potter F.6 XR760 – Two targets pursued at supersonic speed. AI and visual contact obtained. Leader descended and contact lost. Rear aircraft, a Bear D, shadowed. Rear gunner in Bear took many photographs of Lightning.
- 5 June: Fg Off. M. Donaldson F.6 XS938 – Target turned away out of range before interception made.
- 6 June: Fg Off. D. Hemmings F.6 XS935 – Vectored on to target by MRS, then lost contact with MRS. Continued and intercepted Russian Badger D, which turned into Lightning in possible attempt to prevent photography.
- 6 June: Major F. Pieri USMC F.6 XR727 – Target faded before interception.
- 6 June: Flt Lt A. Ellender F.6 XR760 – Two separate targets, Bear D, intercepted. Close escort on second target maintained until ordered to return to base. Crew of aircraft being escorted behaved in a friendly manner.[8]

It had been a busy time for No. 23 Squadron, and in July 1968 command changed to Wg Cdr D. McClen. Williamson, now Grp Capt., moved to become station commander at Gütersloh.

Moving onto June 1971 one of the added benefits of introducing the F.6 was the option to fit the twin 30mm ADEN cannons. The unit was pleased about this and made the following comment:

> History was made in June by the first live guns firing by 23 Squadron Lightnings against the banner and, contrary to many expectations, hits were made. In fact during the first firing on the 27th June, the target was shot off by the CO. Some reasonable scores are hoped for in July.[9]

Due to missing pages within the ORB, the next mention of the cannons comes in November 1972 while the unit was under the command of Wg Cdr W.B.G. Hopkins:

> The finish of the gun firing programme ended on a high note with the best results yet. This was a score of 11.4 per cent returned by Flight Lieutenant D.L. James. As to be expected, the squadron's results improved as more experience was gained. After a disappointing start an average 3.52 per cent was returned. This equated to a total of 218 hits from 6,190 rounds fired. Individual pilot scores are given below.

Pilot	Rounds Fired	Sorties	Hits	%
Wg Cdr Hopkins	416	5	15	3.6
Sqn Ldr Gross	450	5	14	3.1
Sqn Ldr Mace	431	5	18	4.2
Flt Lt Childs	450	5	28	6.2

Pilot	Rounds Fired	Sorties	Hits	%
Flt Lt Doble	450	5	2	0.4
Flt Lt Hamilton	480	5	17	3.5
Flt Houston	540	5	18	3.3
Flt Lt Lea	410	5	17	4.1
Flt Lt McLean	540	5	4	0.7
CPE Robert	540	6	4	0.7
Flt Lt Slocum	418	5	15	3.6
Flt Lt Spoor	540	6	37	6.9
Flt Lt Taylor	270	3	0	0
Flt Lt James	255	3	29	11.4

> Since the gunnery phase, the emphasis has been on night flying, both in Cyprus and at Leuchars. This is to make up our yearly requirement after the summer nights. Training has been varied, including Ops, Profit and low-levels.[10, 11]

In the last week of November 1972, an event occurred previously mentioned in this chapter. Between the 27th and 30th two Jet Provosts and four pilots were attached from RAF Manby to conduct spinning exercises with the squadron pilots. As the ORB states, this was now an annual requirement for all pilots to undertake one sortie.

Further cannon firing occurred in October 1973, and marksmanship had improved from the results noted in the ORB. In November 1972 a total of 6,190 shells had been fired, achieving 218 hits, a percentage of 3.52. Just under a year later, 5,869 30mm shells had been sent towards the banner with 470 hits, equating to 8 per cent.

Looking back to March 1972, the unit received two Lightning F.1As, XM173, XM178 and a third XM182 in July. The aircraft were used for target duties, but by July 1974 all had taken their last flights. As previously stated, fatigue restrictions on the F.6 reduced flying hours and impacted training. This situation and the loss of the F.1As led to the squadron receiving three F.3s, XP706, XP750 and XP751, in exchange for three F.6s as described earlier under the heading of No. 111 Squadron.

The final year of Lightning operations for No. 23 Squadron came in 1975, along with a further change of command as Wg Cdr I. Thomson took over in April. The following May Operation Bolthole was implemented, sending the unit to Wattisham while runway work was undertaken at Leuchars. Shortly after arrival Southern IAF was held for two weeks, but unlike their time up north no live scrambles were undertaken; however, the status quo would soon resume.

At the end of July the squadron returned to Leuchars and Northern IAF was back on the agenda. For instance, on the 29th of the month Flt Lt G. Smith intercepted two Bear-Ds, and in August Flt Lt C.J. Willmer scrambled and photographed a Soviet *Kresta II* Class cruiser shadowing USS *Nimitz* and its support ships.

Having previously won the Dacre Trophy in May 1966 and 1968, the squadron achieved the accolade again with the prize awarded by Mrs Dacre MBE on 12 September 1975. October was the last month operating the Lightning, and it went out in some style with five live scrambles, two of which were rewarded when one Bear-D was intercepted on the 10th by Flt Lt R. Lapraik and two more three days later by Flt Lt G. Smith, both while piloting XR753.

On the last day of the month twelve Lightnings were on site, with eleven moving to Binbrook by 4 November. Cat. 3 damage to one aircraft entailed it staying at Leuchars until repairs could be made. The days of the Lightning for the unit were over, but on 17 November 1975 No. 23 Squadron began forming at Coningsby equipped with the Phantom FGR.2.

No. 56 Squadron

With the disbandment of No. 74 Squadron in August 1971, seven Lightning F.6s - XR759, XR761, XR764, XR771, XR773, XS897 and XS921 - were destined to be taken on strength by No. 56 Squadron. The first pair arrived at Akrotiri from Tengah on 5 September of the same year. The unit's aircraft were in bare aluminium finish with the area over the AVPIN tank and pumps painted white to reflect the heat. Red and white squares were applied on either side of the nose roundels with a large gold 'Firebird' on the tail.

The F.6 was soon making inroads into the F.3's domain. For many years the bane of the Lightning's career again made itself felt on 30 September 1971.

While climbing through 24,000ft, XR764 piloted by Flt Lt R. Bealer, experienced a Reheat 1 warning. He instigated the required drills, but felt the controls stiffen and noted the Reheat 2 warning had illuminated. An ejection in such circumstances was usually inevitable, and this came to pass shortly after when Bealer pulled the face blind handle at 22,000ft. He came down in the sea and was picked up by an SAR helicopter.

With the F.6 becoming established on the island, the squadron continued with Battle Flight. On 27 October Flt Lt C. Taylor was scrambled against two targets at 150 nautical miles, which turned away and were not identified. Over the coming months in 1972, interceptions continued with some of the more interesting ones shown below:

- 21 January: Flt Lt R. Bealer F.6 XS932 – USN Orion was operating with one engine feathered at low level. It was covered in aerials. The weather was poor and the Orion was probably off course.
- 21 February: Flt Lt A. Childs F.6 XR773 – Two UAR Badgers at low level.
- 23 February: Sqn Ldr T. Elworthy F.6 XR773 – Turkish F-100F.
- 2 March: Wg Cdr Farrer F.6 XS921 – Israeli Noratlas at 10,000ft.
- 1 June: Fg Off. C. Cystar F.6 XS921 – Two UAR Badgers.
- 7 June: Flt Lt K. Bryan F.6 XS921 – Four Israeli Phantoms.
- 8 July: Sqn Ldr T. Elworthy F.6 XR773 – Buccaneers.
- 15 August: Flt Lt I. Dixon F.6 XS933 – Israeli C-97 Stratocruiser 60 nautical miles south of Akrotiri at 2,000ft.
- 17 August: Flt Lt K. Skinner F.6 XR761 – Israeli C-130 at 2,500ft.
- 3 October: Flt Lt C. Willmer F.6 XR773 – USAF EC121.[12]

In November 1972 scrambles increased between the 2nd and 29th when twenty-nine Aeroflot Antonov An-12 Cubs and an An-22 Cock were intercepted. During the same month, Wg Cdr Farrer departed to be replaced by Wg Cdr M.E. Bee. Among all the activities there was time for a little downtime: 'A "Monster" Kebab was held in the Limassol on 14 Nov, attended by members of 56 Squadron, 23 and 111 Sqns and several visiting tanker crews, to mark in traditional style the first occasion on which three Lightning squadrons had been assembled at Akrotiri.'[13]

December saw even more intense activity and further scrambles, with thirty-four An-12s and an An-10 Cub intercepted and shadowed. As can be seen, Akrotiri was certainly the place to be if you wanted to use the Lightning for its intended purpose. The ORB for the last month of the year commented:

> Battle Flight: This month the flight carried out thirty-one scrambles, the majority of which were for the purpose of identifying and shadowing Soviet transport aircraft in transit through local airspace. On one scramble on 14 Dec, an Antonov AN-10 Cat aircraft was observed, but on other occasions, only Antonov AN-12 Cubs were shadowed. As in November, unarmed aircraft were used when such

> activity could be forecast. On 22 Dec, a scramble was called to identify a C-47 transport aircraft (suspected Israeli), and a further scramble on 26 Dec was to identify a USN C-130. The remaining two scrambles were for practice purposes.[14]

With the coming of the New Year of 1973, squadron life continued along with further interceptions. Another loss occurred on 3 April when XS934 crashed into the sea near Zygi. A mixture of vibration and fire warning captions illuminating made pilot Flt Lt Greer's mind up and he successfully ejected at 11,000ft. He came down in the ocean and was picked up by helicopter. There was little wreckage for the board of inquiry to work with to establish the cause with certainty, but from the evidence it could have been due to a hot gas leak causing a fire.

During the same month, an Armament Practice Camp (APC) was held between the 9th and 18th at Akrotiri, during which the F.6s carried out air-to-air gunnery for the first time. Initially results were poor, but began to improve as pilots became more skilled at relearning the lost art.

In June six F.6s flew to Valley for an MPC, and on the 26th a Red Top was fired, which proceeded to break up shortly after launch, damaging the Lightning's port mainplane and tailplane. Over the course of the camp further missiles were successfully launched, but there was another hazard that presented itself. On 2 July XS901 suffered a bird strike, preventing it from being moved back to Leconfield with the other five F.6s three days later for a Mini-Adex with No. 11 Squadron. With the exercise complete, the unit's detachment of Lightnings returned to Akrotiri between the 19th and 20th of the month.

The deployment that followed in September 1973 would be unthinkable today. On the 15th Wg Cdr Bee led four F.6s to Mehrabad, Tehran. During the detachment sixty-two hours and forty-five sorties were flown, including IFR observed by the Northrop F-5s of the Imperial Iranian Air Force (IIAF). In addition fighter affiliation was carried out with the F-5s together with four two-versus-two combat sorties with IIAF Phantoms. The F.6s came home on 20 September with the ORB commenting: 'All in all, the detachment was considered to be of interest and value to those taking part.' The Iranian Revolution of 1978/79 put paid to any further deployments as the regime turned hostile to the West, a situation still prevailing today.

The year 1974 began and continued with the normal routines. The loss of F.6 XR759 was narrowly averted on 18 February by some very skilful flying by Flt Lt John Ward, who was carrying out a high-altitude interception exercise as part of standardization checks with the squadron while on the staff of No. 226 OCU. After undertaking a diving attack, the pilot found a control restriction, meaning the stick could not be pulled back further than the neutral position. Luckily he had height on his side and was able to ease out of the dive by applying maximum back pressure on the stick and attaining straight and level flight. After a handling check, the Lightning was set up in a landing configuration and Flt Lt Ward found he could make small nose-up pitch changes by engaging the No. 1 engine reheat.

With judicious use of the throttle and reheat, he was able to adjust his approach angle and land at 240 knots. By anyone's standards this was an incredible feat of airmanship, and he was duly awarded an Air Force Cross for saving his aircraft.

In July concerns grew as tensions between the Greek and Turkish Cypriots again flared up. On the 15th of the month, the readiness state was increased to Defcon Bravo due to a coup staged in the Republic by the Cyprus National Guard backed by the Greek government against the Cypriot President Archbishop Makarios III. He was replaced by Nikos Sampson, who was fanatically anti-Turkish. From the 16th, all Lightnings were serviceable and armed, with the decision taken to evacuate the dormitory towns with personnel obliged to sleep in the squadron buildings.

In response, on the 20th the Turks invaded, prompting the alert being raised to Defcon Charlie from dawn to dusk as its Air Force stepped up activities over the island, with some coming close to the SBA. Typical intercepts were RF-84F Thunderstreaks and F-100 Super Sabres. During the month 110 Battle Flight and operational sorties were flown, of which 104 were between the 16th and 31st with back-up provided by the Phantoms of Nos. 6 and 41 Squadrons and No. 228 OCU, which arrived on the island on 25 July from Coningsby to act in the air defence and ground attack roles.

A second invasion came in August 1974 with the Turkish nation taking 37 per cent of the island before a ceasefire was agreed upon. The ORB commented as follows:

> Battle Flight: The tense situation remained on the island for the first part of the month, resulting in a state that fluctuated between Bravo and Charlie. On 15 August, the Turkish Forces began a second push towards Famagusta, and squadron activity resembled that of the initial invasion in July. When the fighting died down again, the squadron reverted to Defcon Bravo, sharing the task with 41 TAF Phantoms. During the month, there were 39 scrambles; most were to CAP overhead the SBAs, the airspace being severely restricted at the time.[15]

The increase in tensions over the past two months added to the activities, but the departure of Wg Cdr Bee in August was celebrated with a meal of barbecued steak and salad in the Saddle clubhouse, together with a disco. Wg Cdr A.B. Blackley filled his position during the same month, while in the following the AI 23C radar was introduced to the unit's F.6s. By November the situation on the island had eased and the squadron was stood down to Defcon Normal which continued through December. At the end of the month some news was received as detailed in the CO's remarks: 'On 23 December, the squadron was informed that it would deploy to Wattisham in January 75. After the uncertainty of the last few months, this firm decision has generally been welcomed, although it's not to everyone's taste.'[16]

From 7 to 17 January 1975 two Victors from No. 57 Squadron were detached to Cyprus to provide IFR practice before the unit's return to Britain. By the end of the month thirteen F.6s, one T.5 (XS422) and the two Canberras had returned home, leaving XS928 alone at the airfield. This aircraft had previously experienced a titanium fire and was still Cat. 3 when the rest departed. Another T.5, XS452, remained at Akrotiri but was allocated to No. 11 Squadron, which took over the Battle Flight commitment on the island at the end of January 1975.

The return to Wattisham entailed the squadron becoming a mixed fleet of nine F.6s, three F.3s and two T.5s; it also meant the loss of the TFF. After the heightened activity of Battle Flight at Akrotiri, life at the Suffolk airfield was somewhat quieter. Southern IAF was maintained, and on 7 November 1975 two Bear-Ds of the Soviet Naval Air Force were intercepted, shadowed and photographed.

On 4 June 1976 the unit celebrated its diamond jubilee and was awarded the Dacre Trophy for 1975. Flying training continued until the 23rd of the month, culminating in a diamond nine formation being flown. Six days later the Squadron Standard was handed over to the new No. 56 Squadron and its FGR.2 Phantoms. On 17 July the last eight Lightnings left Wattisham and ended the unit's almost sixteen-year association with the aircraft. The final word goes to Wg Cdr Blackley:

> Fortunately, the squadron was kept extremely busy until well into the month, which made it easier to maintain enthusiasm and standards to the end. The Lightning era had ended as it ought to with the squadron performing well and in good heart. I wish the new 56 Squadron success and good fortune.[17]

Lightning F.2A

In 1963 the Air Council's plans for the Lightning Force had been agreed upon, part of which was converting the two F.2 squadrons based in Germany to F.2A standard. The conversion began in September 1966 as a rolling programme in which the F.2s were returned to Warton for the works to be completed. In time the effort would produce an interceptor with improved performance and handling at a relatively low cost. The F.2A was also passed through the Fire Integrity Programme from 1968 through to 1971.

In its original form, it was planned for the F.2A to be fitted with the Stage 3 fin, a larger ventral tank, improved brakes and an airfield arrester hook. After a loan to the Ministry of Aviation, XN795 was returned to Warton on 7 July 1964 for conversion to the proposed new standard; there was no intention initially to fit the CLE wing. However, flight testing by XN795 during 1965 and 1966 concluded that the production F.2A would benefit from utilizing the same wing as used on the F.6, although it was not fitted to the test aircraft. Of note, later in 1972 XN795 tested the 27mm Mauser cannon planned to be used by the Panavia Tornado.

Thirty airframes were converted to full F.2A standard with serials running through XN724, XN726 to XN728, XN730 to XN733, XN735, XN771 to XN778, XN780 to XN784 and XN786 to XN793.

A pair of Rolls-Royce Avon 211 axial-flow turbojets provided power, producing 11,750lb of thrust at sea level and 15,000lb in fully variable reheat. The 211 was similar to the 210, but had modifications to improve engine handling qualities. Fuel was carried in integral wing tanks, flaps and a 610-gallon non-jettisonable ventral, giving a usable supply of 1,326 gallons. It was not envisaged that the variant would be used outside West Germany or would undertake overseas deployments, therefore the capability to fit overwing tanks was not provided. However, it was considered that the aircraft could be used to reinforce the Lightning Force in Britain should the need arise and also to attend MPCs at Valley and APC at Decimomannu.

Dimensions were the same as the F.2 except for wing area, which increased from 458.5 sq ft to 474.5 sq ft. Maximum take-off weight was 39,750lb, landing 34,500lb. Airspeed limitations, with or without missiles, were M1.7/650 knots depending upon which was reached first, and with an IFR probe fitted, M1.7/625 knots. Missile firing was permitted between M0.6/300 knots and M1.7/650 knots at up to 3g or until the onset of mild buffet up to 55,000ft. The minimum speed detailed was 180 knots with flaps and undercarriage up or 140 knots with both down.

The F.2A was fitted with a Martin-Baker Type 4BSA Mk 2 ejection seat, with the Aircrew Manual stating that it should not be flown above 60,000ft. The maximum altitude for which the oxygen regulator and personal equipment were cleared is shown below:

Personal Equipment	Mk 17F	Mk 21B
P or Q mask	50,000ft	45,000ft
P and Q mask with sleeveless jerkin and anti g trousers	-	56,000ft

Regarding g limitations were (positive):

	Up to M0.9	Above M0.9
Ventral empty, 2,300lb/side or less wing fuel	6g	5.5g
Up to 2,000lb in ventral	5.5g	5g
More than 2,000lb in ventral	4g	4.5g
With single missile	4g	4g
Negative: The maximum permissible negative acceleration is minus 3g. Negative g should not be applied for longer than 15 seconds.		

The machine retained the PAS, AI 23 radar and the ADEN 30mm cannon fit which, similar to the F.2, could be configured for the carriage of either two or four cannons. This armament was useful for firing warning shots, dogfighting and should the need arise for ground attack. Unlike the F.3 and F.6, the F.2A could not launch the Red Top, although thought had initially been given for such an upgrade. However, this was not proceeded with.

It was considered by many who flew the F.2A to be the best variant of the breed. It certainly didn't suffer from fire in the same way as the F.3 and F.6, probably due to its cooler-running Avon 211 engines. In service two were lost: XN772 of No. 92 Squadron on 28 January 1971 after failing to recover from a spin (Fg Off. P. Hitchcock ejected at 15,000ft), and XN786 of No. 19 Squadron which suffered damage to the jet pipe and hot gas leak in the air on 4 August 1976. The latter's pilot, Fg Off. C. Rowley, managed to land the aircraft, but the damage was significant and it didn't fly again.

Nos. 19 and 92 Squadrons

The first flight of a production F.2A, XN789, took place on 12 October 1967, with the aircraft delivered to No. 19 Squadron at Gütersloh on 15 January the following year after a stint with the A&AEE at Boscombe Down. Both Nos. 19 and 92 Squadrons were based at the airfield, and the latter received its first example of the variant, XN773, on 26 June 1968. The two units operated a mixture of F.2, F.2A and T.4.

The arrival of XN774 with No. 19 Squadron on 2 September 1970 marked the final F.2A to be taken into service. RAF Germany now had a more capable interceptor within its ranks and one very able to deal with the situations that arose within the ADIZ.

Originally conceived to counter the threat of high-level Soviet bombers, the Lightning's role in Germany was in a different combat environment. It operated at low-level, overland, integrated with missile and gun belts. Gütersloh was 80 miles from the Inner German Border and just outside the 30-mile Buffer Zone, a strip designed to ensure no unintentional contact with hostile aircraft flying in East German airspace. In such an environment, the F.2A's cannons were an ideal weapon for the type of potential threat likely to be faced.

The Lightnings of Nos. 19 and 92 Squadrons began their time with the F.2A in a bare aluminium finish, each with its own markings. The latter's aircraft also sported a blue spine and fin. However, in the early 1970s it was later decreed that the RAFG Lightnings be camouflaged with dark green on the upper surfaces and fuselage sides, with the undersides retaining the natural metal finish. The new scheme was deemed more appropriate for the low-level environment in which the aircraft operated. After repainting, one of No. 92 Squadron's machines, XN793, sported a gold crown on its fin badge and the words 'Flagship 92' on the front fuselage. It gained the name of King Cobra and was the personal aircraft of the unit's CO, Wg Cdr J.B. Mitchell. The story of the two squadrons is taken up in their respective final year of operation.

In January 1976 No. 19 Squadron began the year holding Battle Flight at Gütersloh. On strength were fourteen F.2As and two T.4s (one of which was unserviceable due to a fuel leak) under the command of Wg Cdr R.L. Barcilon. A near disaster came on 15 January when Flt Lt D.R. Carden, piloting XN777, collided with the F.2A of Flt Lt P.R. Cooper while carrying out a Visident at night. Thankfully both aircraft were able to land safely.

Towards the end of the month the Rt Hon. Margaret Thatcher MP visited Nos. 19 and 92 Squadrons accompanied by Air Marshal Sir Michael Beetham KCB, CBE, DFC and AFC. At the time Thatcher was Leader of the Opposition and became the Conservative Prime Minister on 4 May 1979. Beetham had an illustrious wartime career as a Lancaster pilot with No. 50 Squadron, Bomber Command, and completed thirty operations over enemy territory. He was at Gütersloh for a first visit as C-in-C RAFG, during which an aircraft turnaround demonstration was enacted under full nuclear, biological and chemical conditions, followed by a practice Battle Flight scramble.

Two pilots, Sqn Ldr J.A.G. May and Flt Lt Carden, achieved 2,000 hours on Lightnings in February, an event celebrated by consuming a large quantity of champagne. The following month the CO notched up 1,000 hours, again marked by the downing of a vast amount of the French sparkling wine. Aside from the frivolities, the day job continued over the coming weeks with the squadron participating in Battle Flight, exercises and an MPC at Valley, during which eight Firestreaks were fired. At the end of April the CO made the following comment in the ORB:

> Regrettably the squadron's operational training was badly affected by the imposition of a 4.5 maximum G limit. Combat training has ceased and low-level CAP training has been reduced to essential exercises only. It is hoped that a practical solution will be found to the problem so that the Air Defence Force does not lose its low-level air defence capability. Meanwhile the squadron is concentrating on high-level flying.[18]

During May activities continued, including First Hand, the annual tripartite Berlin corridor exercise mounted from Gütersloh, and detachments from the USAF Europe and the French Air Force. A royal visitor came on the 27th with HRH Princess Anne witnessing a practice Battle Scramble. The following month two Lightnings detached to Reims and were hosted by Escadron 2/30 Normandie-Niemen. In return four Mirage F.1s came to Gütersloh. The ORB describes:

> At Reims the squadron flew four 2v2 combat sorties against the Mirage F.1. The results showed that the Lightning was superior at low and medium levels, and

> the F.1 was superior supersonic at high level. The combat honours were shared equally between the squadrons. Socially the squadron enjoyed a full programme including a weekend visit to Paris. On their return, the squadron personnel had great difficulty in remembering the detail of their experiences.[19]

By the end of July the g restrictions imposed due to cracks being found in the airframes had been lifted from ten aircraft, which pleased the CO who commented that he found the previous situation irksome. As a foretaste of what was to come, the first Phantom in No. 19 Squadron markings was seen over Germany in September.

With the approach of autumn a detachment of the unit's Lightnings was sent to Wildenrath on 12 October to hold Battle Flight until the 18th. Also on this day two Jet Provosts and four pilots from the Central Flying School arrived at Gütersloh to provide the prescribed annual spin recovery training.

The following day Fg Off. C.M. Rowley was awarded the Queen's Commendation for Valuable Service in the Air following the hot gas leak incident as previously described while piloting XN786. The ORB states:

> His aircraft had suffered a fire shortly after take-off and severe structural damage to the fuselage, fin and to the Number 1 engine had resulted. The entry in *The London Gazette* read: For his outstanding courage, presence of mind and airmanship when on 4 August 1976, he brought his badly damaged Lightning aircraft safely back to base. Had he abandoned it, the aircraft could well have inflicted considerable damage, death or injury on heavily populated areas.[20]

November was the last full month of flying for the unit, with the final squadron dinner taking place on the 26th. AVM T. Lloyd (Deputy Commander RAFG) and Roland Beamont were in attendance, with the latter flown in a T.4 during the afternoon by Flt Lt P.S. Owen.

The final Battle Flight commitment was taken over from No. 92 Squadron on 15 December and held until 31 December 1976, when it was handed to the unit's Phantoms. During the stint on alert, two interceptions occurred:

- 17 December: Flt Lt Dobson F.2A XN784 – Ordered off to interrogate unknown in KG 484 HDG Northeast at 11,000 feet, speed 170 knots. HH 14 intercepted at 14:31Z. A yellow Cessna. Interrogation showed that no airspace violation had occurred.
- 22 December: Flt Lt Carden F.2A XN784 – Ordered off to interrogate unknown in JA 532 Vector 060 Angels 100. Contact observed in LH 12 heading West at 9,000 feet. Identified as Cessna 172 – IAF, Reg Delta Echo Delta X-Ray. Training flight departed limits, position of intercept LA 22 at 22 11:51Z at 5,000 feet.[21]

With this final scramble complete, there would be just nine more days before the squadron's fourteen-year association with the Lightning ended. The last page of the ORB brings the following closing comment from the CO:

> The final 19 Squadron training sortie took place on 21 December, after which the remaining aircraft were prepared for final disposal. The administrative process of phasing out the squadron is also complete, and the Squadron Standard was handed over to 19 Phantom Squadron at Wildenrath on 30 December. This being the final report from 19 Lightning Squadron, I would like to thank all sections of RAF Gütersloh, without whose assistance and support the squadron could not have succeeded in its task. We wish Gütersloh and 19 Phantom Squadron at Wildenrath the best of good fortune and success in the future.[22]

During February 1976 No. 92 Squadron held Battle Flight and undertook four live interceptions:

- 6 February: Flt Lt G.P. Evans F.2A XN732 – HH 34 scrambled to investigate apparent light aircraft at 9,000 feet squawking 376, as if searching for an airfield to land. The aircraft landed at Greven-Osnabrück, with complete RT failure, before HH34 closed.
- 7 February: Flt Lt C.W. Ilsley F.2A XN791 – HH 22 scrambled to investigate unusual occurrence identified by X-ray by Visselhövede. No contact made, and eventually suspected as balloon or bird flock.
- 17 February: Flt Lt P.V. Boothroyd F.2A XN791 – HH 22 scrambled to identify unknown in KG. Track faded before intercept, eventually tracked to light aircraft below 3,000 feet in Braunschweig area and no ADIZ violation occurred. HH 22 continued on border patrol.
- 19 February: Flt Lt G.P. Evans F.2A XN727 – HH 40 scrambled to patrol LK as a precaution following suspected border penetrations of 3 non-NATO aircraft reported by ATC Bremen to Visselhövede. SOC subsequently designated these penetrations of Bremen FIR and not FRG.[23]

In February, in addition to the Battle Flight commitment, the unit participated in Exercises Mineval, Cold Igloo and Ample Gain, together with Buccaneer and Phantom affiliation. Training continued through March, with Combat Leader, ECM, supersonic interception and IFR on the agenda.

The following weeks continued similarly to those in the early part of the year, with the addition of an MPC in August where eight out of ten missiles were launched. Also this month four members of No. 23 Squadron came for a social weekend on the 13th and later flew back to Wattisham with a healthy respect for German beer.

As stated with No. 19 Squadron, No. 92 had the same g restrictions imposed in April which were lifted in September, resulting in increased electrical problems due to more severe shaking of the airframe. The next month six F.2As and two

T.4s were detached to Royal Danish Air Force base Aalborg from the 12th to the 18th while runway repairs were carried out at Gütersloh. However, bad weather curtailed flying during the detachment.

On the sports and social front Flt Lt Millard, Cpl Phillips, SAC Williams and Jnr Tech Jones represented the station at rugby and Sgt Wright at golf. On the 30th the squadron held an all-rank Halloween Party in one of the hardened aircraft shelters (HAS). The remoteness of the HAS and the general atmosphere must surely have added to the spookiness of the occasion. Gütersloh was one of the first RAF airfields to utilize the HAS, and it is considered that Nos. 19 and 92 Squadrons were the only Lightning units to operate from such facilities as Binbrook not so equipped.

In November a No. 92 Squadron reunion was organized by Flt Lt P. Boothroyd and held on the 13th at Binbrook. Fifteen pilots attended and the event was a tremendous success. For reasons unknown the page for December in the ORB is missing, so it is not possible to state the CO's remarks at the end of the last full year of operation.

As No. 19 Squadron bowed out, No. 92 was left as the last Lightning unit in RAFG under the command of Wg Cdr E. Durham. In January 1977 Battle Flight was held twice and three pilots, Flt Lts J.S. Spoor, P.S. Owen and T.M. Neville, were declared operational, having transferred over from No. 19 Squadron. During the month preparations were in hand to dispose of some of the unit's aircraft, which were to be deployed for decoy duties; these were XN732, XN773, XN787, XN791 and XN792. The following were taken on strength from No. 19 Squadron: XN735, XN771, XN776, XN777, XN781, XN784 and XN793. The F.2As retained were XN726, XN727, XN728 XN774, XN778, XN782 and XN788 and T.4s XM968 and XM995.

January progressed with two stints on Battle Flight and affiliation with Harriers and Jaguars. The month also saw the Harriers of No. 4 Squadron coming to the base to make it their new home (No. 3 Squadron also came in April of the same year).

A dent to the squadron's pride came in February with the loss of T.4 XM968. On the 24th, while being piloted by Sqn Ldr M. Lawrance and with Sqn Ldr Granville-Wright (No. 4 Squadron Harrier pilot) accompanying him and in the downwind circuit, the aircraft suffered a hydraulic failure and loss of control, forcing the two crew to eject. After causing consternation on the ground at the airfield, the errant T.4 seemed determined to come to earth within its confines, but eventually crashed about half a mile from the boundary.

In the squadron's final month of operation, it held Battle Flight twice with three active scrambles (the aircrafts' serials are not shown in the ORB):

- 10 March: Flt Lt R.C. McGowan F.2A – HH 35 scrambled for an unknown in KJ 2020 at 09:39Z. The aircraft vectored 030° at Angels 20 operating with Loneship. Although the radar return faded, a search was flown to no avail.

- 15 March: Fg Off. R.R. Gingell F.2A – At 16:40Z HH 24 vectored 120° at Angels 07 to interrogate an unknown in KG under Loneship control. Radar return faded, and an area search proved unfruitful.
- 18 March: Fg Off. R.R. Gingell F.2A – At 11:48Z HH 40 scrambled to interrogate unknown reported at KG 0530. The aircraft vectored 120° at Angels 10 under Loneship control. The aircraft was identified as a Cessna 210K registered to Herr Hillgruber Hans of Hamburg.[24]

During the morning of 30 March 1977, to mark the end of the Lightning's service with RAFG fourteen F.2As were launched from Gütersloh and in the afternoon XN784 and XN788 were flown to Brüggen for disposal.

On the same day a diamond nine was conducted over Rheindahlen, HQ RAFG, during which Flt Lt P. Owen experienced a problem with XN793. While in the circuit to land, Owen could not get a green locked-down indication for the starboard undercarriage leg. Knowing the perils of trying to land a Lightning in such a configuration, he flew to the ejection area at Dümmer See when suddenly the aircraft shuddered and he had three greens. Returning to the airfield on fumes, he landed safely shortly after. It later transpired that the undercarriage D-door had come off its hinges and had fouled the lowering wheel. The use of the emergency high-pressure lowering system overcame the restriction, allowing the leg to lock into place. For Owen, it had been quite a last sortie!

To close No. 92 Squadron's last month of operation, the final words go to the OC Sqn Ldr M. Lawrance:

> 92 Lightning Squadron was declared non-operational at midnight on 31 March/1 April, and a last pair of Lightnings marked the event by flying a sortie of night practice intercepts controlled by local Air Defence Agencies. Although a sad occasion, all squadron members were in good heart, and the squadron remained fully operational in every respect until it handed over its commitments to the re-equipped 92 Phantom Squadron based at RAF Wildenrath. Thus, another chapter in the squadron's history is finished; a chapter of which all the officers and men of 92 Squadron past and present can feel justifiably proud. All 92 Lightning Squadron members join me in wishing our successors the very best of luck in the future.[25]

To mark the disbandment ceremony, on 1 April 1977 Flt Lt J. Wilde led a final five-ship formation. Disposal of the F.2As began shortly after, with XN728 and XN774 flown to Coningsby to act as decoys. The former would gain a degree of notoriety as the 'A1 Lightning', a moniker it received after being removed to the site of A1 Commercials next to the road from which it took its name. Over the years the aircraft became the focus of souvenir hunters and graffiti artists and was something of a landmark in the local area. It was eventually scrapped with the cockpit saved, which now resides with Darren Swinn at Binbrook where ongoing restoration is being undertaken.

Three further F.2As, XN726, XN727 and XN771, were flown to RAE Farnborough where they were transported to the Proof and Experimental Establishment, Foulness, Essex for weapons testing. Here the airframes were shot at with all manner of guns and munitions. In such an environment it would not be expected for any to have survived, but the cockpit of XN726 was saved and is in the capable hands of Hugh Trevor. After many years of painstaking restoration, it can now be seen on display at the Boscombe Down Aviation Collection, Old Sarum.

Many who flew the F.2A considered it an ideal compromise between the F.3 and F.6 as with its cannon fit it could carry the most fuel, while its Avon 211s, although less powerful, were more economical and cooler running. In the words of Clive Rowley, in Stewart Scott's *The Lightning Force*: 'I think it would be fair to say that the era of the Lightning F.2A in Germany was, in many ways, the heyday of the Lightning. With the addition of the large ventral fuel tank and CLE wings, the aircraft had much increased operational effectiveness.'

Export Lightnings: Royal Saudi Air Force

Unfortunately for the Lightning, the Air Staff and the government initially seemed to consider that the aircraft was nothing more than a stopgap until the nation's air defences were catered for by the surface-to-air missile. History tells us such a situation never came to fruition, but the lack of investment, development and backing for this remarkable M2.0 interceptor ensured its potential within the export market was never truly met. With the support of their governments, the US and France had far more export success with the F-104 Starfighter and Mirage respectively. Despite interest from countries such as Austria, Brazil, West Germany, Japan, Jordan, Nicaragua and Venezuela, the export market for the Lightning was limited to Saudi Arabia and Kuwait.

In 1964 a Yorkshire businessman named Geoffrey Edwards persuaded contacts within the Labour Wilson government to support arms sales to Saudi Arabia. It had earlier come to light that the nation wanted to update the Royal Saudi Air Force (RSAF) after tensions rose in 1962 with the Egyptians and rebels in North Yemen.

Ilyushin Il-28 Beagle bombers and MiG-17 Fresco fighters, considered to be under the ownership of the Egyptians and flown by the Yemeni Air Force, often intruded into Saudi airspace and there was practically nothing the kingdom could do to stop them. Crown Prince Faisal was naturally worried about his country's security and used the nation's oil wealth to update its military.

On 3 July 1964 Lightning F.2 XN730 of No. 19 Squadron was flown from detachment at Akrotiri to Bahrain. From here and with all markings removed, the aircraft was flown and displayed to dignitaries at Riyadh, Saudi Arabia on 4 July by BAC pilot Jimmy Dell. Suitably impressed, the Saudis sent one of their pilots, Lt Hamdan, over to Warton to fly the Lightning. He was let loose on F.2 XN723 following some dual instruction on a T.4. Flying in chase was an RAF F.3 which watched the enthusiastic Saudi put the F.2 through its paces. No doubt inspired by his experience, Hamdan had no qualms about recommending to his government that the Lightning should be purchased for its air force. Therefore on 21 December 1965 a deal was signed worth £100 million with BAC for manufacturing thirty-four F.53s and six T.55s. The contract also included two Lightning T.54s, four F.52s, six Hunter T.7s, BAC Strikemasters and BAC Thunderbird surface-to-air missiles as well as technical and training support from Airwork Ltd.

With the main production contract under way, the kingdom urgently required the supply of aircraft to protect its security in the interim. Therefore two T.4s, XM989 and XM992, were taken directly from the RAF and became 54-650 and 54-651 respectively. The four F.2s, XN767 (52-655), XN770 (52-656), XN796 (52-657) and XN797 (52-568), were extracted from storage at 33 MU for conversion to F.52 at Warton. P.1B Development Batch, XG313, was also sent to Saudi Arabia for ground instruction (shipped by sea). When prepared, the F.52s were flown to their new owner in July 1966 under the codename of Magic Carpet. One, 52-657, was lost during take-off on 20 September and was replaced by XN729 (52-659).

The Lightning F.53 was based on the F.6 with the same dimensions and powered by a pair of Rolls-Royce Avon 302C turbojets producing 12,580lb of thrust at sea level and 16,300lb in reheat. Fuel was carried in integral wing tanks, flaps and non-jettisonable ventral tank, giving a usable supply of 1,275 gallons or 1,200 gallons if cannons were fitted in the ventral. Maximum take-off weight was 42,000lb, landing 34,500lb, emergency 39,000lb. The aircraft was equipped with a Martin-Baker Type 4BSC Mk 2 ejection seat, and the Pilot's Notes from 1983 show an AI 23S radar. The notes also cite the capability to carry a reconnaissance pack and details that the machine should not be flown above 60,000ft.

Airspeed limitations were somewhat complicated and are best explained by utilising a table. As can be seen, the export Lightnings could carry a wider range of under/overwing and external/internal stores and showed the potential EE and BAC envisaged for the aircraft all along:

All configurations without missiles or underwing pylons	The lesser of M2.0/650 knots (700 knots operational necessity only)
With Red Top or Acquisition missiles below 10,000ft	550 knots
Above 10,000ft	The lesser of M2.0/650 knots
Drill missiles	The lesser of M2.0/650 knots
With Firestreak missiles	The lesser of M2.0/650 knots (700 knots operational necessity only)
With or acquisition missiles	The lesser of M2.0/650 knots

With underwing pylons, no stores	M0.9 (The lesser of 650 knots/M1.8 operational necessity only provided that above M0.9, 2in rocket-launchers remain closed, normal acceleration does not exceed 4g, rolling is confined to normal course changing manoeuvres only)
With 1,000lb bombs	M0.9
With Matra launchers – SNEB rockets	The lesser of M0.9/450 knots
With HC or HE SNEB rockets	The lesser of M0.9/520 knots
With 2in rocket-launchers extended	The lesser of M1.7/650 knots
Minimum speed with flaps and undercarriage up	180 knots
Minimum speed with flaps and undercarriage down	140 knots
Taxiing with canopy open	65 knots (taxi plus wind component)

Regarding g limitations were (positive):

Speed/configuration	Wing Fuel		
	Less than 5,000lb (total)	Full	Full
	Empty	Up to 1,000lb	More than 1,000lb
Without pylons (with missiles, 2in rockets or reconnaissance pack) Up to M0.9 – with/without gun pack With/without rocket launchers extended	6g	6g	5.5g (5g with overwing 3,500lb in ventral launchers extended)
M0.9 to M1.7 – with rocket-launchers extended	3g	3g	3g
M0.9 to M1.8 without gun pack	6g	5.5g	5g
With gun pack	5.5g	5g	4.5g

With pylons Up to M0.9 – with/without stores (including single underwing store) And with/without gun pack And with/without launchers extended	5.5g	5.5g	5g
Above M1.8 or with a single missile		4g maximum	
M0.9 to M1.8 – no stores, operational necessity		4g maximum	
Negative – the maximum permissible negative normal acceleration is minus 3g indicated			
Negative g must not be applied for longer than 15 seconds at any one time and a period of 1 minute should be allowed to elapse between successive applications			

The Lightning T.55 was again based on the F.6 but fitted with a twin-seat side-by-side cockpit. It was equipped with Martin-Baker Type 4BSB Mk 2 ejection seats and possessed similar capabilities (or greater if it is considered that a second crew member could act as a weapons operator) to its single-seat stable-mate. Maximum take-off weight was 40,250lb, landing 34,500lb, emergency 39,000lb. Speed and g limitations were similar to the F.53, but the aircraft was not configured to carry bombs, SNEB rocket-launchers or cannons. However, the internal 2in rocket pack could be fitted.

One F.3, XR722 (53-666) and a single T.5, XS460 (55-710) were taken from the production lines and converted to F.53 and T.55 standard. The former had first flown as an F.3 on 23 January 1965 and after conversion to F.53 in November 1966, with 'B Condition' registration G-27-2. The latter initially took to the skies on 2 February 1966 and had flown in the T.55 configuration by 19 January 1967. It was to have a short career and was written off in a crosswind-induced landing accident at Warton on 7 March of the same year.

The T.53s and T.55s were delivered to Saudi Arabia between 1968 and 1969, with serials running from 53-666 to 53-689, 53-691 to 53-699 and 55-711 to 55-716 (the last of which replaced 55-710) where they served with Nos. 2 and 6 Squadrons and the Lightning Conversion Unit. It will be noted that 53-690 is not included; this aircraft crashed on 20 August 1968 before delivery. As a replacement, the last production Lightning, 53-700 (the cockpit survives with Dave Tylee at Gatwick Aviation Museum), was completed and flown to the kingdom on 4 September 1972. The RSAF Lightnings were the only examples of the type to see combat with one, 53-697, lost to ground fire on 3 May 1970 during a reconnaissance sortie near the Yemeni border.

During the 1980s the McDonnell Douglas F-15 Eagle began to replace the Lightning in the air defence role, and by December 1985 the transition was complete. Upon retirement, BAe purchased eighteen F.53s and four T.55s and flew them back to Warton with RAF markings and serials through ZF577 to ZF598 on 14 January 1986. The hope was that the aircraft could be refurbished and sold to Austria to replace Saab Drakens which failed to materialize. Thoughts of conversion to high-speed target drones also came to nothing and disposal became the only option. In time some found new homes in museums, either complete or as cockpits if the main part of the airframe was scrapped. During its time in service with the RSAF and from the available evidence, three F.52s, thirteen F.53s and one T.55 were written off. Information regarding surviving airframes in Saudi Arabia is sketchy and sometimes contradictory, but it's safe to say that some remain extant, including at least one and possibly two T.54s.

Kuwait

The only other export for the Lightning came when Kuwait purchased twelve F.53Ks and two T.55Ks with a contract signed in December 1966. Serials ran from 53-412 to 53-423 for the single-seaters and 55-410 to 55-411 for the twins. Delivery commenced two years later. It was not a happy story as the country's air force struggled with the complexities of the machine. Flying became intermittent as there was no real operational requirement, and in time the aircraft was considered economically unviable. By 1977 the Lightnings had been disposed of and replaced with the simpler Mirage F.1. Examples have survived in Kuwait in various states of repair, although at least one T.55K, 55-410, was destroyed during the First Gulf War (Operation Desert Storm) at Ali Al Salem.

6

Interception Part Four: Into Retirement

Street parties, bunting and an additional public holiday will be how many people remember 1977 as Queen Elizabeth II marked her Silver Jubilee from 6 to 9 June. This was the year the ever-popular Ford Fiesta was released and firemen called for strike action over pay, forcing the government to bring the 'Green Goddess' fire engines out of mothballs. The aviation industry saw the creation of British Aerospace formed from BAC, Hawker Siddeley Aviation, Hawker Siddeley Dynamics and Scottish Aviation.

On the entertainment scene, punk was sticking up two fingers at the musical establishment, while in October Queen released the anthem *We Are the Champions* from their *News of the World* album. Also during this month former Liberal leader Jeremy Thorpe denied allegations of the attempted murder of Norman Scott, and police continued to hunt for Peter Sutcliffe, the so-called 'Yorkshire Ripper'. In December *The Morecambe and Wise Christmas Show* attracted more than 28 million viewers, one of the highest viewing figures for Britain's entertainment industry, while *Star Wars* opened in the nation's cinemas.

In the same year the Lightning Force had reduced from a high of nine squadrons to just two plus a training flight. The Phantom had taken over the Lightning's air defence role from Nos. 29, 23, 56, 19, 92 and 111 Squadrons, while No. 74 Squadron had been disbanded.

It slowly dawned on the Air Staff that the nation's interceptor force was inadequate and reserves were minimal. In 1979 the government announced that it would form a third Lightning squadron from the eighty or so examples available, of which only around thirty F.3s and F.6s were in service. The proposal never came to fruition, but if it had the new unit would likely have been a reformed No. 45 or No. 74 Squadron.

Following this, the Lightning Augmentation Flight (LAF) was formed to keep current previously Lightning-qualified officers below the rank of wing commander who had subsequently been assigned to ground-based duties. Six training courses were conducted annually, but there were no specifically assigned aircraft; instead they were borrowed from the LTF or storage. Aircraft used were marked with a small orange LAF diamond motif applied to the tail. The pilots trained would provide a pool of aircrew that could be used in a time of war, but with the retirement of the Lightning appearing on the horizon, the flight soon disappeared.

The final trio of Lightning units, Nos. 5 and 11 Squadrons and the LTF were now firmly ensconced in their lofty perch high in the Lincolnshire Wolds at Binbrook. Support came from the Aircraft Servicing Flight (ASF) and the Aircraft Storage and Support Flight (ASSF) incorporated within the Mechanical Engineering Air Squadron. Around 1983 the ASSF became the Lightning Engineering Support Flight. It was proposed that the Tornado Air Defence Variant would replace the last operational Lightnings, but delays in service entry ensured that the ageing interceptor would remain in service for some years to come. To enable this, surviving Lightnings underwent Mod 9 works to the wing roots to add 400 hours' fatigue life to the aircraft's service career.

The last two operational squadrons undertook similar roles, tasks and training as previously described for the other Lightning units. Therefore in this chapter Nos. 5 and 11 Squadrons will be explored in less detail to give space for the history of that most hallowed ground, RAF Binbrook.

RAF Binbrook

If you draw a line from the former airfield at Binbrook towards the east, the distance covered before reaching the coast is just less than 17 miles. From the line's end, the cold brown waters of the North Sea appear with nothing between the observer and the Netherlands, some 200 miles distant. Across these waters comes some of the harshest weather imaginable with high winds, rain, sleet and snow. As it hits land, there is no barrier to prevent it from striking Binbrook at its height of 378ft above sea level. No wonder this was a cold and desolate place in winter, but one where the men and women of the RAF toiled to defend the nation during the Second World War and the Cold War. By contrast, it could be a delightful place when the skylarks sing on a summer's day.

RAF Binbrook was one of the last Expansion Period airfields to be built, with construction starting in the spring of 1938. Five C-type hangars were erected along with administration, technical and barrack sites. The landing ground was grass with eighteen pan-type hardstandings. The lack of concrete runways was a drawback, often resulting in a waterlogged landing ground.

On 10 May 1940 Hitler launched his blitzkrieg against France and the Low Countries, which caught the Allies totally by surprise. In short order, the British and French armies were pushed back towards the coast. To try to stem the advance, Fairey Battles and Bristol Blenheims from the Advanced Air Striking Force were sent to bomb bridges, troop concentrations and airfields and, to put it bluntly, were decimated by cannon-armed Luftwaffe fighters and ground fire.

With the reformation of No. 1 Group of Bomber Command on 18 June 1940, it was allocated Binbrook, then still under construction. Early in July Nos. 12 and 142 Squadrons relocated to the airfield after their mauling in France, where they began to mount attacks on invasion barges building up along the French coast. During one of these operations on 1 August, Battle I L5568 from No. 12 Squadron was mistakenly shot down by a Blenheim of No. 29 Squadron near Mablethorpe. The crew, Fg Off. B. Moss, Sgt T. Radley and Sgt B. Long, did not survive and now rest in the village churchyard of St Mary's.

With the Battle of Britain well under way, Nos. 12 and 142 moved to Eastchurch on 13 August 1940 and launched attacks on the ports of Boulogne and Calais. In September the two squadrons returned to Binbrook to convert to the Vickers Wellington, with No. 142 departing to Waltham in November. Their place was taken by No. 1481 Target Towing Flight equipped with Westland Lysanders and renamed No. 1481 Target Towing and Gunnery Flight in January 1942, then No. 1481 (Bomber) Gunnery Flight in the following May. Duties included providing targeting facilities to local anti-aircraft sites and No. 1 Group squadrons, with courses for air gunner leaders, aircraft recognition and the Browning machine gun. The flight left Binbrook in September 1942 for Blyton, but was back with the new name of No. 1481 (Bombing) Gunnery Flight in May 1943 before again departing for Ingham in March 1944.

Operations for No. 12 Squadron started over the night of 9/10 April 1941 with an attack on Emden, resulting in its first Wellington loss in action when W5375 'PH-D' was shot down into the Ijsselmeer at 00:59 hours by a Messerschmitt Bf 110 night fighter piloted by Oblt Egmont Prinz zur Lippe-Weissenfeld of 4./NJG1. All crew were lost, including Wg Cdr V. Blackden, the squadron's CO, and their bombing and gunnery leaders Fg Offs Broughton and Marshall. Over the coming months operations continued, including participation in the '1,000 Bomber' raids on Cologne, Essen and Bremen in May and June 1942. The squadron's tenure at Binbrook ended in September of the same year with its departure to Wickenby, where it continued to mount bombing operations over Occupied Europe until the war's end, initially with the Wellington and then the Lancaster.

After this the airfield went back into a construction phase with the laying of the standard concrete runways found at most heavy bomber airfields, orientated through 04-22 (2,000 yards), 09-27 (1,415 yards) and 15-33 (1,429 yards). A perimeter track was also laid together with the addition of nineteen loop hardstandings.

In April 1943 Binbrook was named as the parent station of No. 12 Base for No. 1 Group. In May of the same year, No. 460 Squadron of the RAAF arrived from Breighton equipped with Avro Lancasters and became the station's sole operational squadron for the rest of the war. The unit had three full flights with up to thirty-six aircraft on strength.

During operations and after undertaking approximately 5,700 sorties, the squadron lost 140 Lancasters, with another 31 written off in crashes, the highest loss rate within No. 1 Group, Bomber Command. As a measure of the losses sustained, just one of the squadron's Lancasters reached ninety completed operations, W4783

'AR-G', G-for-George. In October 1944 the aircraft was flown to Australia and is preserved in the Australian War Memorial Museum. The last operation for No. 460 Squadron was on 25 April 1945 when an attack on Hitler's mountain retreat at Berchtesgaden was mounted. During this raid one Lancaster I, NX585 'AR-M' piloted by Plt Off. Payne RAAF was lost, with the crew becoming prisoners of war. This was the last operational loss from Binbrook during the war, and a memorial to the unit was unveiled in 1974 in Binbrook village.

In July 1945 No. 460 Squadron left for East Kirkby, and at the end of the summer No. 12 moved back in from Wickenby to be later joined in October by No. 101 Squadron from Ludford Magna. During April and May Nos. 9 and 617 Squadrons arrived respectively, with No. 12 leaving for Waddington in July 1946.

Conversion to the Avro Lincoln came for Nos. 9, 101 and 617 Squadrons in the spring and summer of 1946, followed by entry to the jet age with the Canberra in May 1952, June 1951 and June 1952 respectively. Two further Canberra units came to the airfield – Nos. 109 and 139 (Jamaica) Squadrons – which arrived in January 1956 and stayed until disbandment in February 1957 and December 1959. Nos. 617 and 101 Squadrons disbanded in December 1955 and January 1957 to reform later as V-Force units, with No. 9 Squadron departing to Coningsby in June 1959. By December of the same year all flying units had departed from Binbrook, which was then placed under a care and maintenance status.

On 1 April 1960 the airfield was allocated to Fighter Command, but it was to be more than two years before flying recommenced. Following an extension of 500 yards to the main runway, the addition of two Operational Readiness Platforms and the construction of a large Aircraft Servicing Pan, Binbrook reopened on 1 June 1962. In August of the same year, No. 64 Squadron arrived with its Javelin FAW.9s from Waterbeach. The unit stayed until March 1965, after which it became part of the FEAF and deployed to Tengah.

In October 1962 the CFE brought a small fighter fleet of Javelin FAW.8s, Hunters and Meteors, together with the AFDS's Lightning F.1s and a T.4. The station's long association with the iconic interceptor had begun. Also coming in April 1963 was No. 85 Squadron, previously known as the Target Facilities Squadron while based at West Raynham. The unit was equipped with variants of the Canberra and provided aircraft for fighter interception duties from Binbrook until returning to West Raynham in January 1972, with final disbandment coming in December 1975.

Although the Lightning's presence had begun in 1962, the reforming of No. 5 Squadron on 8 October 1965 cemented the type's association with Binbrook into the history books. For just under twenty-three years, the quiet countryside around the Wolds would echo to the sound of reheated Rolls-Royce Avon turbojets as the station took its place at the forefront of the defence of Britain during the height of the Cold War. The airfield had its own QRA (IAF) facility with two Lightnings on 24-hour, 365-day standby, ready to intercept intruders who dared to infringe on or threaten the nation's airspace. On 22 March 1972 No. 11 Squadron moved south from Leuchars and the coexistence of the two units began. The LTF's formation has previously been described in Interception Part Two.

Binbrook entered its final decade of operation in 1980. In Britain, in the years that followed, the music scene was dominated by the New Romantics and electronic music, while Band Aid and later Live Aid sought to feed the world. In 1981 Prince Charles married Lady Diana, and in the following year a short, brutal conflict, the Falklands War, erupted in the South Atlantic. Prime Minister Margaret Thatcher would not sit back and allow an Argentinean junta to get away with its invasion. Therefore, in due course the islands were liberated with a Herculean effort by the British armed forces, boosting Thatcher's popularity and leading to a landslide election victory in 1983. Within a year her resolve was tested again by the Miners' Strike, which lasted until March 1985 and resulted in the defeat of the National Union of Mineworkers and a weakening of the trade union movement. Mrs Thatcher was to win a third term in office in 1987 but with a smaller majority.

For anyone who remembers 22 August 1987, it was a day of low cloud and heavy rain, and it just so happened to be the date of the 'Last Lightning Show', the swansong for the icon and the station alike. The weather had been fine for the previous Friday arrivals as all manner of NATO hardware descended to take up position within the static and prepare for the next day's display. Also in the mix was BAe's F.6 XP693, resplendent in its bare aluminium finish, which had flown in from Warton. However, in line with the well-known law, on Saturday the heavens opened. Thousands came to the airfield, and those there will recall a constant barrage of rain alleviated only by visits to the hangars to observe Lightnings in various states of repair and maintenance.

Despite the conditions and poor visibility, the pilots of Nos. 5 and 11 Squadrons still put on a show seared into the minds of those who witnessed it. As the lead Lightning XR728 'JS' piloted by Binbrook's station commander Grp Capt. J. Spencer thundered down the rain-lashed runway, it turned through 270 degrees to cross over at a right angle to the next aircraft on its take-off run, the process continuing until all participants in the display were airborne. Following the crossover, each machine climbed steeply with the accompanying fluff of condensation appearing above the wings. Upon forming up, a very precise diamond nine was flown consisting of XR728 'JS', XR770 'AA', XR725 'BA', XS904 'BQ', XR753 'BP', XR754 'BC', XR726 'BM', XS928 'AD' and XS919 'BB'. Following on, two singletons, XR771 'AN' and XS929 'BG', flew a high-speed pass, the latter creating an incredible halo around the aircraft in the moist atmospheric conditions as M0.92 was reached. All too soon it was over, and just the memories remained.

The end of the last Lightning squadrons will be discussed further in the following unit histories. However, mention must be made regarding the small group of enthusiasts who frequented Crash Gate No. 3 during the final years of operation. Here a decision was taken to ensure that the Lightning would live on years after its retirement to the present day. The story of these preservation pioneers and others will be told later in this work. However, there can be no doubt about the effect that the Lightning had on people if individuals were willing to devote a huge amount of their time, money and effort to ensuring that the sight and sound of this truly British icon remained for future generations to enjoy.

With the conclusion of the Lightning's operational career with No. 11 Squadron at the end of April 1988, Binbrook was deemed surplus to requirements. However, it acted as a Relief Landing Ground for Scampton. In July 1989 it had a starring role in producer David Puttnam's film *Memphis Belle*. Five Boeing B-17 Flying Fortress aircraft arrived for the filming, one of which was lost when it crashed and burned out on take-off. Fortunately there were no fatalities from the incident.

The airfield finally closed on 12 July 1992, with the Grob Vigilant motor gliders of No. 643 Volunteer Gliding Squadron the last unit to grace the skies above the station. However, it was not the end, as between 1993 and 1997 ex-RAF Jet Provosts acquired by Global Aviation were stored at the airfield before onward sale. The Q-Shed was also used as a paint shop to respray some aircraft. One who was there was Jeff Bell, who recalls:

> I made three or four trips up to Binbrook with an ATC Assistant in an RAF car, complete with a mobile radio pack for comms. We also took a fire appliance and an ambulance with medics. It was usually two JPs at a time with two Tucanos as crew ferry back to Scampton. On arrival, we had to inspect the runway to ensure it was safe to use and then sat on the taxiway awaiting the radio call when the aircraft were inbound. However, one visit was in vain, as the cloud was too low, and all four diverted to Scampton. We did manage a peek up the Tower on one visit, but it had been classed as unsafe due to the arson attack; the approach room was gutted, such a shame. My last visit there was on 21 September 1994.[1]

Once flying completely ceased, the airfield was sold off with the runway removed. The control tower was demolished in 1995 due to concerns of illegal entry to the building and the possible injury to those who should not have been in there in the first place. Today the hangars remain in business use, as do many of the domestic/technical buildings; however, in 2012 the pan was broken up and removed. The Q-Sheds survive, but have been subject to vandalism. The village of Brookenby has formed around the former airfield and utilizes dwellings once used to house RAF personnel.

It is hard now to comprehend what happened at Binbrook as a visit today finds the site quiet and peaceful, a far cry from when the Merlins and Avons roared. However, if thoughts are left to wander, it is not difficult to see and hear the echoes from the past in your mind, as imagination is assailed by a place once filled with happiness, hope, stoicism, courage, sadness and loss, lest we forget.

No. 5 Squadron

At the end of September 1965, Wg Cdr C.R. Gordon wrote:

> The final month of 5 Squadron's existence in Germany has passed quietly and peacefully. I consider that both air and groundcrew have done their job in Germany for the last three years with distinction. All of us on 5 Squadron look forward keenly to following the fortunes of our successors at Binbrook.[2]

On 8 October 1965 No. 5 Squadron reformed at Binbrook following its earlier disbandment at Geilenkirchen where it had been a Javelin all-weather fighter unit. Under the command of Sqn Ldr L.G. Hargreaves, this was the start of the unit's connection to the Lincolnshire airfield that would last for more than two decades.

The squadron formed at South Farnborough on 26 July 1913 and served on the Western Front in the Army Co-operation role during the First World War, where it suffered the first RFC loss on 22 August 1914 when Lt V. Waterfall and Lt C.G.G. Bayly flying an Avro 504 were shot down and killed by the 5th Jaeger Division near Enghien, Belgium. Two days later Lt C.W. Wilson and Lt C.E.C. Rabagliati forced down an Etrich Taube monoplane near Le Cateau-Cambrésis in Northern France with the crew captured. This was the first German Air Service 'kill' for the RFC.

Disbandment came in September 1919, with reformation on 1 February the following year at Quetta in India, again in the co-operation role and equipped with the Bristol Fighter. The unit became known as No. 5 (Army Co-operation) Squadron and served on the North-Western Frontier until June 1940, after which it began working up in the light bomber role. On 21 February 1941, based at Risalpur in India, its role changed to two-seat fighter equipped with the Hawker Audax. Conversion to something a little more potent came in December with the arrival of the Curtiss Mohawk which took up bomber escort, standing patrols and close air support. It continued to operate during the Burma campaign, converting to the Hurricane II in June 1943 and the Republic Thunderbolt Mk I in October 1944. Post-war, the squadron flew the Tempest II and disbanded in August 1947. It was reformed in March 1952 as part of the 2nd Tactical Air Force at Wunstorf equipped with the Vampire FB.5, converting to the Venom FB.1 and FB.4 in December 1952 and July 1955 respectively. A further disbandment came in October 1957, but the squadron was back again in January 1959 as a night fighter unit equipped with the Meteor NF.11, and the following year began an association with the Javelin (FAW.5 and 9) lasting until October 1965 when conversion to the Lightning came. However, it would not be until the following month that the first of the type was received when T.5 XS451 arrived at Binbrook on 19 November. The squadron also had a Hawker Hunter T.7A on strength equipped with an OR946 system.

The first Lightning F.6 Interims (or 'F.3ER' as the ORB describes them), XR755 and XR756, were delivered to No. 5 Squadron on 10 December 1965, and by 6 March the following year a complement of twelve machines had been received. The aircraft were in a bare aluminium finish with red rectangles on either side of the roundel on the nose and a green and black maple leaf on a white disc applied to the tail.

Over the coming months the squadron pilots got to grips with handling, radar conversion, PIs, MPC and exercises including three Lightnings detaching to Gütersloh in May. Of note is this comment from the OC in the March 1966 ORB: 'One heartening aspect has been the high proportion of successful sorties. The extra endurance of the Lightning F.6 helps ensure that the briefed sortie can be achieved, even when bad weather forces a return with sufficient fuel for a long-range diversion.'[3]

In October QRA was held and there was some excitement when, on the 20th, two F.6s scrambled to intercept three Bisons. Flt Lt Ginger met one at 34,000ft, which then descended to 1,000ft above the North Sea. He shadowed it until near the Shetland Islands, but then diverted to Leuchars due to a fuel shortage. Flt Lt Gambold also intercepted a Bison at 38,000ft, but again had to divert to Leuchars due to lack of fuel. Five days later there was a similar occurrence as Bisons were intercepted, this time with photographs taken. These were sent to Fighter Command, who returned a bottle of champagne in return.

Although formed in July 1913, it was not until 25 November 1966 that the squadron celebrated its fiftieth anniversary with an open day at Binbrook. On the day the unit was reviewed on parade by AM Sir Aubrey Ellwood, KCB, DSC, RAF (Ret'd), its former commander from December 1932 to November 1933, in the presence of AOC Fighter Command, Air Marshal Sir Frederick Rosier KCB, CBE, OBE, DSO and station commander Grp Capt. J.O. Dalley, OBE, DFM. The event, in true RAF fashion, was meticulously planned, even down to the car order which included three Austin Princesses, three Ford Zephyrs, a Rover 2000, a Standard Ensign and a Humber.

With the review completed at 12:30 hours it was time for luncheon in the Officers' Mess, where a special anniversary cake was displayed. The menu ran as follows:

- Mushroom Soup
- Grilled Fillet of Plaice
- Roast Beef
- Yorkshire Puddings
- Horseradish Sauce
- Croquette and Creamed Potatoes
- Brussels Sprouts
- Ice Cream Gateau
- Cheese and Biscuits
- Coffee
- Piesporter Weg
- Châteauneuf du Pape

After the meal the squadron was presented with a silver model of an F.6 by AM Sir G. Tuttle, KBE, CB, DFC, RAF (Ret'd) on behalf of BAC. It was planned at 14:15 hours for the assembled guests to be treated to a programme of flying with five Lightning F.6s taking off, followed by a Spitfire, Hunter, F.1A and F.6 display. However, with a familiar theme the weather intervened and the event was cancelled. A static display had been set up, and the ORB commented that the veterans of the First World War who viewed the Lightning were impressed by its complexity. Considering the machines that these brave men once flew, this can come as no surprise. In the evening an anniversary ball was held to which all visitors were invited.

On 3 January 1967 the first full production standard F.6, XS894, came to the squadron and soon all Interims were replaced. There was also a change of command as Wg Cdr J.H.A. Winship assumed the helm.

The extended endurance of the F.6 was tested in January 1968 while the unit was holding Northern QRA on detachment to Leuchars. During a practice scramble, Flt Lt H.E. Hick flew further north than any other Lightning to prove the interceptor's maximum endurance.

A tragic accident occurred on 29 April when the squadron lost one of their own, Fg Off. A. Davey. He had been tasked to fly as one of a pair of Lightnings detailed to undertake an IFR demonstration with a Victor over Scampton. The plan was for the F.6s to join the tanker at 1,000ft over Binbrook. As they began to form up, Davey's aircraft, XS924, on the port side was seen pitching up between 45 and 65 degrees. With speed and the port wing dropping, the Lightning descended steeply and crashed at Beelsby. The pilot did not attempt to eject and was not wearing an anti-g suit, so it's possible that the pitch-up could have caused him to black out. The Board of Inquiry could not fully establish what had caused the accident, but it was considered that a failure with the tailplane control system may have been responsible. He had only been married for around four weeks and is buried in Binbrook's St Mary's churchyard.

In the following years the unit undertook several long-distance flights including Operation Gambroon in May 1968, when four F.6s with overwing tanks flew a 4,000-mile, 8-hour non-stop trip to Muharraq, Bahrain with Victor tanker support.

The Dacre Trophy was awarded in August 1968 (for achievements in 1967). In January the following year Wg Cdr K. Bailey took command, but was replaced by Wg Cdr G. Black in November. In 1970 the Dacre was won again, along with the Huddleston Trophy (retained in 1971), the latter for achieving the accolade of being the best NATO fighter squadron. In June the unit came under the leadership of Wg Cdr G.A. White, while in the same month the two Lightning F.1As of the TFF were absorbed into the squadron's ranks. These operated as targets and display machines until September 1972, after which they were transferred to Binbrook's TFF (disbanded in December 1973). In their place came three Lightning F.3s: XP749, XP764 and XR751.

On 8 September 1970 the squadron experienced its second fatal accident while operating the Lightning. Capt. B. Shaffner USAF was tasked to undertake a TACEVAL, but by the time he was scrambled at 20:25 hours, this had changed to a shadowing and shepherding operation with a Shackleton, a role for which he was not cleared. It was during this exercise it is considered that Shaffner's F.6 XS894 had hit the sea at low speed with a low rate of descent and sank. When the Lightning was recovered two months later, the canopy was found to be attached but not closed and the ejection seat was still in place. It was concluded that, in all likelihood, after hitting the sea the aircraft slowly sank and the pilot had tried to manually abandon the cockpit but had drowned in the process. His body was never recovered.

The squadron's winning ways continued with the award of the Dacre Trophy for the third time in 1971 (awarded in June 1972) and again under the command of Wg Cdr R.D. Lightfoot:

> On 21 May 1979, the squadron heard that it had been awarded the Dacre Trophy for 1978/79. The trophy is awarded to the fighter squadron that achieves the best overall standard during the year of its operational, training, and engineering commitments, and obviously, it was won despite stiff opposition from the F.4 squadrons. It is perhaps fitting recognition of the large amount of work put in to maintain and improve our operational efficiency whilst equipped with ageing aircraft.[4]

From the autumn of 1975, the metal finish of the unit's aircraft gave way to a matt dark green and dark sea grey camouflage applied to the upper surfaces and fuselage sides. The markings were also toned down and reduced in size. In their final years, variations of an 'air superiority' grey colour scheme were applied to the Lightning fleet while some aircraft retained camouflage. In 1984 three F.6s received 'shark's teeth' markings while participating in an APC at Akrotiri.

The final two fatal Lightning losses in RAF service came while serving with No. 5 Squadron. On 13 July 1984 Flt Lt D. Frost piloting F.6 XS920 was undertaking combat training with USAF Fairchild A-10 Thunderbolts in West Germany. During manoeuvring, Frost's aircraft came into contact with power lines and crashed near Häuslingen, giving him no time to react or initiate an ejection.

The following year on 6 March, while undertaking air combat training over the North Sea, Fg Off. M. Ramsey's F.6, XR772, entered a spin, forcing him to eject. The pilot came down in the sea but did not survive, and he was recovered by an RAF SAR helicopter with an unopened parachute. The Lightning impacted around 20 miles north-east of Skegness, and some parts of the airframe were salvaged including the uppermost part of the fin. In June 1987 to commemorate the end of the Lightning era, the fin tip was presented to Binbrook Primary School, along with a memorial plaque where it remains to this day. The artefact carries the markings of Nos. 5 and 11 Squadrons on its port and starboard sides respectively.

The squadron's last year of operation began in 1987 commanded by Wg Cdr D.A. Williams. With the disbandment of the LTF in April, two F.3s, XP741 'AR' and XR716 'AQ', were used by the unit to fulfil the year's display commitments. The pilot was Flt Lt J. Fynes, and on 25 September he flew his last public display at Honington and a final routine at Binbrook four days later. (The subsequent fate of the two F.3s was previously detailed in Interception Part Two.)

The ultimate Southern QRA was held in October, while on 23 November, an F.6 was fitted with overwing tanks to extend range and allow participation in trials with the AI 24 Foxhunter equipped F.3 Tornado, which was experiencing development problems with its radar. The ORB comments:

> On 26 November Flt Lt A.M. Page flew XR724, which had been specially prepared in overwing tank fit, for a Ministry of Defence (MoD) sponsored trial at BAe Warton. Two sorties were flown with Tornado F.3 A.03, the radar development ac, in order to assess the radar signature of the Lightning in this fit and to see if the required time on task for a suitable target could be met: the sorties went well.[5]

In time, the trials would see other Lightnings participating in the programme, extending the time that the type would be seen in Britain's skies. Also, in November 1987, Wg Cdr Williams, having flown his last sortie in a Lightning, handed over command to Sqn Ldr D.G. Lloyd. On 2 December two Lightnings piloted by Flt Lts M. Chatterton and P. Sutton flew in formation with a pair of Tornado F.3s of No. 5 Squadron (Designate) over Binbrook and Coningsby. At a parade commanded by Wg Cdr E. Black, OC No. 5 Squadron (Designate), the unit's Standard was handed over by Flt Lt Sutton to those who were to come after. The squadron had received its first Lightning on 19 November 1965 and, with the above-mentioned event, became the longest operator of the type.

With the station standing down on 22 December 1987 for the Christmas Grant, No. 5 Squadron effectively marked this as the final day for the unit's Lightnings, leading to a postscript in the ORB:

> On 31 Dec 87 No 5(F) Sqn ceased to exist after 22 years of continuous operations with the Lightning. This was the longest period of operation of a single aircraft type in the history of the Sqn. 5(F) Tornado will officially form in Mar. 88 and it is hoped they will carry on the traditions of a great Sqn. We wish them luck at the end of an era – *Frangas non flectes* ['you may break, but not bend me'].[6]

No. 11 Squadron

Netheravon airfield in Wiltshire can trace its history from the earliest days of the RFC coming into existence in 1913. Here, on 14 February 1915, No. 11 Squadron was formed and equipped with the oddly configured Vickers F.B.5 Gunbus. The unit would fly throughout the First World War and operated the Nieuport, Bristol Scout and Fighter. Disbanding in December 1919, reformation came in January 1923 at Andover in the light-bomber role in Britain and later in India. In the early years of the Second World War it flew the Blenheim and undertook operations in Egypt, Greece, Crete, Palestine and Iraq.

While in India in August 1943 the squadron converted to the Hurricane IIc, an aircraft it would operate in the attack and escort role until June 1945 when

Spitfire XIVs were taken on strength, followed by Spitfire F.18s later in 1946. Disbandment came in February 1948, but the unit reformed in October of the same year at Wahn in Germany as part of the 2nd TAF. The squadron again disbanded in November 1957 but, in the intervening years, was equipped with the Vampire F.B.5, Venom FB.1 and 4.

Reformed again in January 1959 at Geilenkirchen, it was now assigned to the night fighter role and initially operated Meteor NF.11s until replacement came with Javelin FAW.4 and 9s in 1960 and 1962 respectively. The unit would be the last to fly the large delta-wing fighter in the European theatre and finally disbanded in January 1966.

On 1 April 1967 the Lightning age was entered as the squadron reformed at Leuchars under the command of acting CO Sqn Ldr P.S. Collins. Here it would go on to share the policing of Britain's most northerly defence zone with No. 23 Squadron.

Deliveries of the F.6 began in April. The aircraft were in a bare aluminium finish with the unit's black rectangle, superimposed with a yellow diamond on either side of the nose roundel. The fin was adorned with a pair of buff-coloured eagles upon a white disc.

In June Wg Cdr D.R.K. Blucke took over command in time for the unit to undertake its first QRA commitment on the last day of the month. Blucke certainly had aviation in his blood as his father was AVM R.S. Blucke CB, CBE, DSO, AFC*, whose career began in April 1918 when he joined No. 63 Squadron as an observer.

Blucke (senior) later trained as a pilot and had a distinguished service career, notable in the summer of 1940 when he commanded the Blind Approach Training and Development Unit, tasked to utilize its Ansons to trace and determine the direction of Luftwaffe *Knickebein* beams used to guide its bombers to their targets. In June 1942 he was made OC of Holme-on-Spalding Moor and, a year later, Ludford Magna, home to No. 101 Squadron, Bomber Command. From here he often flew operations, winning an AFC for piloting a severely iced-up and almost uncontrollable Lancaster III, JB142 'SR-Y', to Mannheim on 5 September 1943, where he successfully bombed the target. With the rear turret out of action and the elevator trimming gear jammed, Blucke managed to return safely to base, aided by one of the crew members. His last assignment was as AOC Training Command, a post he took up in January 1952, retiring shortly after at his own request. He lived to the age of 91 and died in October 1988.

Blucke (junior) went on to become a group captain and station commander at Coningsby. On 9 August 1974 he was piloting Phantom FGR.2 of No. 41 Squadron when, at low level undertaking a training flight, his aircraft collided with Piper Pawnee crop-sprayer registration G-ASVK in the vicinity of the villages of Hilgay and Bexwell, Norfolk, killing the pilot P.K. Hickmott. The Phantom crashed inverted, taking the lives of Blucke and his navigator Flt Lt T. Kirkland, both of whom are buried in Coningsby Cemetery.

Like other Lightning squadrons, No. 11 also conducted long-range deployments including a flight of more than 9,100 miles from Leuchars to Singapore on 6 January 1969.

On 4 March 1970, the unit experienced its first fatal loss while flying the Lightning. Flt Lts G. Clarke and T. Doidge (piloting F.6 XS918) were undertaking PIs when the latter received Reheat 1 and 2 warnings. The pilot decided to eject at 19:00 hours, which was successful and he came down in the North Sea, 9 miles from the coast. The SAR helicopter dispatched was unable to locate him, and it was not until 01:00 hours the next day that a lifeboat picked him up, by which time he had died of exposure.

As ever, QRA/IAF was an important role for the squadron and was especially so for Flt Lt S. Gyles on 23 April 1970 as he reflects upon his memories of the day:

> The 23 April 1970 was to be a QRA/IAF/Battle Flight day like no other I had experienced during my first eighteen months of operational flying, nor anything I would see again when I left air defence in 1980 for a buckets of sunshine role with the Tornado.
>
> I was Q2 to Sqn Ldr Chalky White when, at about 02:30 hours, the squawk box crackled. For those who do not know, we had an open hotline connecting Leuchars with Buchan Radar near Aberdeen. There were a number of hot feeds around the base, including Ops, ATC, squadron ops, and the QRA sheds. Whenever Buchan came online, there was always a short crackling sound preceding the broadcast. We jumped instantly from our slumbers. The controller came online to say that a couple of unknowns were on their way. Expect to come to cockpit readiness shortly. So we got togged up into immersion suits, roused the ground crew, and Chalky went outside for a quick 'pipe'.
>
> Sure enough, a few minutes later, the box crackled again: 'Leuchars, this is the Buchan Master Controller. Alert 2 Lightnings', and so off launched Chalky on quiet procedures into the pitch-black moonless night. I was stood back down to ten minutes.
>
> About thirty minutes later, the box crackled once more. I was about to run, but it was a situation report. The Master Controller informed us that Norwegian radars were picking up a lot of activity. We could be getting busy. A while afterwards, I became aware of lights coming on in our squadron buildings. Then Chalky returned, parked his machine, lit his pipe and came inside. I asked him what he had got, and I gave him the updates. He told me he thought he got behind a Badger, but it was so dark he could not be certain. He then got on the phone to speak to higher authorities. Just then, the box crackled once more: 'Leuchars, this is the Buchan Master Controller. Alert 2 Lightnings and as many more as you can muster. We have eighty tracks inbound.' I remember Chalky looking at me and saying: 'Off you go, Steve. I'll follow as soon as I'm turned round.' And with that, I was off. Scrambled on silent procedures, just given a point in the North Sea about 400nm north to aim for. As I came out of the sheds, I saw the Victor crew running from their transport to their aircraft on the ORP. I saw the whole station coming to life, with lights coming on in all the hangars. Then I was gone. Darkness except for a hint of dawn in the Far East.
>
> When I finally switched on my radar, I was swamped with returns out to 60 miles. They were still coming on the top of the scope as I started my turn in

> behind on the nearest four-ship of Badgers. At the same time, another four-ship went across my canopy about 1,000 feet above on a ninety. A glance to the north and all I could see were black dots everywhere. Apparently, about forty of the contacts I saw were believed to be tankers and soon after turned away to the north. The remaining forty stayed in the area for a few hours. The tanker and another 11 Sqn Lightning joined me, but it wasn't Chalky. I immediately recognised the voice as Graham Clark. Several years later, he would leap out of a Lightning on a Cyprus detachment. Later, he would become OC 74 Sqn on the F.4. We stayed there mingling for about two and a half hours and were eventually replaced by 43 Sqn's F.4s, yet to be declared operational and then went back home for breakfast.
>
> Eight hours stand down, then back into the sheds for the night, this time as Q1. They allowed me some sleep before the alarm went off around 08:00 hours for another scramble. Bit like 16 September 1940, I guess. No enemy to be seen, just a solitary Danish Neptune. Still, I shouldn't complain. My tally in the previous ten days was twelve intercepted and about another sixty sighted.[7]

As the Phantom began to take over the Lightning's air defence commitments, No. 11 Squadron was displaced from its Scottish home and moved to Binbrook to join No. 5 on 22 March 1972. From then on, the two units operated together from the airfield for the next sixteen years.

The squadron was to experience its second fatal loss on 7 April 1975 during a detachment to Akrotiri. On the day Sqn Ldr D. Hampton was piloting F.6 XR762, which came down into the sea off Cyprus. With a lack of material evidence, it was not possible to establish the cause of the crash.

In August 1979 celebrations were held to mark twenty-five years of the iconic interceptor. At Binbrook Nos. 5 and 11 Squadrons contributed to the event, adorning nine Lightnings in the markings of each squadron that had flown the type over the years. Despite the weather curtailing but not entirely stopping the planned aerial activities on 3 August, more than 200 former Lightning pilots and guests attended, including Roland Beamont and Sir Frederick Page.

While the Lightning's usual prey was high-flying, fast-moving targets, every eventuality needed to be catered for. Therefore on 13/14 November 1985, two F.6s were detached to RNAS Yeovilton to carry out affiliation with Boeing Chinook and Sud Puma helicopters: 'The problems of operating a fast jet against very slow and low-level targets were thoroughly examined, and suitable tactics were explored. The opportunity was also taken to carry out medium-level PIs under the control of the RN Fighter Direction School based at RNAS Yeovilton.'[8]

With the disbandment of No. 5 Squadron, No. 11, under the command of Wg Cdr J.C. Jarron, became the last operational Lightning unit. On 6 January 1988 an F.6 fitted with overwing tanks was sent to Warton piloted by Flt Lt Page to participate in radar trials with the Tornado F.3 in what was to become a regular commitment. Also during the month Dissimilar Air Combat Training (DACT) took place with Tornado F.3s of No. 29 Squadron and Northrop F-5 Tiger IIs of the

527th Tactical Fighter Training Aggressor Squadron from Alconbury. A detachment was also sent to Gütersloh for DACT with Harriers from No. 4 Squadron.

As is well known, throughout its career the Lightning was prone to catching fire, and in its last month of operation the element was to claim a final victim. On 11 April F.6 XR769 was engaged in air combat training with three other Lightnings over the North Sea. The adversaries were Phantom F-4J(UK)s of No. 74 Squadron. As the combat unfolded, Flt Lt D. Coleman piloting XR769 issued a Mayday after loud bangs were heard and the Fire 1 caption illuminated. Assistance came from Flt Lt I. Black, who took up position on the Lightning's port side and noticed flame issuing near the No. 1 engine compressor. Coleman headed back to Binbrook, but the fire persisted. The options were limited, forcing the pilot to eject after turning his aircraft away from the coast. The final ejection from a Lightning was successful, with Coleman picked up by an SAR Wessex around fifteen minutes later. Many attendees, including the author, at the 'Last Lightning Show' in August 1987 would have seen this aircraft undergoing maintenance in Hangar No. 3. Who would have thought it would be at the bottom of the North Sea in just under eight months?

To the very end of its operational days the Lightning held QRA at Binbrook, therefore in its last two months it is very apt that four live scrambles were initiated:

- 24 March: Flt Lt McDonald-Webb F.6 – No contact made.[9]
- 25 March: Flt Lt Sutton F.6 - Two Russian Bear Ds intercepted.[10]
- 20 April: Flt Lt McDonald-Webb F.6 – ORB gives no further detail.[11]
- 27 April: Flt Lt J. Carter F.6 – Two Russian Bear Ds intercepted.[12]

Around an hour before the last live scramble, as detailed above, Flt Lt D. Smith piloting XS903 also launched to fire the final two Red Top missiles at the Aberporth range against a GAF Jindivik drone towing a flare.

Interestingly, just over five years later, a Russian Air Force Tu-95MC Bear-H was escorted by a No. 43 Squadron Tornado F.3 as it landed at RAF Fairford for static display in that year's Air Tattoo. How many Lightning pilots who had intercepted this iconic Leviathan over several decades would have thought that such an event was ever likely to occur? The Cold War was over, although an aggressive posture set up in recent years by the Russian Federation under Putin's rule has seen a reignition of tensions between East and West.

With the end now only two days away, on 29 April 1988 Grp Capt. J. Spencer (former CO of No. 11 Squadron), Wg Cdr J.C. Jarron, Sqn Ldr Alderton and Flt Lt Page flew a four-ship formation for the benefit of photographers (or 'budding Lord Snowdons' as the ORB describes them), to make up for the lack of opportunities from the very wet open day. Also on this day a Hangar Party was held to celebrate twenty-eight years of operations and the closure of No. 11 Squadron, with 700 ex-Lightning personnel joining the event. In the evening the squadron officers hosted 200 guests at a 'Gin Mine' in the Officers' Mess. The next day the frivolities continued, with 300 officers attending a reunion party in the mess. The following morning some officers were heard uttering the immortal words 'I'll never drink again.'

Twenty-eight years of RAF Lightning operations were now at an end, and the final words go to OC Wg Cdr J.C. Jarron:

> Well, that's it! The end of the Lightning. Operationally, the squadron marked the last day of QRA in fine style with a scramble to fire two Red Top missiles on Aberporth range, followed shortly after by another scramble which resulted in the interception of two Soviet Bear D aircraft. Socially the Lightning was seen off in true fighter style with a vast catalogue of 'Last Lightning' events culminating in the Lightning Reunion on 29/30 April. As was intended, 11 Squadron (Lightning) stayed up front and operational right to the end. I trust our Tornado counterparts will do as well. We wish them well.[13]

Not Quite the End

As previously noted, delays with the reliability of the Tornado ADV's AI 24 Foxhunter radar contributed to its delayed entry into service and the problems dragged on. On 8 and 11 April 1988 XS904 and XR724, with overwing tanks fitted, flew from Binbrook to Warton to participate in the trials programme. Over the coming years the F.6s (joined later by XS928 and XR773) were operated by BAe (Military Division) on behalf of the MoD (Procurement Executive), and all contributed to acting as high-speed target aircraft for the Tornado and Foxhunter-equipped Buccaneer S.2B XX897. A further S.2B, XV350, was also flown for the trials and was utilized in the IFR role when flying with the Lightnings. As well as the ex-Binbrook F.6s, BAe also flew its own example, XP693, within the programme. With the exception of this aircraft, the other four F.6s were low on hours, necessitating XR724 being flown to Shawbury for storage in July 1990; XR773 was brought in as a replacement. It was unusual to see any of the last airworthy Lightnings participate at air shows; however, an exception was XS904, which flew to the International Air Tattoo at Boscombe Down over the weekend of 13/14 June 1992 for a stint in the static park. The programme concluded in December 1992 with the Lightnings sold into preservation, which will be discussed in the final chapter.

The Final Lightning Movements at Binbrook

With No. 11 Squadron now converting to the Tornado F.3 at Leeming, Binbrook's days as an operational station were over but Lightnings continued to fly. In May and June 1988 the last airworthy examples residing at the airfield flew out to preservation with new owners or to take up duties at other RAF sites as ground-based airframes. Below are the flights and their destinations:

- 18 May F.6 XS903 Yorkshire Air Museum
- 19 May F.6 XS929 Akrotiri
- 23 May F.6 XR753 Leeming
- 13 June F.6 XS928 BAe Warton (Foxhunter trials)
- 14 June F.6 XS922 Wattisham
- 22 June F.6 XR754 Honington
- 24 June F.6 XR728 Lightning Preservation Group Bruntingthorpe
- 27 June F.6 XR773 Boscombe Down (for storage and later Foxhunter trials)
- 28 June F.6 XS899 Cranfield
- 29 June T.5 XS452 Cranfield
- 29 June T.5 XS458 Cranfield
- 29 June T.5 XV328 Cranfield
- 30 June F.6 XS898 Cranfield
- 30 June F.6 XS923 Cranfield

Aside from the above, F.6 XS898 undertook one last display commitment at North Coates Armed Forces Day on 25 June 1988. As well as the flyers, grounded airframes remained on site and many of these found a new life in preservation while others were scrapped. To enable the road journey to new homes the Lightnings were dismantled, which often entailed wings being cut off and then remounted once the new destination was reached. One was T.5 XS420, which was to become a major focus of the author's life some thirty years after the aircraft had last flown.

As with the ending of all stories, it's nice to have a twist in the tail as the departure of XS898 and XS923 was not quite the end of aerial activity for the Lightning at Binbrook. On 23 July 1992 F.6 XR724 was flown to the airfield from Warton by BAe test pilot Peter Gordon-Johnson for preservation after purchase by the Lightning Association.

Today many people visit museums where the defender of Cold War skies can be viewed. I have often listened into conversations that can span several generations. Granddad recounts a tale of being in awe of the shiny new jet when, as a young man, he had seen the machine hurtling skywards with an earth-shattering sound at one of the SBAC shows. His son recalls a day at Binbrook during an exercise when the Wolds rang to the sound of Avons. The grandson? Well he wishes he had seen and heard what his elders describe. Luckily for him, due to the efforts of those in the preservation world, he can at least hear what a Lightning sounds like even if he can't as yet see one fly. However, this has not gone without considerable effort, expense and dedication from groups and individuals who have strived to ensure that the Lightning's legacy lives on. The following chapter will examine where the seeds of preservation were sown and the memories of some of those involved.

7

Preservation

Quick Reaction Alert

Britain in the mid-1970s when the Cold War was still at its height. It's 1.00pm on a Sunday, families are sitting down to their traditional lunch and all appears quiet and normal. As Father carves the joint, Mother enters with bowls full of roast potatoes and vegetables while the two boys squabble over some trivial matter, which to them seems vitally important. 'You two, settle down and come to the table; it's time to eat, not fight.' The orders from the matriarch are heeded and without a word calm prevails as she is not one to be argued with.

On a military airfield somewhere in England, the sound of skylarks disturbs the silence as they ascend into the tranquil blue sky with their insistent song ringing out before swooping back to earth and resting from their exertions. The QRA shed doors are closed and nothing stirs on this Sunday afternoon. The airfield is deserted and could almost be abandoned.

Suddenly there is a flurry of activity as a klaxon sounds. Air and ground crew rush out of the adjacent crew room. The Q-Shed doors slide open to reveal the purposeful shape of a fully-armed F.6 Lightning. The pilot ascends the access ladder and, aided by the ground crew, straps himself into the cockpit. With his finger spinning indicating start, the 'weee-phut' of the AVPIN starter is heard as the resultant smell of its pungent exhaust drifts from the open doors. With one Avon 302 spooling up the other is brought to life and the whine reaches a shrill crescendo. The canopy is closed and locked, the ground power is disconnected and the interceptor is ready to taxi. Inching forward and with a quick stab on the brakes, the Lightning gathers pace, joins the main runway and is away with reheats glowing, leaving a thunderous chorus in its wake. Slowly the calm of the English countryside returns as if nothing had happened in those frantic minutes.

Buchan Radar advises the pilot that an unidentified contact is being tracked 80 miles off the east coast and he is to intercept and identify. A little later he calls up and says he is in formation with a Tupolev Tu-16 Badger at 25,000ft and requests instructions. The response: shadow the aircraft and report its tail number.

The Soviet machine continues on its track, and the interceptor's pilot is instructed to return to base. The Lightning is next seen taxiing back to the Q-Shed where the ground crew await their charge. Mission over, the pilot raises the Lightning's canopy and awaits the access ladder to be attached. For him, it's just another day at the office. The F.6, XS904, is pushed back into the shed, ready for the next time hostiles might encroach on Britain's airspace.

This was a regular occurrence in the Cold War years, but remember the opening line to this chapter: Britain in the mid-1970s. The QRA described above occurred on 15 July 2012, more than twenty-four years after the Lightning retired from RAF service. How was this possible? Well it all sprang from the seed of an idea planted at Crash Gate No. 3, Binbrook in the final months of the Lightning's operational career. From this the Lightning Preservation Group (LPG) was born, which led to the erection of the former Wattisham Q-Shed at Bruntingthorpe and the ability to re-enact a period QRA when many thought that such a scene would never again be witnessed.

The thought of keeping a supersonic interceptor in a working or even static condition would fill most individuals with a sense of dread, but thankfully some took on the challenge. What follows gives an insight into their vision, aspirations and commitment.

The Pioneering Trio

It is fair to say that the days of Lightning preservation began with the last flights of the P.1As, WG763, on 7 December 1959 and WG760 on 18 February 1961. Unlike some aircraft following the Second World War such as the Stirling and Whitley which were lost forever to future generations, the two P.1As survived to take up ground-based roles. WG760 was dismantled and sent by road to No. 8 School of Technical Training (SoTT) at RAF Weeton in June 1962, where it acquired the maintenance airframe serial 7755M. Just over three years later it moved to No. 4 SoTT, St Athan, and in 1966 to 71 MU Bicester. In the same year came a move to Henlow, where it joined WG763 (7816M) which had arrived in 1963. Both went on to be used as backdrops to the Officer Cadet Training Centre parade ground, which was also based at the site.

In July 1982 WG760 moved to Binbrook and appeared at the station's Open Day on 28 August, followed by dismantling in January 1986 and a road trip to the RAFM Cosford for display, where it remains to this day. WG763's turn to relocate came in August 1982 when it was transported to the Greater Manchester Museum of Science and Industry to take up duties as an exhibit. In early 2022 the P.1A was transferred to the Boscombe Down Aviation Collection at Old Sarum, Wiltshire, and is currently on public view.

The third airframe produced for the Lightning project, P.1B XA847, flew for the final time on 21 April 1966 when it was delivered to RAE Farnborough for gravel bed over-run trials. After surviving the ordeal, a move to Henlow for storage came in June 1969, followed by allocation to the RAFM Hendon in 1972 where it remained until May 1988. With the recently retired F.6, XS925, available for display, the decision was taken to dispose of XA847. As the P.1B was the first British aircraft to reach M2.0, it is an important part of the nation's aviation history, therefore the swap seems nonsensical.

Placed on the MoD's disposal list, XA847 was purchased by Wensley Haydon-Baillie and transported for storage at Southampton Docks. In September 1994 it appeared as a static exhibit at the SBAC Show Farnborough and was later sold to Portsmouth Marine Salvage, who moved it on to a private buyer in Suffolk in October 1998. Although not on public display and in a dismantled state, at least this important machine survives.

As time passed other early marks of the Lightning found their way into preservation as gate guardians or museum pieces, often resulting from having become ground instructional airframes. However, as the end of the Lightning's operational career approached, private individuals and groups made enquiries, with plans emerging to ensure that the interceptor was preserved, not just as a static airframe but also in a live condition.

Until the cessation of Lightning operations, airframes that had survived the scrap man's attentions had done so mainly due to official intervention as, after retirement, redundant machines took on ground-based roles such as airfield decoys or went into storage. With the interceptor's service days over, official tenders were produced, thus allowing the sale of the Lightnings to the highest bidder. Many of the preserved examples we see today came from this process. But what compels a group or an individual to take on what would appear to be an onerous and expensive task? Well, for the LPG, it all started at Crash Gate No. 3, Binbrook.

Want to own a Lightning?

Binbrook was the last bastion of the Lightning and, in its final years, attracted a regular group of enthusiasts who would video, photograph and record the interceptor's activities. Observing an active military airfield is very special as you can never be sure what may turn up within the daily routines. The advent of the airband radio allowed transmissions to be listened to, and the clipped measured responses from the Lightning pilots to ATC's instructions were noted. There was also the chance that something exotic or unusual would call up to heighten the excitement. If there were an exercise on, like Priory or Elder Forest, the lane leading to the crash gate would be filled with cars as enthusiasts jostled for position to see the action.

No one likes change, especially when it becomes apparent that your favourite pastime will soon end with the phasing out of the Lightning and the closure of its base. You want more than just memories, but saving the object of your fascination is surely just a pipe dream, isn't it? Well it would appear not.

Richard Norris is one of the founding members of the LPG, and on one summer's day at his home I asked him where his interest in aviation started and how he became so involved in Lightning preservation:

> When I was young, Chris, my older brother, and I lived in Hatch End. One day, our neighbours announced that they were going to the 1961 Farnborough Air Show and would we care to go with them. Although Chris and I were more interested in railways, we liked things with wings and accepted their invitation. After a road trip in a Mk 9 Jaguar, we arrived at the airfield and had a thoroughly enjoyable day viewing displays by V-Bombers, the [Fairey] Rotodyne, Scimitars, Sea Vixens and Bristol 188. The Mosquito really knocked me out though; I'd never seen a piston-engined aircraft fly so fast. Aside from this, the thing that sticks in my mind is nine shiny silver Lightnings with a tiger emblazoned on their tails. After a stream take-off, they gave a wonderful display and landed with brake chutes deployed.
>
> One distinct memory I have is when we drove out past where the FAST [Farnborough Air Sciences Trust] museum is now; I recall looking at the parade of small shops opposite and seeing a lot of shopkeepers with platform brooms, sweeping up plate glass. I imagine the nine Lightnings were responsible for the damage, and the insurance companies would be busy the next morning.[1]

Around 1981 Richard was an area sales manager in the hardware and garden furniture trade. This job, in part, took him out on field visits to monitor the activities of sales representatives. It was during one such trip that he found himself in North Lincolnshire, and an association with Binbrook and the Lightning began:

> It was a hot day, and some colleagues and I were sitting on Cleethorpes seafront having a cup of tea after the day's work. The sky was azure blue, and an ear-shattering noise was heard as we drank the tea, drawing our attention skywards. Overhead was the unmistakable shape of two Lightnings heading out over the North Sea. This surprised me as I thought the type had been retired from RAF service in the twenty years since I'd last seen one.
>
> In the evening, while at my hotel, I studied a road atlas and found Binbrook. Although I wasn't that interested in aircraft then, the name rang a bell because it may have a connection with the Lightning. I asked locally and was informed that this was the case.
>
> I drove to the airfield, reached the main gate, and asked if I could see a Lightning. It was a beautiful summer evening, and the chap at the entrance said I was in luck as there was an exercise on. He directed me to Crash Gate No. 3, where there were a few people, which I learned after was the norm. I stood and watched and remember later phoning Chris, asking if he knew the Lightning

was still in service. After this, we got the bug for the aircraft, all through a chance cup of tea on Cleethorpes seafront.

Over the coming years, Richard and Chris would spend a lot of time at Binbrook:

We often stayed for several nights at a delightful bed and breakfast named Hoe Hill near Swinhope. Some of the exercises were great and very memorable. On airfield defence, the Lightning would loiter three or four miles away, waiting for traffic, which could be Hunters from Yeovilton, Luftwaffe Phantoms or NATO-member F-16s. Then all hell would break loose as we saw the Lightnings hot on the tails of the hostiles. It looked like they did remarkably well, considering the age of the machine, but it still had the agility, if not the weapons fit and avionics, to deal with the more modern adversaries. The pilots' ability and the machine's power ensured they did well, with the crowd punching the air as they roared overhead. It was exciting to watch this, but in the mid-1980s, the fight was moved out over the North Sea, but they were heady days at the gate.

Among the regulars were my son Nick and me, Chris, Hugh Trevor, Bob Tuck, the late Peter Talbot and Tony Hulls, who all became LPG members. The great thing about the location was there was only a very low fence, giving excellent views. There was the occasional security patrol, but often they would stop and talk to you; it was all very friendly. We never thought that one day we might be involved with some of the pilots as they taxied past, some giving a friendly wave.

As I previously mentioned, Chris and I were keen on steam engines, and we would have loved to have preserved a mainline locomotive when they were retired in 1968, but we weren't old enough and didn't have the means. However, by mid-1987, Chris and I were thinking about the Lightning's retirement coming in April of the following year and what would happen to the aircraft.

Next, I went to Alconbury Air Show, where two F.3s, an F.6, and a T.5 were in attendance. I asked the ground crew what they thought a Lightning might sell for. They had no real knowledge but suggested maybe £5K for a single-seater and £3K for a twin. This sparked an idea, and the thought processes started of whether we should be doing something to preserve a Lightning.

I remember attending an Air-Britain presentation on the Lightning in the spring of 1988 with Bob, Peter and Hugh. Here, Roland Beamont gave a talk on the aircraft's history, and after I spoke with him, I told him of our thoughts and plans, to which he responded, 'Whatever will you do with it?' but he thought it admirable that we were thinking of trying. You've got to start with the dream.

Back at the crash gate, the thoughts began to gather pace in our minds, and we talked to a few people who considered the plans a good idea and somebody ought to do something. The next step was to get on the tender system with the MoD. Having achieved this, we received all manner of lists of parts, etc, but we didn't want a spare wing spar or a navigation light, we wanted a complete aircraft. Of course, we would be all over such a list now with the benefit of hindsight. First to come up were the decoys that had been at Binbrook for years, but these had been spares recovered, so we passed up on this opportunity.

The disposals office was in Harrogate, and Chris and I decided to travel there to meet and have a chat with a chap named Mr Trodden. His secretary, Kathy Alderson, greeted us and proclaimed we should preserve a Hunter, a far nicer-looking aircraft than the Lightning. However, we met for around an hour, and the pair seemed intrigued by what we proposed in wanting to preserve a piece of Britain's aviation heritage. At this stage, there didn't seem to be much in the way of preservation going on, but we learned that crash gate veterans Stewart Scott and John Jackson of the Lincolnshire Lightning Preservation Society had acquired an F.3 (XP706) and had it towed by a tractor out of Binbrook early on the morning of 20 December 1987 to the airfield at Strubby.[2]

Towing a Lightning along a public road may seem to be an unorthodox means of transporting an airframe but earlier, on 15 December 1987, an even more unusual event had occurred. On this day a USAF Sikorsky MH-53 Jolly Green Giant helicopter was seen and heard over Binbrook as it descended to airlift F.3 XP701 to its new home at the Kent Battle of Britain Museum, Hawkinge. Around three years later the aircraft was scrapped, with the cockpit going to the Robertsbridge Aviation Society. Continuing with Richard's story:

The people at Harrogate thought they could sell a Lightning by what was known as a Private Treaty, but this didn't come to fruition and the open tender system prevailed. We were invited to Binbrook for a viewing day with other interested parties. One airframe that stood out was [F.6] XR773, which had recently been to St Athan and was pristine, but this one was withdrawn and was sent to Boscombe Down as a reserve for the British Aerospace radar trials.

One group considered they could get a Lightning flown to them in Scotland, where it would land on a long straight road next to where they wanted to preserve it. We felt this highly unlikely but thought we might stand an even chance of acquiring an airframe. In due course we put a bid in, by which time the group consisted of twelve people. We were later informed we had been successful, and XR728 was allocated.

Running parallel to the bidding process, I sought somewhere to home the Lightning and considered the airfield at Little Staughton. However, Tony Hulls suggested Bruntingthorpe in Leicestershire as he knew its owners, the Walton family, were interested in aviation, and there was a 10,000-foot runway. I contacted David Walton and told him we were thinking of preserving a Lightning, to which he replied Airfix or Revell. When I said this would be a complete airframe, which we hoped could be flown in, he was very interested in the plan. Later, we announced we had acquired the aircraft and agreed with David to deliver it by air. Arrangements were made for ATC and fire cover to be provided, and on 24 June 1988 [F.6] XR728 arrived piloted by Flt Lt Chris

Berners-Price from 11 Squadron. It was amusing that he flew in in an M2.0 fighter and returned to Binbrook in a Mini Metro.

So we were now the proud owners of a Lightning, but it came with stipulations that certain parts were to be recovered, such as the ADEN cannons. To arrange this, OC Eng from Binbrook, Sqn Leader (possibly Wg Cdr) Blackburn contacted me, and during the call, he advised that initially the Avons were to be recovered, but as the RAF did not need them, they could remain in place. This changed our perspective as we now had a live aircraft.

Chris had a conversation with Ray Nightingale at Binbrook, who worked on Lightnings, and he advised that if you have the engines, it's best to keep them running at set intervals, known as anti-det runs. We recognised we didn't have the required skills to do this, so we started putting out feelers for anyone who could help. In due course, Ray and experienced engineers Roly Elliot and Peter O'Callaghan came, followed by further skilled personnel and pilots who assisted the civilians.

With the end of the BAe radar trials, the chance to bid for another Lightning came. I had discussions with Barry Pover, who was very active in trying to keep an example airworthy in Britain. The LPG did not have the means to fly a Lightning, so it was agreed we would bid on [F.6] XS904, which had the highest hours and fatigue index. This allowed Barry to go for the lower-hours airframes [F.6s] XP693 and XR773. He was successful, and the pair was flown to Exeter on 23 December 1992. Our bid for XS904 was accepted, and this was delivered to us by Peter Orme on 21 January 1993, marking the last military flight undertaken by a Lightning.

The third part of the story was the acquisition of the Q-Shed from Wattisham. This was a passion from when we were at Binbrook. We went into the facility a couple of times when it was live, which was a real hairs down the back of the neck moment with the two F.6s waiting fully armed, ready to go. To me, it summed up the Cold War era.

One day, I had a call from one of our honorary members, Mick Cameron, an armourer at Wattisham, advising me that the Q-Shed was to be demolished to make way for an SAR [Search and Rescue] hangar. It was agreed this building would make a superb addition to our activities at Bruntingthorpe and provide much-needed cover for the Lightnings. With the help of John Spencer, who was taxiing for us at Bruntingthorpe, we got our name on the tenders as a point of contact for companies undertaking the demolition and reconstruction works. This meant they had to speak with us to discuss the structure's future. Trafalgar House Construction was selected to undertake the works, and they liked our proposal of saving the Q-Shed and donated it to the LPG on the understanding it would be rebuilt to its original condition.

Dismantling of the shed, which was no easy task, started in the winter of 1993. Once at its new home, our thoughts turned to reconstruction, but we received quotes far over what could be afforded. Therefore, we put the word out in the enthusiast world about our aims and objectives, and it struck a chord with people who liked the idea and considered it the perfect Airfix kit. Through donations and a lot of support, we managed to finish the building by 2010.

I suppose the fourth piece of the jigsaw came when we heard [F.3] XR713, then at Leuchars, was coming up for disposal. We put in a successful bid and then had the task of correctly dismantling the aircraft and transporting it to Bruntingthorpe. Once back down south, we rebuilt XR713 with the help of a team of apprentices from BAe. It was then repainted into the markings of 111 Squadron on the port side and 56 to starboard.

Reaching 2020, we had over thirty years of fast taxiing the F.6s and QRA re-enactments. In March the same year, a new Cold War Jets Collection museum was set up, combining the aircraft of the various resident groups. At present, the runway is not available, but open days and other events have been reintroduced, including static running the Lightnings into reheat. All this has been made possible due to a very dedicated and active membership, together with the loyal backing of our valued supporters. Over and above this, none of this would have been possible without the encouragement and support of the Walton family. We pinch ourselves every day that the dream has become a reality.[3]

The Cranfield Lightnings

It will be recalled from the previous chapter that six of the remaining airworthy Lightnings at Binbrook – F.6s XS898, XS899, XS923 and T.5s XS452, XS458 and XV328 – were purchased by businessman Arnold Glass and flown to Cranfield. He planned to keep examples of the interceptor airworthy, but the concept failed to reach fruition. In time, the three single-seaters and XV328 were scrapped, with their cockpits surviving and entering preservation. The other twin-seaters were more fortunate and remained intact thanks to the efforts of Tony Hulls.

In June 2022 I met with Tony, and he recalled his time at Cranfield:

My interest in aviation came from radio-controlled aircraft, which I've flown for many years, and in 1982 my friend's daughter, who worked in ATC at Binbrook, told me an air show was planned for that year, which I attended. This was one of my first experiences with the Lightning, and I was gobsmacked by the aircraft and its performance. I then started to visit Crash Gate No. 3 every week, where I got to know fellow enthusiasts. We would usually arrive by about 8am and wait for something to happen. You could see the Lightnings being prepared on the pan, and they would taxi out past us and then take off; the noise was lovely. I bought a motor home to enable me to spend more time there and mounted a swivel chair on its roof to give 360-degree visibility. I also started to video the action; my wife Margaret and I spent many happy hours at the airfield.

As the Lightning's days were ending, a few of us regulars at the gate said we ought to keep one of these. Then Richard Norris contacted Harrogate, which started the ball rolling, and we formed the LPG. As you know, the group acquired XR728, and I remember well when it flew into Bruntingthorpe, as on the day Barry Sheene [professional motorcycle racer and TV presenter] was there attending an event organised by the truck dealer Ford and Slater. He came up to us and said, 'Christ, what the hell is this thing?' He'd never seen anything like it and then stated, 'Anybody who is faster than me, then I'm very interested.' So that was the start of Lightning preservation for me, and I spent many hours at Bruntingthorpe.

Over the years, I got to know a lot of people, including Arnold Glass and became aware of the six Lightnings at Cranfield. I used to visit the aircraft, which were very forlorn and in a terrible state. One day, I asked Arnold if I could clean one up, and he agreed, allowing me to choose T.5 XS452, which I picked as I considered a twin-seater would give me a chance to sit beside the pilot. Help came from Nev Martin, Barry Pover, Ray Nightingale and Baz Livesey (ex-BAe Warton), and in time, we powered up the aircraft and attempted to get an engine running. When Ray pushed the start button, the Avon began spooling up, which was quite remarkable as it hadn't run for at least five years (this took place in 1993). Cranfield then allowed us to put the aircraft in a hangar, enabling tasks to be carried out, including taking an engine out and refitting. It was an interesting time made even more so as I was just an ordinary man off the street doing something like this. We were able to taxi the aircraft, and Baz and I had several trips up and down the runway.

In time, Arnold decided he wanted to part with the Lightnings, and I received a phone call from Barry Pover telling me the aircraft were going to be sold at Sotheby's on the following Saturday. I'd promised on this day to video my daughter's friend's wedding, so I had to carry on with the commitment. My friend Pete Walker came to my rescue and went to Cranfield to bid on XS452. He phoned me in the evening and told me no one had shown any interest in the other aircraft, but he had bought the T.5 on my behalf after speaking with Sotheby's, stating that I needed to pay in cash on the following Tuesday. I then thought how am I going to raise the money? But with the help of a loan from my son Mark, I did and duly settled the bill, paying him back over a period of time.

I went down to the aircraft, set up a tripod and videoed myself giving a speech, stating this is my aeroplane, and it's all down to me, and I'm going to make it work. I contacted the authorities at Cranfield and asked them if they could tow XS452 to Pete's hangar as he was allowing me to park it there. After this, we had many happy hours tinkering and running the Lightning up and down the runway. I had a lot of help from people, including those already mentioned together with Keith Hartley (pilot), Liam Hughes (pilot/engineer) and Tim Latham, all of them tremendous people who knew the aircraft inside

> out. Brian Carroll (pilot) was also involved, and he gave both the LPG and me a great deal of assistance; he offered a huge amount of help within the world of Lightning preservation.
>
> One day Keith brought Mike Beachy Head, and the pair went for a trip down the runway. Upon their return, Mike stated he had to have the aircraft and how much did I want for it? I had an idea of its value, and Mike agreed to my offer and paid a deposit. After this, we didn't see him for two years.
>
> In the meantime, the other single-seaters were scrapped, but XS458 survived as a Cypriot had previously bought it, but his intention to take it to Cyprus fell through. With Nev's help, a deal was struck, and he lent me the money to buy the T.5, which I paid back when Mike sent me some funds. In time, we got the second Lightning running and took them both down the runway, and everything worked well.
>
> The original intention was to fly XS452 out to South Africa, and we prepared the aircraft for flight, but the Civil Aviation Authority (CAA) said no. We were then faced with taking the whole thing to pieces and shipping it abroad in containers, which was a monumental task. It took us three weeks to dismantle and eighteen months for the new owners to reassemble it. I had the privilege of being invited to Thunder City to see her fly, and what a day that was. It was me who had saved her, so that was very special.
>
> We had some great times and created a lot of memories, but when my wife died, I really felt I couldn't continue with all the energy and responsibility that was needed to keep XS458 alive. Russell Carpenter approached me, and he was keen on taking on the project, so in due course we came to an agreement for him to take her on. Over the years that followed, Russell and his team have done a fantastic job of keeping the aircraft in taxiable condition and, in doing so, allowing many paying enthusiasts to experience a run in a fast jet. (At the time of writing, XS458 remains at Cranfield.)
>
> My time with XS458 cost me a lot of time, money and effort, but I enjoyed every minute of it.[4]

Listening to Richard and Tony, it was truly humbling to hear of the vision, time, effort and money that went into the early days of Lightning preservation, coupled with the dedication of many individuals who made a seemingly impossible dream a reality.

More Preservation Candidates

With the winding up of the Tornado AI 24 Foxhunter radar trials programme, the Lightning F.6s that participated were put up for sale by tender and sold as detailed below:

- XR724: The Lightning Association, flown to Binbrook by Peter Gordon Johnson (BAe test pilot) on 23 July 1992.

- XR773: Barry Pover, The Lightning Flying Club (LFC) – registered G-OPIB and flown to Exeter on 23 December 1992.
- XP693: Barry Pover (LFC) – registered G-FSIX and flown to Exeter on 23 December 1992.
- XS928: Barry Pover (LFC) – purchased as a spare source and donated to Warton as a gate guard.
- XS904: The Lightning Preservation Group – flown to Bruntingthorpe on 21 January 1993 by Peter Orme (BAe's Deputy Chief Test Pilot), escorted by a Tornado F.3.

The LFC had been formed with the hope of keeping the Lightning in the air in Britain, but sadly this was not to be. The CAA's strict safety stipulations, endless rules and regulations pushed costs to unsustainable levels and effectively stymied the club's chance of achieving its goals. Therefore the towel was thrown in as gaining a permit to fly the former interceptor would not be possible in Britain.

While the quest to keep a Lightning airborne in Britain failed, two T.5s, XS451 (South African registered as ZU-BEX, previously sold to Barry Pover and residing at Plymouth Airport) and XS452 (ZU-BBD), together with F.6s XP693 (ZU-BEY) and XR773 (ZU-BEW) were bought by Mike Beachy Head around 1997 and shipped to South Africa. Here they flew with Thunder City, based at Cape Town Airport, as part of a fleet of aircraft, allowing many enthusiasts to experience a flight in a fast jet. Unfortunately tragedy struck on 14 November 2009 when XS451 crashed during an air display at Overberg following an in-flight fire, claiming the life of pilot Dave Stock. A very detailed report relating to the accident is available, and it is not the intention to go into this here.

The death of Mike Beachy Head in May 2017 signalled the end of the venture. In the years following there has been much speculation about the collection's fate, but the best advice is to keep an eye on the aviation media, which will surely have all the answers in time. However, F.6 XP693 returned to Britain in July 2023 for preservation at Binbrook.

The world of Lightning preservation does not always remain static, and occasionally moves take place to new owners or organizations. Over the years Damien Burke's website thunder-and-lightnings.co.uk has been a reliable source of tracking these changes, along with many other types of classic Cold War aircraft.

Since the end of Thunder City, there have been no airworthy Lightnings anywhere worldwide. The situation may change as time progresses; however, it is safe to say that no such flight will be within the skies of the aircraft's origin. That aside, preserving the Lightning has a strong, loyal and determined foundation within the nation of its creation, and there is nothing to indicate that interest in the iconic interceptor is abating.

The Gatwick Lightning F.53

There can be no doubting the dedication and effort freely given by many involved in Lightning preservation. However, the Gatwick Aviation Museum's restoration of F.53 53-671 (ZF579) deserves special mention.

In the spring of 2000, the late Peter Vallance purchased the ex-Saudi Lightning and transported it to Gatwick. Previously owned by Marine Salvage of Portsmouth, the aircraft's cockpit was one of eight parted out (dismantled) and sent to Luxemburg to be used as a 'Rapier spacecraft' in the 1999 film *Wing Commander*. In the making of the feature it wasn't meant to be damaged, but upon return it was found that a 6ft section of the wiring loom had been cut through and was missing.

Undeterred, over the next sixteen years the museum's volunteers set about reconstructing 53-671 and painstakingly reconnecting the wiring. On 21 September 2016 their work was rewarded when an engine run was undertaken, probably the first time since the aircraft last flew in January 1986.

Since then, on selected open days visitors have been able to witness the only F.53 in the world that is able to run its Avon 302s. Resplendent in an all-metal finish, this is a truly remarkable and unique experience.

My Life with a Lightning: Richard Hall's Story

To say it rained would be an understatement: it rained in the morning, it rained in the afternoon, and just when you thought it might stop, it rained again. There are few places more dismal than an airfield when the weather is against you, but there we stood, Mike Potten and I, having travelled for four hours from the south of England to the Wolds of Lincolnshire, the date 22 August 1987. As a well-known law dictates, the weather on the day before had been fine and sunny. Video footage of the arrivals for the event confirms this, and guess what? The skies were blue and the weather fine as classic Cold War warriors carried out run and breaks before entering the circuit downwind to land. The next day was another story because as the much-anticipated Last Lightning Show got under way at Binbrook, the heavens opened.

The conditions were somewhat apt on this day as, after all, the Lightning was an all-weather interceptor, but the climate was certainly trying the patience. Never mind though; we'd arrived, so we were going to make the best of it. At the time it didn't seem like much fun, but as the rose-tinted glasses of time changed the perspective, it was agreed that the day was one of the best we had ever experienced. Others I've met since who attended on the day say a similar thing, and they too wouldn't have missed it for the world.

The Lightning is an icon among aviation enthusiasts, and to see one perform at an air show was quite something to behold. The sheer power, noise and agility were, when once seen, never to be forgotten. So to be given the chance to see a diamond nine formation flown in marginal conditions was a truly awe-inspiring prospect.

Away from all the action and to afford some protection from the rain for the bedraggled spectators, a number of the hangars were accessible. The Lightnings within were either stored or being subject to routine maintenance. I'm not sure if Hangar No. 5 was open on the day, but in here T.5 XS420 was stored. If I'd known then what impact this aircraft was to have on me two and a half decades later, I would not have believed it. I was within yards of a future project, but in this instance our first meeting was not to be. This would take place at the Royal International Air Tattoo (RIAT) in 2003 and again on 17 October 2010 during a visit to FAST.

Constructed at Warton, XS420 first flew in the hands of D.M. Knight on 23 January 1965. Following this, it was assigned to No. 226 OCU at Coltishall, arriving there on 29 April of the same year. Here the aircraft was to suffer an accident which could have seen the end of its career. On 31 January 1973 a reheat malfunction to one engine resulted in a failure to become airborne and a subsequent aborted take-off. Contemporary photos show that the aircraft had run off the end of the runway and buried its undercarriage in the soft earth. Thankfully the Category 3R damage wasn't severe and repairs were carried out.

So the usual question from those who visit XS420 is 'How did you come to own a Lightning?' Well, put it this way: it was not something that was on my bucket list. The original plan was to acquire a Lightning cockpit, but as with all such schemes, unexpected events came into play. For some years Mike Potten had wanted to obtain a cockpit to take as a travelling exhibit to air shows. He asked me if I wanted to be involved, and I agreed it would be a nice idea. Mike set about finding a cockpit, and soon a possible candidate came on the scene. Negotiations took place, but to cut a long story short, they failed. On the day I received the news that the plan would not go ahead, I was visiting the Yorkshire Air Museum, Elvington. Mike texted me to advise that the owners of the cockpit did not want to sell. I was gutted, and my thoughts were that we would never get another chance to acquire a Lightning cockpit.

I was staying in Lincolnshire overnight and driving back to the 'Red Lion' in Revesby, and I passed near Binbrook. I decided to visit the airfield and walk out to the QRA sheds. As I stood on the last remaining piece of Runway 04, I looked out over the approach and thought, 'Well, that's another dream gone', but little did I know what was about to transpire.

The next day on 17 June 2012 I went to Cockpit-Fest at Newark Air Museum and started talking to a chap about the failure to obtain the cockpit. He told me there was an exhibitor who had a Lightning for sale at the event and that I should go and take a look. Sure enough, there was a board showing XS420 as being up for grabs so I spoke to the owners, Neil and Heather Airey of Lakes Lightnings. Neil informed me the aircraft had only been put on the market that very weekend, and I had been the first to show an interest. Not believing my luck, I spoke to Mike and asked how he felt about owning 50 per cent of a whole Lightning.

At first he seemed a little hesitant, but when I advised him what the chances were of obtaining a complete airframe in good condition at a reasonable cost and located 30 miles from home at FAST, his view changed. This decision ultimately ended up with Mike and I being the proud and rather bewildered owners of one of the Cold War's most iconic aircraft.

The pair of us set to work on XS420 as there was a fair amount of cosmetic restoration that needed to be done. Mike also looked into obtaining parts for the cockpit as when the aircraft was acquired, it was empty save for two ejection seats, the port rudder pedals, the starboard throttle, one control column pedestal and some smaller items and switches. However, as time progressed Mike decided he wished to pursue his interest in flight simulation, which led to me taking sole ownership of the T.5 in May 2013. It was now time to start looking at some of the more serious work that was required to conserve and maintain the aircraft.

Lightnings do not travel well in anything other than air, so when XS420 was moved by road from Binbrook, the wings were cut off to make transportation possible. It is feasible to dismantle the airframe so that the wings can remain intact, but in this instance they were subjected to the cutter's wheel. The aircraft then went through the hands of several owners, but was eventually purchased by Murray Flint who began the task of stripping it back to a natural metal finish. During his ownership he was approached by the RAF, who enquired if the Lightning could be displayed at the RIAT Fairford, which in 2003 would celebrate 100 years of flight. In return for the loan, the RAF arranged for Serco to repaint the aircraft at Cranwell into an all-silver scheme similar to the bare metal finish it sported upon first entering service in 1965. At the conclusion of its static display appearance at Fairford, XS420 moved to FAST and was, in due course, sold to Neil and Heather Airey.

Following the aircraft's arrival in 2003, a repair was made by laying thin metal plates over the cuts in the wings. These were to remain in place for the next ten years. A neater way of doing this needed to be found, so I decided to fabricate plates that could be slotted into the wing's upper surface. Six 5mm thick aluminium plates were required, three per wing, and these were hand-cut by jigsaw from one large sheet. The pieces were then filed to match the profile of the cuts. This was a long, tedious job as the cuts were very ragged, entailing a great deal of filing, swearing and blisters until a good fit could be achieved. The panels, when finished, were then drilled, tapped and screwed into position.

One of the major milestones for the aircraft was achieved in October 2013 when the cockpit was opened for the first time in many years. Initially the canopy was lifted with some gentle persuasion as it was found that part of the locking mechanism had seized. Once freed off, it took four FAST volunteers to raise the canopy and secure it in the open position. At a later date, a manual hydraulic pump was externally rigged up, enabling pressure to be applied to the canopy ram, which lifted with no problems. This was a testament to British engineering as it is unlikely that the ram had been under pressure for more than twenty years and it worked flawlessly. A self-contained hydraulic pump was then fitted in the avionics bay behind the cockpit, which allowed the canopy to be lifted with a minimum of effort. A genuine ram lock was also obtained to ensure that the cockpit could be safely worked upon when the canopy was open. To ensure that the interior stays dry and sunlight is kept off the Perspex, a purpose-made cover was commissioned and, in due course, fitted.

The cockpit itself had had most of the items removed before the aircraft arrived at FAST. The ejection seats were still in place, minus rails, but the instrument panel, main crates and most other items were missing so there has been an ongoing search to locate parts. Aerojumbles, eBay, people's garages and lofts have all yielded results including a complete AI 23 radar. The Lightning preservation community is a close-knit group, and there has been help on hand in the quest which has proved to be extremely useful. There has been help from the LPG who supplied a starboard radar hand controller, and from Dave Tylee from the Gatwick Aviation Museum who sourced a number of wing panels that have allowed those that were cut or had become corroded to be replaced. There has also been assistance from many other sources and individuals. However, one item missing was the main instrument panel, which was harder to obtain than the proverbial hen's teeth.

To overcome this it was necessary to have a new panel made from scratch. Access was available to a genuine T.5 panel, and this was used as a pattern to fabricate an exact laser-cut replica. When completed the panel was tried for size in the cockpit and was found to fit perfectly with all the fixing points lining up. It was then spray-painted to the correct colour of dark sea grey with all the lettering that was present on the original being etched onto the replacement. Most of the instrumentation had been obtained for refitting, but there was another major piece missing: the crates that hold the aircraft's direction, attitude and height/rate of climb instruments, necessitating a new set being fabricated from scratch by a local engineer who had previously built similar items for other Lightnings.

One problem with a T.5 in being a two-seat trainer is that some cockpit equipment such as the throttles and stick tops are duplicated and also individually configured to port and starboard. This situation compounds the issue of obtaining parts as there were only twenty-two built, but on the whole the hunt has been successful, albeit spread over a long period of time. Patience is certainly a virtue when restoring an old aircraft.

A man who had patience in abundance was former RAF Crew Chief Derek Parks, who undertook much of the work in the early days of rebuilding XS420's cockpit. To get the panel, crates and ejection seats refitted, missing floor panels required fabrication; luckily the T.5's cockpit is a little bigger than that of a single-seater. This made the working environment a bit easier to manage but not much; however, as they say, every little helps. I'm told that working within, for instance, an F.2A cockpit is like being trapped in a car boot, but seeing Derek squashed into the confines of the T.5's office certainly gave me cause for great respect. With the floor back in he then installed the panel, crates, instrumentation and seats, a painstaking job indeed; remember this when you read what is to come a little later on.

Aside from cockpit work, as part of the ongoing maintenance regime fuselage panels are regularly removed to free off and grease Dzus fasteners. On the rear of the panels there are often serial numbers of Lightnings other than XS420. Several long-lost members of the family have been found living on in a small way within the aircraft. One panel came from F.3 XR715 which crashed on 13 February 1974 as described in Chapter Four. A couple of panels have been found to be from aircraft that have made it into preservation elsewhere. It is very much hoped that the current owners of these airframes won't want their panels back as it could leave XS420 with a few difficult holes to fill.

One thing I've learned with regard to the restoration of old aircraft is that when you're looking for parts they never appear, and when you least expect them to appear they do. Who was to know that after Derek had refitted XS420's replacement instrument panel the original one, complete with crates, would come up for sale? There was no hesitation on my part in acquiring the items as the chances of others appearing were practically nil. It was, therefore, with a little trepidation that one day I said to Derek, 'What kind of mood are you in?' 'Why?' he says. 'Well, you know all that work you've undertaken in fitting the new panel and crates?' 'Yes,' he retorts, and while standing at a safe distance I respond, 'How do you feel about doing it all again?' Luckily he was in a good mood, and he duly removed the fabricated panel and crates and replaced it with the originals and all the instruments; no mean feat and several weeks' work. You would think there would not be much call for a second-hand, non-genuine Lightning T.5 panel and crates, but you'd be wrong as the parts sold to a chap within a week who was creating his own cockpit section from scratch.

With the acquisition of the panel and crates came various components that were not available elsewhere and a multitude of instruments. It's strange as parts will often come out of the blue. One such occasion was when I was attending the Yeovilton Air Day in July 2015. As I watched the display, the mobile phone chimed to say there was an e-mail, the contents of which asked if I would be interested in purchasing a T.5 instructor's stick top (starboard). The port stick top (I do have one) is rare, but they occasionally come up on eBay. However, the instructor's is seldom seen for sale. I didn't need asking twice, responding in the affirmative, and the top was duly purchased. Another very scarce part of the jigsaw had fallen into place.

A similar situation also occurred while I was at RNAS Culdrose Air Show in 2016 when a phone call came through saying a T.5 engine start panel was available again and this is an extremely elusive part. I've only seen one outside of a Lightning cockpit and that's the one I now have. The housing for this panel was missing from XS420, but in 2019 one came on the market and has also been obtained; again, it's the only one I've ever seen for sale.

Not all work has been focused on the cockpit. Since arrival at FAST in 2003, XS420's flaps had been in the deployed position where when on the ground they should be stowed retracted and I wanted to address this. The port flap was not much of an issue as it could be pushed into the up position where it stayed in place (something to do with hydraulic lock, I'm advised). The starboard flap was a different matter entirely as on the inboard end there was no bracketing or ram; this had all been lost when the aircraft's wings were cut off years ago. The flap had to be taken off to effect a repair, which necessitated the removal of some of the upper and lower wing panels. These had not been removed in decades, and the panels were held in place by hundreds of screws, many of which were inevitably seized. Derek came up with an ingenious tool that allowed practically all the screws to be undone so they could be reused to refasten the panels at a later date. The flap was duly removed with help from fellow FAST members and new bracketing was fabricated. It was then refitted and held in place by Acrow props – a vertical support system – while the final attachments were made to allow it to hold its own weight in the up position. This was not as easy as it sounds as the flap not only had to be supported in weight, but there was also a requirement to retract it. To achieve a satisfactory outcome, a 16mm threaded bar and heavyweight lifting eye (0.8 tonne safe working load) were attached to the original fixings on the flap. In essence, the bar and eye acted as an artificial jack, which was used to pull the flap into the correct position; it also allowed for fine adjustment to ensure that it was correctly aligned with the wing surfaces.

After the flap work was completed, all the wing panels and their fixings were reinstated. This allowed for the preparation and painting of the upper wing root plates, which had been fitted some years ago. The completion of this major work has considerably tidied up XS420 and helped improve the aircraft's overall appearance.

One of the areas of importance with the T.5 was to give the aircraft a bit of life, and a way to achieve this was to reinstate the navigation, landing and anti-collision lights. It was decided that a new 12-volt Direct Current (DC) system would suffice to give the desired effect. The existing 28-volt DC wiring was in poor order so new cables were run in to serve the outer wings, undercarriage legs, rear fuselage and spine. The system was powered using a 240-volt Alternating Current (AC) to 12-volt DC inverter, with the wing tip and spine anti-collision lights served by a custom-made flasher unit. The external lights on a Lightning are not that spectacular compared to some other aircraft; nonetheless, when energized, they do create a pleasing spectacle, especially as the light fades on a winter's evening.

With the external lighting complete, it was time to get power into the cockpit. Installing twin 1.6mm cables from a 240-volt AC to 24-volt DC inverter from the support shed was one of the most unpleasant jobs I've undertaken on the aircraft as achieving this entailed crawling internally the length of the fuselage. Never have I encountered so many sharp edges, sticky surfaces and places to bang your head; thank goodness for the invention of the bump cap, is all I can say.

Once the cables were in place, the plan was to power up the auxiliary and standard warning panels together with the attention lights. The last of these items was missing, but with the help of Al Stepney, who served with the RAF as an Electronic Mechanic (LMECH) working mostly with flight simulators, the problem was solved. He 3D-printed a pair of light housings and wired up all the components with light-emitting diodes (LEDs). The end result was superb, with the systems operating as they would in service, including audio when the test sequence is initiated. He also manufactured P-lights, again LED lit, and restored the twin undercarriage indicators and volt meters so they could be made to operate. When XS420's cockpit was opened for the first time in many years in 2013 it was cold and dead, but now it is very much alive, all thanks to Al.

It has been some years since XS420 was externally restored, and overall the finish is bearing up well. However, while the paint is holding up the lacquer is suffering from the effects of sunlight on the south-facing elevation. This has resulted in certain areas flaking and it has proved to be very difficult to match the silver paint with which the airframe is coated. Recently the use of an aluminium paint manufactured by Blackfriars has allowed the worst affected areas to be repainted with no startling difference between new and original finishes. With any aircraft kept outside, it is an ongoing battle with the elements, but one that has to be accepted. I now sympathize with those who used to have to paint the Forth Bridge.

As time passed the search for missing components continued, and rare items occasionally surfaced. In August 2019 the rarest of rare made an appearance and presented an opportunity that could not be missed: a genuine mint condition T.5 crew access ladder. This was the first time I'd seen one for sale and the price was a bit on the high side, but as is often stated, 'Where are you going to find another one?' The problem was that the ladder was more than 9ft long, which made transportation interesting. The answer was to hire a 3.5-tonne Transit van, and after a 400-mile round trip to Norfolk, the ladder is now safely ensconced in one of the containers at FAST.

Recently an interesting offer was made to me to obtain the avionics equipment removed from XS420 some thirty years ago. After a trip to King's Lynn to pick up the parts, they have now been refitted and allow some of the panels to be opened to show the black boxes that lurk in the depths of the fuselage. Once again, it is very satisfying to reunite items removed many years ago with the original donor.

There is a saying that no man is an island, and this is certainly the case within the world of aircraft preservation, especially when you are the sole owner of an ongoing project. I can attest to the fact that a lot of time, dedication, effort and money go into keeping XS420 in one piece, but without the help of others the task would have been almost impossible. So it was in early 2022 that a very welcome message was received from Martin Blades who offered his assistance. I wasn't sure where Martin's skills lay, but it soon became very apparent he was a dab hand at electronics. He also works with the LPG and Lightning T.5 XS458 based at Cranfield.

Very soon after his arrival he set to work changing the aircraft's external lighting from the standard 12-volt bulbs I had installed to LED, which cut down on power consumption, increased brightness and added to the display on sunny days. Previously, as stated, I had run twin cables through the fuselage to power the cockpit undercarriage indicators and warning panels. However, Martin had other great ideas to bring further life to the aircraft. In due course he wired up a sound system and one day recently, with the press of a button on the engine start panel in the cockpit, the sound Don Knight heard some fifty-eight years earlier was recreated as XS420 once again basked in a simulated engine start. The hiss of the AVPIN and the low whine of the Avons spooling (recorded at the LPG) has brought a smile to many a visitor's face since, as those who recollect the days of the Lightning and those too young to remember are treated to an interactive experience of just what it was like to have been there.

Over time it is hoped to bring more of XS420's systems to life, and there are plans to wire up the multitude of the cockpit's P-lights, which will be a long and arduous task. Another exciting project Martin has completed is reproducing the functional operation of the B-Scope. The simulation shows the different stages of operation, from search and acquisition to missile launch and breakaway; there is also the ability to operate the sequence from the radar hand controller. Opportunities to see a B-Scope working are few, so this is a genuinely fascinating project. If this was not enough, he has also powered up a Red Top missile-seeker head and the Light Fighter Sight to show their operational functionality again, giving visitors another rare opportunity to witness.

One particular aspect of conserving a Lightning that gives great satisfaction is the times when those who had an association with the type pay a visit. Over the years former personnel have come to FAST to share their memories of working with an aircraft that had, to say the least, an interesting service record. Some talk of what it was like to fly, and others of the trials and tribulations of trying to maintain it. One or two have spoken of their membership of the Ten Ton Club, the entrance to which is achieved by travelling at 1,000 mph in a Lightning.

Coupled with this are the many visitors who come along and get the chance to sit in the cockpit. I've lost count of how many have said their day had been made for being given the opportunity to get up close and personal with an icon. Such comments make it all worthwhile when you see the genuine enthusiasm directed towards an aircraft that left service all those years ago.

One visit in July 2016 was of particular note when a small group of Lockheed Martin F-35 Lightning II air and ground crew from the United States Marine Corps visited FAST one weekday following their participation in the previous week's Farnborough Air Show. A couple of the pilots sat in XS420's cockpit and were amazed by its analogue complexity over the glass-equipped offices they were used to.

Of course, some from the wider world don't understand why anyone would want to save a lump of metal. With such sentiments, I feel the bigger picture is being missed when you see the enjoyment that aircraft preservation, whether flying or static, gives to so many people.

Aside from the above, it can be the simplest of things that leave a lasting, meaningful impression. One day I was looking at one of the items of equipment in the avionics bay, which, on its maker's plate, had been stamped English Electric Co. Ltd Aircraft Equipment Division, Bradford. It suddenly struck me that this referred to the former Phoenix Dynamo Manufacturing Co. Ltd, whose factory was in Bradford and was one of the companies that formed English Electric in 1918. Phoenix has a heritage dating back to the days of steam electrical generation in the late nineteenth and early twentieth centuries. As an interceptor, XS420 was capable of achieving M2.0 and climbing to over 60,000ft. Yet within the parts that make up this iconic thoroughbred can be found a connection dating back to the heyday of Victorian engineering. Food for thought, I'd say.

The Cockpiteers

Aside from the preservation of complete airframes, some equally enthusiastic individuals and volunteers within museums dedicate their time and efforts to conserving cockpits. Long after the rest of the aircraft has been scrapped, the pilot's office lives on sometimes static but also as mobile trailer-mounted exhibits. Many drivers would look aghast and may wonder if they could believe their eyes when a truncated Harrier, Hunter, Sea Vixen or Scout, to name but a few, passes them on the road on its way to some event.

The interest in cockpits is celebrated each year at Cockpit-Fest held at Newark Air Museum, where owners display their pride and joy for others to admire, with prizes awarded in recognition of their endeavours. However, Newark is by no means the only place to see these artefacts from times past, as being transportable they can often be found at air and country shows throughout the nation, giving an important educational insight to the enthusiast and public alike into the world of aviation history.

It will come as no surprise that the Lightning is a popular and much sought after cockpit for collectors. Many have survived long after the rest of the airframe has been scrapped. The keepers of these pieces carry out restorations to a very high standard and lavish much time, money and dedication to their cause. They then share their efforts for others to enjoy.

To give an insight into the trials and tribulations of Lightning cockpit ownership, I spoke to long-time LPG member Hugh Trevor:

> I remember going to air shows in the 1970s, where I always considered the Lightning to be the most impressive performer. In 1975, I was living in Manchester, and there was an air show at Binbrook. I didn't have a car, so there was a tortuous train journey to Lincoln and then a bus up through the Wolds to get to the airfield. I had with me a stills camera, a Super 8 camera and a

cassette recorder for sound. The Rothmans-sponsored aerobatic team was there with its Pitts Specials, and shortly afterwards, the commentator announced in a very public school voice: 'Ladies and Gentlemen, if you look to your right now, you will see two F.3 Lightnings of 5 Squadron, sponsored by Her Majesty's Government, taking off to intercept the two F.6 Lightnings of 11 Squadron you saw departing earlier.'

Over the years, I continued to visit Binbrook and have some great memories and film footage, but I was under the impression you shouldn't take photos at an operational base. However, in 1983, I went to the Abingdon Air Show, where I spoke with Flt Lt Dave Frost from 5 Squadron, who was on static with his F.6 XS928 'BJ'. He told me there was no problem with going to the crash gates to take images or video. Using his advice the following year, I discovered the locations and would often spend two or three days at Binbrook while on holiday, observing proceedings, usually in the pouring rain. Dave was a lovely guy who was killed in July 1984 when he hit power lines piloting F.6 XS920 while chasing a [Fairchild] A-10 in West Germany.

Later, I attended an event in London where Roland Beamont gave a talk. Here, I met Richard Norris, who told me that a group had been formed to save a Lightning – which I subsequently joined and, as they say, the rest is history.

Along with participation with the LPG, I started to attend aerojumbles and bought bits and pieces of Lightning, including an ejection seat. These were in the days before eBay, and all manner of items could be obtained at a reasonable price. Around this time, Tanks and Vessels Industries of Rossington, near Doncaster, had bought Lightnings from the decoy line at Binbrook, and it was planned some would be sold as cockpits. I decided to bid for one as it would allow me to free up some space in my house and place the parts I'd accrued where they belonged. After some negotiations, I bought F.6 XS932's cockpit, but it was still attached to the airframe. However, with some help from members of the then Grimsby Lightning Group, which included Phil Wallis, the task of its removal was completed, but not without incident. Phil winched down and removed the missile pack, allowing access to the hydraulic pipework. He then fitted a hand pump, the plan being to retract the nose wheel to enable the removal of the cockpit to be completed at ground level, which would be safer for all involved.

So everyone jumped on the tailplane, the airframe sat on its tail, the forward undercarriage leg was retracted, and the instruction 'one person jump off' issued. Unfortunately, *which* person should jump off was not specified, and two or three people jumped; accordingly, the nose came crashing to the ground, and Trevor Garrod, who was straddling the rear fuselage, almost went into orbit. Thankfully, the cockpit wasn't damaged, but as the potential owner, I found it to be an interesting moment. With the front fuselage removed behind the transport joint using Stihl saws, it was then transported to Bruntingthorpe in December 1992, later moving to Shoreham, which is closer to where I live, followed by a stint at FAST.

> The opportunity then came to purchase F.2A XN726's cockpit, which had been used as a target at Shoeburyness. For obvious reasons, it was in a far worse condition than XS932, with the canopy off, quarter-light smashed, and holes sustained through bullet and shell strikes. However, with something in that state, anything you do makes it look better, and I found it more satisfying to work on than my first cockpit.
>
> I then sold XS932 to Neil and Heather Airey of Lakes Lightnings [later acquired by Richard Scarborough] and found out Neil went to the same comprehensive school (at a different time) as I did in Ulverston, Cumbria. So when I came to complete the deal, I wore the school tie.
>
> One day, while at an event at Popham, I bumped into Sqn Ldr John Sharpe, who was involved with the Boscombe Down museum project, and I asked him if there was any room for a Lightning cockpit. He said yes, as they didn't have one, so it was transported to the airfield and later to the Boscombe Down Aviation Collection at Old Sarum, where it is now on display.[5]

Hugh appears modest about the restoration of XN726, but to take a cockpit from a dilapidated condition to one that equals or is better than when it was in service is quite remarkable. He, of course, will be the first to admit he has had a lot of help from some equally dedicated individuals who have given their skills and time to achieve the desired result. The attention to detail is something to behold, especially when one is invited to view the cockpit's interior, which is complete with functioning lighting and an Avon start sound system. The shock cone has been partially sectioned to allow the AI 23 radar to be seen in situ, which is a rare, if not unique, opportunity.

After all the hard work, Hugh is now able to relax a little and enjoy the fruits of his labours. However, with aircraft preservation, whether it be a whole airframe or a cockpit, there is always something to do, so he won't be hanging up his spanners or cleaning cloths just yet.

Future Custodians

Few things in life can be relied upon, but if there is one certainty, it is that time moves on. Relentlessly advancing, sweeping all before it, nothing can stand in its way. This presents a problem to preservationists as to who will look after their pride and joy when the time comes. Anyone, whether a group or individual, with a historic artefact under their care, be it an aircraft, classic car, railway locomotive or stately home, is merely a custodian and never truly the owner. Therefore it is obvious that the younger generation needs to follow the old to ensure that years of previous effort are not consigned to the scrap heap.

The above applies equally to the world of Lightning preservation as we are all getting older and want to ensure the icon survives for those who come after to enjoy. I met with Mike Patterson, who is one of the younger generation and has recently entered the world of aviation conservation. He has acquired F.6 XS933's cockpit and has taken it to Binbrook where an ambitious restoration is planned. I asked him why he wanted to get involved:

> I've had an interest in aviation from my earliest years, partly through attending air shows but also driven by my father's involvement with radio-controlled flying. I recall vividly watching a Lightning at an air show when I was young take off and disappear up into the clouds at what seemed unbelievable speed. A few visits to Bruntingthorpe in later years for the fast taxi runs again showed me the power of this aircraft, which had my ears ringing and left me wanting more.
>
> A chance visit to Binbrook to see the Lightning Training Flight guys then got me talking to some of the XR724 [under the care of the Lightning Association and now in ground running condition] engineers, and I realized that mere mortals with no RAF background can join in with preservation too.
>
> In the beginning, I wasn't looking for a full cockpit. I planned to build a Lightning simulator, so I was seeking out instruments and parts. The complex shape of the structure for building a 'sim' from scratch then led me to look for any of the half cuts that had previously been used in the film *Wing Commander*, but of the known examples left, these were either not for sale, in very poor condition or both.
>
> After searching for parts for a few years, a contact in the Lightning world told me of a set of instruments I might be interested in, but they did come with a little bit more attached. After a few e-mails and phone calls, the original owner, Steve Jones, sent over some pictures and asked if I was interested in a viewing. So I took to the road, and 200 miles later, I found a Lightning cockpit sticking out of a hedge, looking like a strange crash scene, but in great condition. After climbing around, over and into XS933, I decided that this was the one for me and started negotiations to purchase her.
>
> That was the easy part done; the next hurdle literally was the aforementioned hedge, which had grown a little in the twenty years since her arrival and now required the services of a crane. A few months later, waiting for the ground to be firm enough for a lifting company to be brave enough to hoist her over the hedge, she was on the move to her new temporary home at Binbrook, where the Lightning whisperer, aka Mr Darren Swinn [a veteran of the Lightning preservation world], offered to help with the restoration.
>
> The intention for XS933 is to do a full restoration of the cockpit interior and make as many instruments operate as possible, eventually with a simulator link so she can 'fly' again. I hope to take her to shows once I've found a suitable trailer to mount the cockpit for road transportation.[6]

As if to emphasize the need to pass on the baton of preservation to a younger generation, I heard with sadness that Steve Jones, the former owner of XS933, passed away in February 2024.

The Collectors

While some may consider that the world of Lightning preservation revolves around complete airframes and cockpits, this is far from the case. Not everyone has the means or the space for large-scale projects, but owning just a small part of the icon is within their grasp. Such items can range from a stick top, radar hand controller, B-Scope, one of the numerous instruments or gauges from the cockpit, a fuselage panel, a fin or a piece of aluminium skin.

Items often appear at aerojumbles or online auctions and sit nicely on a mantelpiece or within a man cave, where they give the owner immense joy and satisfaction knowing that this is a part of aviation history that once attained M2.0.

The chance to obtain a fuselage panel is very rewarding, as these are often marked with the serial number of the donor aircraft. For those with an investigative nature, knowing an identity gives a chance for further research and to piece together the machine's history. The Operations Record Books, along with the Aircraft Movement Card, will provide more insight. Before long, the researcher will know far more about the artefact they possess, and a long-forgotten Lightning will, in a small way, come back to life, and after all, isn't that what the world of preservation seeks to achieve either in a large or small scale?

No matter if you own a complete Lightning, a cockpit, a light fighter sight, a fuel contents gauge or a tiny piece of fuselage skin, the preservationist has committed either time, money, effort or in some cases all three to ensure that the creation of Petter and Page lives on, not just for now but way into the future. Long may their endeavours prevail!

Appendix I

Lightnings Built, Written Off and Preserved

Variant	Number Built	Written Off	Airframes Preserved	Cockpits Preserved
P.1A	2	0	2	0
P.1B Prototype	3	0	1	0
P.1B Development Batch	20	4	3	2
F.1	19	4	1	0
F.1A	28	11	4	3
F.2 (1)	13	5 (2)	0	1
F.2A	31	2	4	3
F.3 (3)	70	24	5	5
F.6 Interim	16	8 (4)	2 (5)	3 (6)
F.6	39	18	15	7
P.11	2	1	1	0
T.4	20	8	2 (7)	0
T.5	22	4 (8) (9)	8	3
F.53	34	14 (10)	15	6 (11) (12)
F.53K	12	3	9	0
T.55	6	1	2	3 (13) (14)
T.55K	2	1	2 (15)	0
Total	339	108	76	36
Structural Test Airframes				
P.1A	1 (16)	0	0	0
F.1	1 (17)	0	0	0
Total	2			

(1)	XN767, XN770, XN796, XN797, XN729 to RSAF as F.52 52-655, 52-656, 52-657, 52-658, 52-659.
(2)	XN796, XN797, XN729 were written off in RSAF service.
(3)	F.3 XR722 to RSAF as F-53 53-666.
(4)	Seven F.6 Interim written off after conversion to full F.6 standard.
(5)	XR753 and XR755 were preserved after conversion to full F.6 standard.
(6)	Three F.6 Interim cockpits – XR754, XR757 and XR759 – were preserved after conversion to full F.6 standard.
(7)	XM989, XM992 to RSAF as 54-650, 54-651, both preserved in Saudi Arabia.
(8)	XS460 to RSAF as T.55 55-710 (crashed before delivery).
(9)	XS451 was written off in South Africa in November 2009.
(10)	Includes XR722 after transfer to RSAF.
(11)	ZF587 (53-691) survives as a cockpit parted out from its fuselage and wings, which are stored.
(12)	ZF590 (53-679) survives as a cockpit parted out from its fuselage, which is stored.
(13)	ZF595 (55-714) survives as a cockpit parted out from its fuselage.
(14)	ZF596 (55-715) survives as a cockpit parted out from its fuselage and wings.
(15)	55410 – Wreckage present Ali Al Salem.
(16)	WG765
(17)	XM168

While best endeavours have been taken to ensure the accuracy of the above information, caution should be exercised regarding the ex-RSAF and Kuwaiti airframes and cockpits. While researching, it was noted that some listed as preserved have not been seen for some time with locations unknown, meaning that their continued existence cannot be guaranteed. In other cases, cockpits have been parted out from the fuselage and wings, with the various sections surviving separately.

With reference to Nos. 13 and 14 above, a private collector has acquired the cockpit of ZF595 (55-714) and has fitted it to the wings and fuselage of ZF596 (55-715) and, in doing so, has created a complete airframe.

Appendix II

Surviving Lightning Airframe and Cockpit Serial Numbers

Variant	Complete Airframes	Cockpits
P.1A	WG760, WG763	Not applicable
P.1B Prototype	XA847	None survive
P.1B Development Batch	XG313, XG329, XG337	XG325, XG331
F.1	XM135	None survive
F.1A	XM172, XM173, XM178, XM192	XM144, XM169, XM191
F.2	No complete airframe survives	XN769
F.2A	XN730, XN776, XN782, XN784	XN726, XN728, XN795
F.3	XP706, XP745, XR713, XR718, XR749	XP701, XP703, XP743, XP757, XR751
F.6 (including Interim)	XP693, XS897, XR724, XR725, XR728, XR753, XR755, XR770, XR771 XR773, XS903, XS904, XS919, XS925, XS928, XS929, XS936	XR747, XR754, XR757, XR759, XS898, XS899, XS922, XS923, XS932, XS933
P.11	XL629	None survive
T.5	XS416, XS417, XS420, XS422, XS452, XS456, XS458, XS459	XS421, XS457, XV328
F.52	XN767 (52-655), XN770 (52-656)	None survive
T.54	54-650 (XM989), 54-651 (XM992)	None survive

F.53	53-670 (ZF578), 53-671, 53-672 (ZF580), 53-675 (ZF581), 53-681 (ZF583, 53-682 (ZF584), 53-684, 53-685 (ZF591), 53-686 (ZF592), 53-687, 53-692 (ZF593), 53-693 (ZF588), 53-696 (ZF594), 53-698, 53-699	53-676 (ZF582), 53-683 (ZF585), 53-688 (ZF586), 53-691 (ZF587), fuselage, wings and tail also survive, 53-700 (ZF589), 53-679 (ZF590) fuselage also survives
F.53K	53-412, 53-415, 53-416, 53-417, 53-418, 53-420, 53-421, 53-422, 53-423	None survive
T.55	55-713 (ZF598), 55-716	55-714 (ZF595) fuselage also survives, 55-715 (ZF596) fuselage also survives, 55-711 (ZF597)
T.55K	55-410 (wreckage), 55-411	None survive

Appendix III

Roll of Honour

The piloting of fast jets is never without risk as any aviator will attest, and some who take to the skies pay the ultimate price. The following is in memory of the sixteen pilots (including one from the USAF) who were lost while flying the Lightning in RAF service:

Flt Lt Alan Garside: No. 111 Squadron – F.1A XM186 – 18 July 1963
Fg Off. George Davie: No. 92 Squadron – F.2A XN785 – 27 April 1964
Flt Lt Glyn Owen: No. 74 Squadron – F.3 XP704 – 28 August 1964
Fg Off. Derek Law: No. 56 Squadron – F.3 XR721 – 5 January 1966
Fg Off. Alan Davey: No. 5 Squadron – F.6 XS924 – 29 April 1968
Fg Off. Peter Thompson: No. 74 Squadron – F.6 XS896 – 12 September 1968
Flt Lt Tony Doidge: No. 11 Squadron – F.6 XS918 – 4 March 1970
Fg Off. John Webster: No. 74 Squadron – F.6 XR767 – 26 May 1970
Flt Lt Frank Whitehouse: No. 74 Squadron – F.6 XS930 – 27 July 1970
Capt. Bill Shaffner USAF: No. 5 Squadron – F.6 XS894 – 8 September 1970
Fg Off. Phil Mottershead: No. 29 Squadron – F.3 XP736 – 22 September 1971
Flt Lt Paul Cooper: No. 29 Squadron – F.3 XP747 – 16 February 1972
Sqn Ldr David Hampton: No. 11 Squadron – F.6 XR762 – 7 April 1975
Flt Lt Mike Thompson: LTF – F.3 XP753 – 26 August 1983
Flt Lt Dave Frost: No. 5 Squadron – F.6 XS920 – 13 July 1984
Fg Off. Martin Ramsey: No. 5 Squadron – XR772 – 6 March 1985

Endnotes

Chapter 2

1. McClelland, T., *English Electric Lightning* (Hersham: Chevron Publishing, 2009), p.13.
2. Scott, S.A., *English Electric Lightning, Volume One: Birth of a Legend* (Peterborough: GMS 2000), p.1.
3. McClelland, T., *English Electric Lightning* (Hersham: Chevron Publishing, 2009), p.16.
4. Beamont, R., *Testing Years* (Book Club Associates, by arrangement with Ian Allan Ltd, 1980), p.96.
5. The National Archives, *AIR 8/2168*, p.3.
6. *Ibid.*, p.9.
7. Text written and permission given for publication by Colin Murray.
8. Beamont, R., *Testing Years* (Book Club Associates, by arrangement with Ian Allan Ltd, 1980), p.117.

Chapter 3

1. www.britpolitics.co.uk/quotefinder/churchill-winston-the-battle-of-france-is-over
2. Text written and permission given for publication by Dennis Brooks.
3. Cossey, B., *Onward and Upward: The Life of Air Vice-Marshal John Howe, CB, CBD, AFC* (Barnsley: Pen & Sword, 2008), p.139.
4. The National Archives, *AIR 27/2794*, December 1960, p.3.
5. Cossey, B., *Onward and Upward: The Life of Air Vice-Marshal John Howe, CB, CBD, AFC* (Barnsley: Pen & Sword, 2008), p.154.
6. Scott, S.A., *English Electric Lightning, Volume One: Birth of a Legend* (Peterborough: GMS 2000), p.179.
7. Text written and permission given for publication by Colin Murray.
8. The National Archives, *AIR 27/2935*, August 1961, p.3.
9. *Ibid.*, October 1964, p.2.
10. *Ibid.*, December 1964, p.6.
11. *Ibid.*, February 1965, p.4.
12. The National Archives, *AIR 27/2967*, June 1961, p.3.
13. *Ibid.*, June 1961, p.2.
14. *Ibid.*, September 1961, p.2.
15. *Ibid.*, April 1963, p.2.

16. *Ibid.*, December 1963, p.2.
17. *Ibid.*, June 1964, p.2.
18. *Ibid.*, August 1964, p.1.
19. *Ibid.*, August 1964, p.3.
20. *Ibid.*, April 1964, p.2.
21. Text written and permission given for publication by Brian Clifford.

Chapter 4

1. https://www.theguardian.com/culture/gallery/2012/sep/29/1962-year-pictures
2. scottbouch.com/aircrew-uk-oxygen-mask-p-q-type-series.htm
3. The National Archives, *AIR 27/2909,* October 1962, p.3.
4. *Ibid.*, April 1963, p.3.
5. *Ibid.*, July 1964, p.1.
6. *Ibid.*, August 1964, p.1.
7. *Ibid.*, December 1964, p.1.
8. *Ibid.*, September 1965, p.2.
9. The National Archives, *AIR 27/2958,* June 1963, p.3.
10. Text written and permission given for publication by Dennis Brooks.
11. Text written and permission given for publication by Colin Murray.
12. Text written and permission given for publication by Dave Rowberry.
13. *Ibid.*
14. *Ibid.*
15. The National Archives, *AIR 27/2952,* April 1964, p.2.
16. The National Archives, *AIR 27/3102,* August 1966, p.2.
17. The National Archives, *AIR 27/2912,* November 1964, p.3.
18. *Ibid.*, May 1965, p.5.
19. The National Archives, *AIR 27/2967,* April 1965, p.3.
20. *Ibid.*, October 1965, p.1.
21. The National Archives, *No. 111 Squadron Operations Record Book*, December 1967, p.3.
22. *Ibid.*, February 1968, p.5.
23. *Ibid.*, December 1968, p.2.
24. *Ibid.*, May 1970, p.1.
25. Scott, S. A., *English Electric Lightning, Volume Two: The Lightning Force* (Peterborough: GMS 2004), p.153.
26. The National Archives, *AIR 27/3091,* December 1968, p.2.
27. *Ibid.*, March 1969, p.1.
28. *Ibid.*, May 1969, p.1.
29. The National Archives, *AIR 27/3051,* March 1967, p.3.
30. *Ibid.*, July 1967, p.3.
31. *Ibid.*, December 1967, p.3.
32. *Ibid.*, August 1968, p.1.
33. *Ibid.*, September 1969, p.2.
34. *Ibid.*, May 1971, p.2.
35. Text written and permission given for publication by Steve Gyles.
36. The National Archives, *AIR29/3670, Annex F to F540, RAF Coltishall*, November 1969.
37. Text written and permission given for publication by John Ward.
38. Text written and permission given for publication by Clive Hammond.
39. The National Archives, *AIR 27/3266,* October 1974, p.1.
40. Text written and permission given for publication by Ian Brett.

Chapter 5

1. AP 101-1003, 5&6-15A *Aircrew Manual, Airframe Limitations,* p.5.
2. The National Archives, *AIR 27/3102,* May 1969, p.1.
3. *Ibid., Annex 9 to 74 S F540*, pp.1-10.
4. *Ibid.*, November 1969, p.1.
5. *Ibid.*, July 1971, p.2.
6. The National Archives, *AIR 27/3041,* May 1967, p.4.
7. *Ibid., Form 541*, May 1968, p.4.
8. *Ibid., Annex A to Form 540,* June 1968, pp.1-3.
9. *Ibid.*, *AIR27/3041*, June 1971, p.2.
10. *Ibid.*, November 1972, p.1.
11. *Ibid.*, November 1972, p.2.
12. The National Archives, *AIR 27/3091, Form 541,* January to October 1972.
13. *Ibid.*, *AIR27/3041*, November 1972, p.3.
14. *Ibid.*, December 1972, p.1.
15. The National Archives, *AIR 27/3306,* August 1974, p.1.
16. *Ibid.*, December 1974, p.3.
17. The National Archives, *AIR 27/3448,* June 1976, p.2.
18. The National Archives, *AIR 27/3417,* April 1976, p.4.
19. *Ibid.*, June 1976, p.2.
20. *Ibid.*, October 1976, p.2.
21. *Ibid., Form 541,* December 1976, p.1.
22. The National Archives, *AIR 27/3417,* December 1976, pp.4-5.
23. The National Archives, *AIR 27/3458, Form 541,* February 1976, pp.1-2.
24. *Ibid.*, March 1977, pp.1-2.
25. The National Archives, *AIR 27/3458,* March 1977, pp.4-5.

Chapter 6

1. Text written and permission given for publication by Jeff Bell.
2. The National Archives, *AIR 27/2898,* September 1965, p.3.
3. The National Archives, *AIR 27/3011,* March 1966, p.3.
4. The National Archives, *AIR 27/3394,* May 1979, p.3.
5. The National Archives, *AIR 27/3820,* November 1987, p.2.
6. *Ibid.*, December 1987, p.3.
7. Text written and permission given for publication by Steve Gyles.
8. The National Archives, *AIR 27/3731*, November 1985, p.1.
9. The National Archives, *AIR 27/3826,* March 1988, p.2.
10. *Ibid.*
11. The National Archives, *AIR 27/3826,* April 1988, p.1.
12. *Ibid.*, p.2.
13. *Ibid.*, pp.3-4.

Chapter 7

1. Transcribed from an interview between the author and Richard Norris.
2. *Ibid.*
3. *Ibid.*
4. Transcribed from an interview between the author and Tony Hulls.
5. Transcribed from an interview between the author and Hugh Trevor.
6. Text written and permission given for publication by Mike Patterson.

Bibliography

Primary Sources

Beamont, R., *English Electric P1 Lightning* (Shepperton: Ian Allan Ltd, 1985)

Beamont, R., *Testing Years* (Book Club Associates by arrangement with Ian Allan Ltd, 1980)

Beamont, R. and Reed, A., *English Electric Canberra* (Shepperton: Ian Allan Ltd, 1984)

Boiten, Theo, *Nachtjagd Combat Archive 1939–12 July 1941: The Early Years, Part 1* (Walton-on-Thames: Red Kite, 2018)

Brown, E., *Miles M.52: Gateway to Supersonic Flight* (Stroud: Spellmount, 2012)

Brown, T., *Flying with the Larks: The Early Aviation Pioneers Of Larkhill* (Stroud: The History Press, 2013)

Campbell-Smith, D., *Jet Man: The Making and Breaking of Frank Whittle, Genius of the Jet Revolution* (London: Head of Zeus, 2020)

Caygill, P., *Lightning Eject: The Dubious Record of Britain's Only Supersonic Fighter* (Barnsley: Pen & Sword, 2012)

Chorley, W.R., *Royal Air Force Bomber Command Losses of the Second World War 1944* (Midland Publications, 2008) and others in the series

Claisse, Maurice, *1942 – Farnborough at War* (Elvetham Publications, undated)

Cornwell, P.D., *The Battle of France: Then And Now* (Old Harlow: After The Battle, 2007)

Cossey, B., *Onward and Upward: The Life of Air Vice-Marshal John Howe, CB, CBD, AFC* (Barnsley: Pen & Sword, 2008)

Davies, G., *From Lysander to Lightning: Teddy Petter, Aircraft Designer* (Stroud: The History Press, 2014)

Delve, K. and Sheehan, J., *The Greatest Multi-Role Aircraft of the Cold War*, Vol. 1 (Stroud: Fonthill Media Ltd, 2022)

Ellis, K., *Testing to the Limits: British Test Pilots since 1910, Addicott to Huxley* (Manchester: Crecy, 2015)

Ellis, K., *Britain's Aircraft Industry: Triumphs and Tragedies since 1909* (Manchester: Crecy, 2021)

Ellis, K., *Wrecks and Relics: 28th Edition* (Manchester: Crecy, 2022) and others in the series

Halley, J.J. (ed.), *Royal Air Force Aircraft XA100 to XZ999* (Tunbridge Wells: Air-Britain, 2001) and others in the series

Holmes, H., *The World's Greatest Air Depot: The US 8th Air Force at Warton 1942–1945* (Shrewsbury: Airlife Publishing, 1998)
Jackson, A., *Avro Aircraft since 1908* (London: Putnam, 1990)
James, D., *Gloster Aircraft since 1917* (London: Putnam, 1987)
James, D., *Westland Aircraft since 1915* (London: Putnam, 1991)
Jennings, M.D., *Royal Air Force Coltishall: A Fighter Station* (Cowbit: Old Forge, 2007)
Lanchbery, E., *Against the Sun* (London: Cassell, 1955)
Lightning Preservation Group, *Lightning Legend* (Bruntingthorpe: 2016)
Lindsay, R., *Lightning* (Shepperton: Ian Allan Ltd, 1989)
Longworth, J.H., *Test Flying in Lancashire: Military Aviation at the Leading Edge, Volume 1: WW1 to the 1960s* (BAe Systems, 2012)
McClelland, T., *English Electric Lightning* (Hersham: Chevron Publishing, 2009)
Mould, G., *The Lightning Conversion Units 1960–1987* (Billericay: Prospect Litho Ltd, 1993)
Price, A., *Spitfire at War* (Shepperton: Ian Allan Ltd, 1974)
Rawlings, J., *Bomber Squadrons of the RAF and Their Aircraft* (London: McDonald, 1964)
Rawlings, J., *Fighter Squadrons of the RAF and Their Aircraft* (London: McDonald, 1969)
Royal Air Force Historical Society, *The Canberra in the RAF* (RAFHS, 2009)
Scott, S.A., *English Electric Lightning, Volume One: Birth of a Legend* (Peterborough: GMS 2000)
Scott, S.A., *English Electric Lightning, Volume Two: The Lightning Force* (Peterborough: GMS 2004)
Smith, J.R. and Kay, A., *German Aircraft of the Second World War* (London: Putnam, 1982)
Taylor, H.A., *Fairey Aircraft since 1915* (London: Putnam, 1974)
Temple, J.C., *Wings Over Woodley: The Story of Miles Aircraft and the Adwest Group* (Bourne End: Aston Publications, 1987)
Trevor, H., *Lightnings Live On* (Bruntingthorpe: LPG, 1996)
Watkins, D., *De Havilland Vampire: The Complete Story* (Budding Books, 1998)
Wilson, T., *English Electric Lightning, Genesis & Projects* (Horncastle: Tempest Books, 2021)
War Diary of the English Electric Company Ltd, March 1938–August 1945 (undated)

The National Archives: Air 8, 27, 29; DEFE 13, 58, 280; T225

Online Sources

http://www.britpolitics.co.uk/quotefinder/churchill-winston-the-battle-of-france-is-over
http://radarpages.co.uk/mob/rotor/rotorarticle1.htm
https://www.raffca.org.uk/art_ControllingTheLightning.php
https://www.rafweb.org
https://scottbouch.com/aircrew-uk-oxygen-mask-p-q-type-series.htm
https://www.theguardian.com/culture/gallery/2012/sep/29/1962-year-pictures
https://www.thunder-and-lightnings.co.uk